CW01034729

WINSTON CHURCHILL

IN 100 OBJECTS

WINSTON CHURCHILL
IN 100 OBJECTS

Phil Reed
&
Anthony Richards

Greenhill Books

IN PARTNERSHIP WITH

Greenhill Books

Winston Churchill in 100 Objects

First published in 2024 by Greenhill Books,
c/o Pen & Sword Books Ltd,
George House, Unit 12 & 13,
Beevor Street, Off Pontefract Road,
Barnsley, South Yorkshire s71 1HN

This edition published in 2024
by Greenhill Books

www.greenhillbooks.com
contact@greenhillbooks.com

ISBN: 978–1–80500–024–2

CIP data records for this title are available from the British Library

Printed and bound in China by 1010 Printing International Limited

Typeset in Minion Pro Regular 9.7/12.2pt

Contents

Introduction

In my early days as Director of the Churchill War Rooms, one of the wartime secretaries to General Hollis, who had responsibility for establishing the Rooms in 1938–9, recounted to me how, when newly married and short of cash, she and her husband would 'go and buy a memory'. It didn't matter how cheap and seemingly insignificant it was – be it a ride on the top deck of a bus or a walk by the lake in a London Park to feed the ducks – it was just something that one day they could look back on as a memento of their lives together.

In a similar way in any tourist spot on the planet you are bound to encounter a swathe of souvenir shops and stalls. Regardless of the relevance of the items they are touting, tourists will often use them to acquire some recollection of that place and their experiences there. The very word 'souvenir' is French for memory or reminder and we all like to look back on our travels or some past experience, and these artefacts act as prompts for our memory. Who hasn't listened to a piece of music and been transported back to a time or an occasion in the past? Many people retain and cherish simple objects from their past which preserve memories and stories.

Souvenir shops in almost every major city in the word will offer postcard images and other visuals of what we see as iconic landmarks of those places – the Tower of London, Rome's Colosseum, or Paris's Arc de Triomphe, for example. The images are instant reminders of each site. So it is often the case too with famous people: the Beatles are instantly recognisable by their trademark haircuts; Napoleon Bonaparte will be forever pictured with his arm tucked inside his jacket; Charlie Chaplin will always be a skinny tramp in a bowler hat and ragged trousers.

But no figure of modern times is so readily identifiable by a vast array of images and objects that people immediately recognise and associate with them as Winston Churchill. In his early political career a cartoonist latched on to a rather ludicrous hat that he was seen wearing on a beach in Lancashire and for years his most cartooned form was in a variety of hats. Churchill, the master of spin, translated art into reality and ensured he had a wide

The newly commissioned Churchill in his 4th Hussars uniform at the outset of his career.

Stalin, Roosevelt and Churchill at the Tehran Conference in December 1943. This was the first meeting of the US and Soviet leaders, but as an assiduous traveller Churchill had met Stalin twice before and Roosevelt several times.

range of hats and thus encouraged the spread of images of himself and ever-greater recognition. As his fame grew – with no small amount of encouragement from Churchill – the hats were replaced by other items, most significantly his cigars, which became a *sine qua non* for Churchill whenever he appeared in public or the media, so much so that a popular song *The Man with the Big Cigar*, though not written with Churchill in mind, became widely identified with him.

Churchill deliberately and shamelessly flirted with the media throughout his life in an effort to make his name known, with the result that a host of images and objects connected to him have become totemic: his suits, his polka-dotted bow ties, his 'siren suits', even his slippers. Each item, however, is not only a part of his image. Emblematic of the man, they all have

back stories that give intriguing insights into his personality, his attitudes and, of course, his style.

Churchill held, at various times, all the high offices of the British government except for Foreign Secretary, he won a Nobel Prize for his writings and oratory, and he was a painter of some talent (enough to merit inclusion in the Royal Academy Summer Exhibition). He was a legendary consumer of cigars and champagne, and, as his friend Lord Birkenhead is often quoted, was 'easily satisfied: he liked the best'. All his clothes were hand-made by the finest tailors, his cigars were Cuban and his favourite drink was vintage Pol Roger champagne.

Despite his penchant for a rich lifestyle, he had an empathy for, and a fair under-standing of, the common man and, in his days as a Liberal politician, helped produce government policies that many would now think of almost as 'socialist' (though he would turn in his grave at such an accusation). His was a life rich in its variety and conducted on what we might now call high octane: his energy, resilience and capacity for work astonished his staff and amazed his doctors. It is fair to say that there has never been anyone quite like him and, while he has always had detractors, his achievements continue to excite real admiration across the world and at every level of society, not least amongst other world leaders. His neologisms and characterful expressions continue to populate the English language and be used and quoted almost as much as Shakespeare (of whom he was a great admirer).

Inevitably, he has been the subject of hundreds of books – by the year 2000 at least 52 biographies of him had been published and countless more have been since – as well as press and scholarly articles, TV programmes, feature films and even comics. His reputation remains firm, despite growing numbers of detractors, mostly arguing from the standpoint of current attitudes and values and with little regard to the age within

which he grew up. So what more can be said and why might another 'Churchill book' be worthy of publishing?

Firstly, 2024, marks the 150th anniversary of his birth, and his fame shows no sign of diminishing. In deciding to produce yet another book about Churchill in this anniversary year, we wanted to bring Churchill alive for a modern generation and to use objects connected with Churchill, some well-known, but many unexpected and at first puzzling, as prompts both to tease curiosity and to give insights into his life. The images will not only illustrate those aspects of his life that are widely known and recognised, but also facets and details that might be less well-known, even to many of those who avidly sweep up any new publication about him.

Many people have essentially one image of Churchill in their minds, namely as a balding, corpulent, jowly figure, from the era of the Second World War. But the lock of his hair reminds us that, as a young boy, he had a full head of red hair, while other depictions show him as a handsome individual, with Yousuf Karsh's photographs also providing a real insight into his indomitable spirit, in contrast

Visiting the combat zone. Churchill and General Brooke (*left*) at General Montgomery's headquarters in Normandy, 12 June 1944.

Churchill with his Chiefs of Staff in 1945: (*L to R*) Portal, Brooke, and Cunningham. Behind are their principal staff officers, Generals Hollis (*left*) and Ismay.

to the Graham Sutherland eightieth birthday study, showing how age had made its mark. Oddly, other things that might have taken a toll on his health – his copious drinking and cigar smoking for example – appear not to have done and the favoured champagne and cigar stubs remind us of these intrinsic elements of his lifestyle. It is sometimes overlooked that Churchill was from an aristocratic family, with tastes to match, though a large part of the luxuries he enjoyed were obtained on credit! After the Second World War his money worries melted away, as his memoirs earned him vast sums, a point illustrated by his purchase of a series of race-horses, a hobby that any owner can tell you is not an income generator, but a massive financial drain. It was a hobby he shared with Her Majesty Queen Elizabeth II, for whom he had the deepest admiration and affection, something that persuaded him to accept the nation's highest honour, the Order of the Garter, in 1953, to add to an already vast array of awards from across the globe. These remind us not only of the stature he held globally, but also of the degree of real bravery he showed as a soldier.

The book is intended as a handy companion, dipping into which will produce surprises, provoke discussion and maybe even bring a smile to one's face. In any event, the stories behind the objects will reveal sides to Churchill's life and persona that have been overlooked or neglected and will shine fresh light on aspects of the man, despite his being one of the most recognisable figures in modern times and being seen as a global icon. Above all we hope that this companion volume will help people better understand the man widely recognised as Britain's greatest statesman and help ensure that this reputation continues, and his memory lives on.

PHR

The statesman, as painted in 1942, by the Hungarian artist Arthur Pan.

The Objects

1 | Lock of Churchill's Hair

Winston Leonard Spencer Churchill was born, prematurely, at Blenheim Palace, the home of his grandfather, the 7th Duke of Marlborough, on 30 November 1874. His father was an eminent Conservative politician, the apogee of whose political career was his appointment as Chancellor of the Exchequer in August 1886.

Like so many British aristocrats, with impressive titles, but relatively little by way of financial resources, Lord Randolph had married an American heiress. Jennie Jerome was the daughter of a wealthy financier, Leonard Jerome; they married

A lock of Churchill's hair, carefully preserved in an envelope from Blenheim Palace, the place of his birth.

at the British Embassy in Paris on
15 April 1874. Together the couple lived
a hectic and spendthrift social life, and,
in common with many of that class, were
happy to allow a nanny and his schools to
oversee their son's upbringing.

They did, belatedly, move him from
his first school, St George's Preparatory
School in Ascot, after it was discovered
– by his nanny, Elizabeth Everest, or
'woomany' as Winston called her – that
the headmaster had a habit of beating

Churchill photographed in 1881, at the age of seven.

Churchill was born into the aristocracy.

the young Churchill till he bled. With such absentee parents, Mrs Everest was Churchill's confidante, and he often spoke to her about his troubles.

The distance between the young Churchill and his parents became even greater when they informally separated in 1886, when Winston was just eleven years old. It is doubtful that he was aware of his parents' philandering – Lord Randolph carried on his consistent rakish behaviour, while Jennie Churchill, a legendary beauty, took a series of lovers, that gave support to the theory that Winston's brother Jack might not have been Randolph's son.

Lord Randolph's political career took several wild curves, not least when he involved the Prince of Wales (the future King Edward VII) in a court case and society scandal, leading to Randolph's effective exile to Ireland for three years from 1877, to serve as Private Secretary to his father, the 7th Duke, who was Lord Lieutenant and Viceroy of Ireland. Lord Randolph was a wilful and generally rebellious individual (traits inherited by his son, Winston), who, in 1886, after just five months in office as Chancellor, misjudged the strength of his position, by offering the Prime Minister, Lord Salisbury – not for the first time – his resignation, over the Army and Navy budgets.

On this occasion the Prime Minister accepted the resignation and with that

Lord Randolph's top-level political career was at an end.

Churchill's father was a very strict parent, a perfect illustration being the occasion when Winston confessed how he had lost and, at great expense found and had repaired, a watch given to him by his father. Lord Randolph's only response was: your brother Jack never lost his. When Churchill was finally (at the third attempt) admitted to the Royal Military College at Sandhurst for cavalry training, his father was furious, utterly dismissing his son's ability, while decrying him for the costs a cavalry officer would incur. Nevertheless, throughout his life Churchill lionised his father, wrote a rather uncritical biography of him and generally set him on a pedestal. There is no final proof of a widely held belief that Lord Randolph died of syphilis, though his philandering makes it credible. He died at the young age of forty-five on 24 January 1895. Churchill long thought that he too would die young and was ever in a hurry to fulfil his potential (he also died on 24 January, but in 1965 at the age of ninety).

His mother married twice after Lord Randolph's death, on both occasions to unsuitable partners, continued to spend more money than she had, and to enjoy society and all its pleasures and distractions, till her death in June 1921.

PHR

2 | Churchill's Toy Soldiers

Churchill displayed an interest in all things military from a very early age, in line with so many other young boys of that era. According to his autobiography, his earliest memories were of his grandfather, the 7th Duke of Marlborough, unveiling a statue in 1878 amid a parade of soldiers on horseback; such trappings of a military life must have made quite an impression on his young mind.

This fascination with soldiery was most clearly displayed through Churchill's large collection of toy soldiers, which he began to amass from childhood. Made from solid metal and usually imported from France or Germany, such objects were an expensive purchase and therefore largely remained the plaything of boys from wealthy families. The last decade of the nineteenth century saw something of a craze for metal soldiers, following new production methods which made the figures cheaper to make, although on the whole it was still only the more privileged children who could amass a substantial collection. By Churchill's own estimate, his own assortment of troops amounted to nearly 1,500 figures.

Indeed, Churchill believed that his affection for the tiny lead figures was the main reason that he embarked on a military career. His father's decision to send Winston to the Royal Military College at Sandhurst appears to have been made upon witnessing his fourteen-year-

old son's fascination with deploying his toy soldiers into carefully formed lines of attack, and from that point on Winston's education was directed towards a military career. As an aside, Winston himself recognised that his father's decision may also have been influenced by what he himself thought of as his poor educational record, making him unsuitable for any other profession.

The popularity of toy soldiers during this era no doubt played a major role in fostering a keen interest in all things military among British schoolboys. The emphasis on soldiers' colourful appearances and bravery encouraged a romantic view of the military world and war, which was of course significantly removed from the often harsh reality of

A selection of Churchill's toy soldiers, which he kept carefully throughout his life.

Toys from Churchill's childhood remained firm favourites in his adult life.

life in the Army. The planning of military campaigns could be seen as more of a safe puzzle to be solved, in a consequence-free world, rather than a matter of real life and death. Such affection for toy soldiers undoubtedly inspired many young British men to volunteer for military service in South Africa at the end of the nineteenth century and for the campaigns of the First World War, in pursuit of an honourable means to serve their country.

Churchill's fascination with his toy soldiers did not end with his childhood. In fact, as the years went on, he expanded his collection regularly and was known to play with them as an adult, using the figures as a means of escapism when opportunity permitted. The surviving large collection of soldiers, which are still on display at Blenheim, reflects Churchill's affection for the small objects which so influenced the course of his life.

APR

Churchill dressed for public school, in a photo probably dating from 1889.

3 | Hand Cast of Jennie Churchill

Churchill's childhood was characterised by a certain detachment on the part of both his parents. His mother took a back seat in his upbringing, with her child's daily care largely down to his trusted nanny, Mrs Everest, in a manner common to many other children of the aristocracy. Yet Jennie Churchill would remain an object of admiration for her son, and somebody who would provide a strong support to him as he began to follow in his father's footsteps towards a career in politics.

Since marrying Lord Randolph in 1874, Jennie had come to embrace the political sphere in which her husband moved and encouraged his ambitions as far as she was able. Despite their marriage suffering numerous difficulties, mainly due to both partners pursuing their own extra-marital affairs, their political union remained a strong factor in Randolph's success. Remaining popular and well-known in British society and its elite political circles, Jennie would promote her husband's worth at numerous opportunities, exploiting family links as well as her extra-marital contacts. Although her numerous romantic affairs were common knowledge, her warm personality and intelligence ensured that she remained a widely admired society figure.

After Lord Randolph's early death in January 1895, Jennie focussed her support on her son, Winston. Although his desire to enter politics was undoubtedly inspired by his father's career and an aspiration to follow the same path, it would be his mother who would serve as Churchill's main supporter during his early campaigns. She worked with her many contacts to build his reputation as a young politician, appealing for financial support

Churchill's mother proved herself to be one of his most ardent early supporters.

to fund his campaigning and encouraging press interest. Such was their relationship, working together on equal terms, that Churchill referred to them both as more brother and sister than mother and son.

Churchill also benefited from Jennie's American ancestry. She was born in Brooklyn in 1854 and enjoyed the reputation of a young debutante among the society parties of New York and also Paris, before meeting Randolph at an engagement on the Isle of Wight. When Churchill began to undertake promotional tours of North America, it was often Jennie's name and reputation which opened doors and encouraged coverage in the local press.

Her motherly instincts also served to deter Churchill from following the same path of extravagant socialising and rowdy behaviour practised by

Randolph, while her appreciation of party politics and the mood of the electorate meant that she would help to guide her son as best she could, in order to ensure popular support. As an aspiring politician keen to build on his father's legacy, Churchill needed Jennie's help and took full advantage of it. Her influence continued until her death in June 1921, although since Churchill's marriage to Clementine in 1908 it would be his wife that would gradually take over the position of chief supporter and social influencer.

This cast of Jennie's left hand was commissioned from the sculptor Herbert Haseltine in June 1914. Following her death in 1921, the cast was offered as a gift from the artist to Churchill, who displayed it at Chartwell for many years.

APR

Churchill pictured with his mother,
in an image from the late 1870s.

4 | Churchill's Christening Robe

Churchill was not a religious person. Although christened into the Church of England in an era when the Anglican Church enjoyed a powerful influence on all aspects of society, it was not long before he came to question the faith which he was expected to follow as an obedient Victorian schoolboy.

His christening robe, now in the possession of Churchill's Irish relatives, the Leslie family in County Monaghan, Ireland, is a lasting memento of this first religious occasion in his life.

Churchill's beliefs would be influenced at a very early age. After the family

pushed him towards a more secular view of the world and encouraged further questioning of traditional Christian thinking. Reade in particular was a widely influential writer, whose portrayal of Jesus as a prophet rather than the actual Son of God had swayed the beliefs of many Victorian contemporaries such as Sir Arthur Conan Doyle and H. G. Wells. By the age of twenty-three, Churchill was declaring in a letter to his mother that he no longer followed Christianity or any other form of religious belief.

But Churchill was careful not to make his views too well known, particularly at a time when the Conservative Party was

---

Churchill would come to place his faith more in Providence than God.

---

travelled to Dublin when he was two, the strongly anti-Fenian views of his nanny Mrs Everest ensured that the young Winston developed a clear distrust of the Catholic Church. His schooling at Harrow was similarly influential, incorporating regular daily attendance at chapel – and three services on Sundays – which proved enough to generate a feeling of discontent within him towards organised religion.

Such disgruntlement helped increase his alienation from religion when, still as a young man, Churchill was stationed in India with the 4th Hussars. It was during his military service at Bangalore that he began to read works by authors including Charles Darwin, Edward Gibbon and William Winwood Reade, all of which

so closely linked to the Anglican Church. He speculated that his secular attitude was perhaps due to the lack of a traditional university education and its atmosphere of questioning and debate amongst peers. His wife Clementine had been a regular church-goer before their marriage, but lapsed somewhat after meeting Churchill, while the only one of their friends to be particularly religious was Lord Hugh Cecil, who acted as Churchill's Best Man.

Instead of a traditional religious faith, Churchill would retain what could be described as a semi-religious belief in Providence. He came to accept that Fate had marked him out as a person with a special purpose to fulfil, which funnily enough might indeed appear to have been the case, considering how he managed to survive several close brushes with death throughout his long life. His particular interpretations still allowed him to hold Jesus in high regard, but as a teacher rather than a Messiah.

Churchill also continued to believe strongly in the right of individuals to practise religious freedom and alternative faiths, and his writing and speeches made frequent reference to religious phrasing. Words such as 'providence' and 'fate' would regularly appear in his oratory, although often being deployed where others might have said 'God'; when God was referred to, it tended to be for jocular or self-deprecatory reasons rather than in an inspiring reference to the divine.

APR

The robe in which Churchill was christened, in 1875.

5 | Harrow School Punishment Book

In common with others of their class, Churchill's parents sent their children to boarding school at an early age, leaving the teachers to care for and develop their sons. It was not at all unusual for boys in that era to see little of their parents and Winston was no exception, even being farmed out to relatives at Christmas in 1881.

Winston's first school, where he was enrolled at the age of seven in 1882, was St George's Preparatory School in Ascot. Churchill received regular (and bloody) beatings from the Headmaster, Herbert Sneyd-Kinnersley, and as a result was finally removed from the school. His next school was in Hove, near Brighton, where he wrote to his father that he was a little disappointed that he did not visit his son when he came to town. It was at Hove that Churchill began to read voraciously and developed his capacity for memorising long tracts of prose and poetry, not least by writers who are now considered hard work to read, such as the historians Edward Gibbon and Thomas Macaulay.

It was a skill that would stay with him for the rest of his life and impress people as he would suddenly recite some ancient lay, some music hall ditty, or even songs from the American Civil War when touring the battlefields there with President Roosevelt during the Second World War. Certainly it served him well at his next school, Harrow, where he won a number of recital competitions, famously doing so on one occasion, when, shortly before the examination, a few dozen more lines were added to the requirement. His behaviour at Harrow continued in the manner that had become his custom at St George's. A recent biographer, Andrew Roberts, describes his behaviour there as 'one long feud with authority' and the punishment book for Harrow and his school reports show him to have been exceptionally naughty, receiving regular

The Harrow School 'punishment book' records 'Spencer-Churchill' (half-way down the left page) as having been flogged for 'breaking into premises and doing damage'.

28

Churchill's education was typical of that of most boys from wealthy Victorian families.

---

beatings as a result. His school days certainly set the seed of rebellion that remained a hallmark of his whole life. He described his life at Harrow as the worst five years of his life, claiming that, though he approved of public (private) schools, he never wished to go back to one. He summarised his education by saying that although he was always eager to learn, he did not always appreciate being taught.

In his writings and conversations Churchill was fond of exaggerating and mythologising about aspects of his life, especially his schooling, and the myth that his school reports were consistently bad comes from the man himself, but is not borne out by the records, which show that he was indeed bad at maths and science, but excelled at history, English and music (he trained on the cello for a short part of his life). Whatever the case, there is no doubt that he was not sorry to leave Harrow to join the Royal Military Academy at Sandhurst, although that too was an institution where, if you were not considered 'the right stuff', you would be brutally ostracised. Churchill was lucky

to find a number of Old Harrovians at the College and took to military life, even with its rigorous and banal routines, from day one.

When he graduated from Sandhurst and was posted to India – where, because of the climate, peacetime soldiering tended to be a purely morning occupation – he read as much as he could get his mother to send to him and it was in this period that he taught himself most. Despite his occasional regrets at not having a university education – and he wholeheartedly believed in the benefits that a university education could bring – he demonstrated a truly exceptional breadth of knowledge, a vast vocabulary and a recall that was a source of astonishment to others all his life. It was these elements that enabled him to write such epic works as his *Life of the Duke of Marlborough* and *A History of the English-Speaking Peoples*, both of which he dictated, with little recourse to written source materials.

PHR

Harrow School Chapel, where Churchill would have attended regular services.

6 | Empire Theatre Programme, 1894

Churchill loved the theatre from a very early age, with some of his earliest recorded memories being attendance at pantomime performances in Dublin, then later enjoying the Gilbert and Sullivan operetta *HMS Pinafore* on the London stage. He also played with a toy theatre and cardboard actors while at school at Harrow, writing to his parents in a plea for further accoutrements to embellish the model.

Churchill's school days also saw him develop an interest in Shakespeare, as he came fourth (out of 25) in the competition for the Lower School Shakespeare Prize of 1888. This fascination with the Bard continued on into adulthood, to the point where Churchill could recite famous passages by heart and quotes from plays would invariably appear throughout his various speeches and writings. He also included theatrical allusions in his many historical works, as if historical personages were actors on a stage.

During his military training at Sandhurst, Churchill would regularly take trips into London with his fellow officer

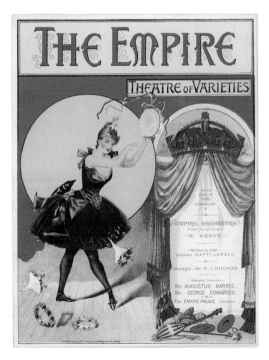

A programme for the Empire Theatre of Varieties, dated 5 November 1894.

A postcard photo of the Empire Theatre, taken around 1905,
some ten years after Churchill's protest.

cadets to visit the theatres and music halls. One of his favourite haunts, the Empire Theatre of Varieties in Leicester Square, had become the centre of a scandal in November 1894 when the social reformer Laura Chant urged the London County Council to deny the theatre management's latest request to renew its licence. Chant and others believed that many London theatres were places of immorality, with the promenade area in the Empire's auditorium in particular being used by sex workers to meet clients and many of the men involved being drunk.

After much deliberation the Council decided to renew the Empire's licence but only on the understanding that its promenade area would be obscured

Churchill enjoyed the theatre throughout his life.

by screens and no alcohol would be sold in the auditorium, yet this led to considerable public protest by regular theatregoers, including Churchill, who believed that the restrictions were too harsh on those with a legitimate desire to socialise.

After a group of young men urged on by Churchill and others tore down the promenade barriers, he is reported to have delivered what was, in effect, a maiden public speech, about the dangers of government interference in people's social habits. How much of this was actually more related to a simple youthful desire for fun remains debatable, yet in subsequent years Churchill remained involved in debates over theatre licensing as well as the censorship of plays.

Even as leader of the nation during the Second World War, Churchill found time to show his support for the theatre. In March 1941 he questioned the wisdom of the Treasury's decision to close theatres on Sundays, while he maintained regular correspondence with such theatrical luminaries as Noël Coward, George Bernard Shaw and Terence Rattigan. He would also commonly visit actors in their dressing rooms to congratulate them after a performance.

With his own easily identifiable image and oft-quoted remarks, Churchill would surely have been well-suited to appearing in a theatrical performance of his own.

APR

7 | Oxfordshire Hussars Uniform

Churchill was very fond of a form of false modesty in looking back over his life, which itself gave strength to a number of myths about him. His own father, Lord Randolph, helped to perpetuate such myths by disparaging his son's intelligence, knowledge and capacity for work, and was not surprised to find it took Winston three attempts to win a place at Sandhurst. Churchill's preference for the cavalry similarly disappointed his father, who wanted his son to join a prestigious infantry regiment – and at the same time avoid the massive expense a cavalry officer's position involved (horses, saddlery, stabling, endless uniform elements).

It was Churchill's real wish to join the cavalry, as it embodied all his romantic just over forty years earlier. The regiment's history undoubtedly fed his romantic aspirations, but Churchill's career strategy saw the Army as no more than a stepping stone, a launch pad, bringing glory and medals won in battle, to enable him to make a name for himself and so attain his real ambition, a life in politics.

His first professional use of firearms introduced him to the standard rifle of the British Army, the Lee-Enfield and the standard hand-gun – which officers traditionally bought for themselves – the Webley Wilkinson revolver, now on display in London's Churchill War Rooms.

Faced with two and a half months of leave in October 1895, Churchill sought adventure and excitement. His attitude to fighting was purely romantic, imagining the excitement of hearing bullets whizzing

---

Churchill's romantic fascination with the military inspired his early career.

---

heroic notions of riding into battle. He proved his father – by then too ill to appreciate it – wrong by graduating in December 1894 twentieth out of 130 cadets and second in the riding class, a skill and a love that stayed with him for the rest of his life – he became an excellent polo player and, after the Second World War, took up ownership of race-horses.

In February 1895 Churchill joined his first regiment, The 4th Queen's Own Hussars, which had famously taken part in the calamitous and foolhardy Charge of the Light Brigade in the Crimean War past while experiencing the thrill of narrowly escaping death.

Thus began Churchill's legendary and real fearlessness, as he connived a position during his leave period as a reporter/observer of the Spanish government's attempt to suppress a rebellion in Cuba. Here, he came under fire for the first time – but enthused about the exhilaration of surviving and being able to write about the experience.

In 1895, Churchill wrote that the more he learned about soldiering, the less inclined he was to pursue it. Developing

Churchill inspects troops of his old regiment, the 4th Hussars,
while in Loreto, Italy, in August 1944.

an interest in journalism before aspiring to follow his father into politics, Churchill used his family connections and influence to join the Malakand Field Force on India's North-West Frontier, nominally as a reporter, but in fact still fighting, bravely and often recklessly. His next sortie, using his connections once more, was to Kitchener's army fighting in Sudan towards the end of 1898, while his eventful experience of the Second South African or Boer War the following year would generate enough public support to get him elected as a Member of Parliament for the first time.

Despite leaving the Army in 1900 to pursue a career in politics, Churchill never lost his interest in military matters as well

as his love for horses and the cavalry. He therefore quickly sought a commission in the reserves, and the logical regiment for him to join was the local one for Blenheim, the Oxfordshire Hussars. Many of his family had already served with the unit, and Churchill joined the regiment as a captain in January 1902, being promoted to major three years later and remaining in command of the Henley squadron until the beginning of the First World War. Shown here is his Oxfordshire Hussars dress uniform, currently on display in the Churchill Museum at the Cabinet War Rooms.

PHR

8 | Webley Wilkinson M1892 Revolver

Churchill was a trained professional soldier, who had first-hand experience of four wars between 1895 and 1900, as well as the First World War, and so was accustomed to handling firearms. By the end of his life he had acquired some twenty-four weapons, of which, by then, he still owned seventeen.

The earliest weapon that we know he owned was a .455 in. Webley-Wilkinson Model 1892 revolver, which he acquired as a cadet at Sandhurst Royal Military Academy in 1894 and which he used while serving (and fighting) with the 4th Hussars on the North-West Frontier of India in 1896.

It was usual for British Army officers to choose and purchase their own personal weapons and, in November 1898, he also

acquired two 7.63 mm Mauser C96 pistols from John Rigby & Co at a cost of £5 5s. (£5.25). The same gunmaker's records show that by 1902 he also owned a third Mauser and a Webley .450 WG Target revolver.

Churchill had seriously injured his shoulder when disembarking at a

Churchill owned many different weapons throughout his life.

particularly slippery wharf in India in 1891, an injury that troubled him all his life. He took part in what is generally considered to be the last full-scale cavalry charge by the British Army, at Omdurman, just north of Khartoum, on 2 September 1898, when 400 men of the 21st Lancers took on what they believed to be 700 Dervishes, but which transpired to be around 2,000. Normally Churchill as a cavalry officer would have wielded a

In February 1914, when First Lord of the Admiralty, Churchill was presented with a Canadian Ross Model 1910 Mk III rifle by the Canadian Minister of Militia and Defence. The Canadians had been hoping to have their rifle become the standard issue rifle of the British Army, but it was found less able to withstand the rigours of trench warfare than the Lee Enfield .303, which continued to be the standard rifle of the British Army until the 1950s. Churchill nevertheless kept the Ross till the end of his life.

Churchill was a keen game shot, taking time out while in South Africa in 1900 as a war

sabre in such an engagement, but his shoulder injury prevented him from holding and swinging one. His first intention was to take his Webley, but he appears to have mislaid it and instead took a Mauser. It was a wise choice, as the Mauser simply required easily installed replacement clips, whereas the Webley needed a slow reloading of the chamber. It is doubtful that he would have survived the battle had he not had his Mauser and a good supply of replacement clips.

After the war in Sudan he acquired as a memento a heavily carved and decorated Italian Vetterli-Vitali Model 1870/87 rifle, which was said to have belonged to the Mahdi (the Sudanese Islamic leader). He kept the rifle his whole life and it is also now held by the Imperial War Museum.

correspondent for the *Morning Post*, to take part in a shoot, and hunted game while visiting East Africa in 1907 in his capacity as Deputy Colonial Secretary. In the UK he took part in many game shoots throughout his life, on the landed estates of his society friends and relatives, including the Duke of Marlborough, the Duke of Westminster, Lord Spencer and Lord Astor. His regular gunmaker was James Woodward & Sons of 64 St James's Street, London, who made his Mannlicher sporting rifle, which he used regularly and he remained a faithful customer of theirs and subsequently of Purdey when they took over Woodward in 1948.

In one of the most famous images of Churchill he is seen holding a Thompson Model 1928A1 sub-machine gun, generally referred to as the 'Tommy gun', which was taken of him while visiting the Home Guard at Hartlepool in 1940. The picture shows him in a striped suit, a homburg hat and a bow tie, looking suitably gangster-like (and it is said that Chicago ex-gangsters taught British troops how to use the gun). The Nazis got hold of the picture, air-brushed out those around him, and used it as the basis for a poster labelling him a 'mass murderer'.

Churchill sports his characteristic cigar and bow tie while posing with a Tommy gun.

Salisbury Plain with General Eisenhower, though he did own a Mk III version, which was presented to him, probably by Sterling Armaments, who also gave him one of the earliest Lanchester sub-machine guns in March 1941 and an L2A3 Sterling, which was a type used by the British Army from 1952 to the 1990s. Engraved with a quotation from his 'we shall fight on the beaches' speech, the Sten Mk III remained with him until his death.

Churchill never personally owned a Tommy gun, nor a Mk II Sten gun, with which he was photographed in 1941 at Shoeburyness and, in 1944, when visiting

PHR

A well-used Mauser C96 pistol.

9 | Elizabeth Everest's Grave

One of the most prominent women in Churchill's life was his nanny, Elizabeth Everest, the woman who was the confidante to whom he poured out all his troubles and who, during his early years, was his most intimate companion.

When Mrs Everest visited him during his schooling at Harrow, despite her lowly social position, he paraded down the main street with her and accompanied her to her train home, in the face of snobbish mockery from his fellow pupils. She was closer to Churchill than anyone and, after she was dismissed by his parents when Winston reached the age of nineteen, he kept in touch with her, visiting her as she was dying and paying for her nursing. After her death in July 1895, Churchill arranged for her funeral and burial in the City of London Cemetery, ensuring the upkeep of her grave for the rest of his life.

The other most influential women in Churchill's life were undoubtedly his mother Jennie and wife Clementine. Though often on opposite sides of an argument, not least a political one, as Clemmie was an avowed Liberal, he had nothing but unalloyed respect and devotion for her. His letters to his wife

A now-obscured part of the inscription confirms that Winston's younger brother Jack joined him in remembering Mrs Everest.

throughout his life are imbued with a deep passion and love and he was giving vent to his true feelings when, in 1935, he wrote that his marriage was 'the most fortunate and joyous event' of his life.

Before he married he had proposed to a number of women, among them the actor Ethel Barrymore and, most famously, Pamela Plowden, whom he described as the most beautiful woman that he had ever laid eyes on, while she said of him: 'The first time you meet Winston, you see all his faults and the rest of your life you spend discovering his virtues.' All of them turned him down, though he remained lifelong friends with each of them.

Nowhere in his life is there a suggestion of sexual impropriety. An attempt in 2018 to prove that he had an affair in the 1930s with Lady Castlerosse was based on entirely spurious evidence, with no foundation in truth.

On several occasions in his life, Churchill allowed his tongue and his joy in the use of language to speak not just loosely, but inappropriately. One episode seems to have been at the end of a long discourse by Churchill at dinner

– a common practice of his – when the first woman to sit in the house of Commons, the American-born Nancy Astor, rebuked him with the remark that, if he were her husband, she would poison his tea, to which he replied with one of the most famous put-downs in the modern era: 'If you were my wife, I'd drink it.' Nancy Astor had her revenge in the House of Commons, when Churchill complained that he found the 'intrusion' of a woman into the House of Commons as embarrassing as if she 'had entered my bathroom and I had nothing to protect myself with except a sponge'. 'Sir, you are not handsome enough to have such fears,' she replied.

The first of these exchanges is slightly apocryphal, though always attributed to Churchill and is almost certainly a variation on a joke that had been around since the late nineteenth century. Similarly, when the Labour MP for Liverpool Exchange, Bessie Braddock, confronted Churchill in 1946 with the remark: 'You are drunk, and what's more you are disgustingly drunk.' Churchill replied: 'You are ugly … but tomorrow

Churchill's respectfulness towards women sometimes wavered in the political arena.

I will be sober.' The authenticity of the exchange has been vouched for by his bodyguard, Ronald Golding, but it is almost certain that he was enjoying playing with language and his legendary memory, as it is again a bowdlerised version of a quip by W. C. Fields, which Churchill must have known. Certain it is that Churchill had respect for Bessie Braddock, one of the country's leading campaigners against poverty, poor housing and poor health care, appointing her in 1953, even though she was a vocal member of the opposition, to be the Chair of the Royal Commission on mental health.

PHR

A colourised photo of Elizabeth Everest, taken in 1875 when Churchill was one year old.

10 | Churchill's Sudan Campaign Medal

Military service with the 4th Queen's Own Hussars seemed never to be enough for Churchill, as he continued to court danger at every opportunity. He had already sought out a chance to visit Cuba as a reporter for a few weeks covering the fighting there at the end of 1895 and, in September 1897, joined the Malakand Field Force,

again notionally as a war correspondent. Such sorties were largely made available to Churchill by exploiting his family connections.

In late 1897 and early the following year, he began to investigate the possibility of joining the expedition to the Tirah region on the North-West Frontier of India. When his attempts proved unsuccessful, he instead pursued

Churchill's desire to be at the centre of any action led to his volunteering for service in the Sudan.

the idea of joining General Kitchener's campaign to retake Sudan. Churchill was permitted by the War Office to join the expedition, but at his own expense and risk. Obtaining a temporary commission with the 21st Lancers, he again chose to incorporate civilian work as a war reporter, this time for the *Morning Post*, to finance his adventure.

After arriving in Cairo on 2 August 1898, Churchill travelled up the Nile with the expeditionary force and was present for the Battle of Omdurman on 2 September. This would include personal involvement in the 21st Lancers' famous cavalry charge, which proved to be the final such large-scale attack ever made by a British cavalry regiment. While on reconnaissance near the city of Khartoum the regiment spotted a few hundred enemy Sudanese troops and the 400-strong Lancers charged in to attack. But it turned out to be a trap, as the riders were counter-attacked by a larger force of some 2,500 enemy infantry.

There followed fierce hand-to-hand fighting in which Churchill, in command of a troop of twenty-five Lancers, had to resort to using his Mauser automatic pistol to save himself. He later described the battle as surely the most dangerous two minutes of his life. He well deserved the Queen's Sudan Medal awarded to participants in the campaign.

The overall battle proved to be a decisive one, bringing the British campaign to re-conquer Sudan to a successful end. Their victory had demonstrated the superiority of a well-disciplined army equipped with the latest weaponry over an enemy force twice its size but with outdated arms. This triumph of technology over manpower perhaps influenced Churchill's future thinking, encouraging his strong advocacy of mechanisation in both world wars.

Churchill's experiences inspired him to write *The River War: An Historical Account of the Reconquest of the Soudan* in 1899, covering the history of the campaign. Originally published in two volumes, *The Times* reviewer described it as containing material sufficient for two good books and one bad one, with the bad one being the more interesting.

APR

11 | Boer 'Wanted' Poster, December 1899

The last of Churchill's youthful excursions as a war reporter was to South Africa, where the Second Boer War had just begun in October 1899. Recognising the demand back in Britain for on-the-spot coverage of the conflict, while also satisfying his own need to be at the centre of any excitement and danger, Churchill arrived in Cape Town on 30 October, as a journalist representing the *Morning Post*.

Barely two weeks after his arrival, on 15 November, Churchill found himself part of a scouting expedition in the British Natal Colony. The armoured train in which he was travelling was ambushed and partially derailed by a Boer force, who surrounded it and laid siege, while Churchill, unarmed, led efforts to get the train operational again. Although part of the train finally escaped, some British personnel were left behind, including

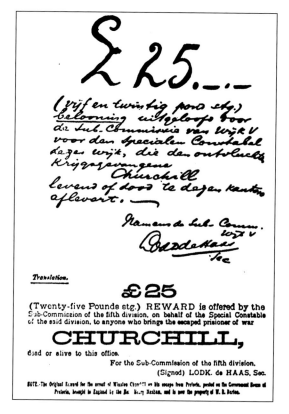

This poster offers a reward for the return of Churchill, following his escape from captivity in December 1899.

Photographed immediately after his capture, Churchill stands on the right, apart from a group of other British prisoners of war.

Churchill, and the survivors were taken prisoner. Although Churchill was present in a civilian role as a journalist, he was in uniform (although had left his gun on the train, by most accounts) and was therefore treated as a prisoner of war. Recognised by the Boers as coming from a privileged ran for freedom. Unfortunately the two fellow-officer prisoners with whom he had colluded did not follow; the guards had become suspicious and their opportunity to escape had passed. This presented a significant problem for Churchill, since his colleagues had the map, compass and

---

Churchill's experiences during the Boer War added to his increasing celebrity status.

---

background, he was also seen as a potentially valuable bargaining chip.

Taken to Pretoria and imprisoned in a converted schoolhouse, Churchill immediately started planning an escape. Initial ideas about a mass breakout were soon deemed unrealistic, and so instead he concentrated on studying the routine of the guards to spot an opportunity to flee. On the night of 12 December he scaled the ten-foot wall around the prison and rations required for the 300-mile journey to freedom. But he set off regardless on the long trek to Portuguese East Africa.

Hitching a ride briefly on a freight train, he then walked for many miles in the wilderness experiencing great hunger and thirst. Eventually having to resort to finding assistance, by great fortune the first person he asked happened to be one of the few Englishmen in the Transvaal region, John Howard, who was

HOW I ESCAPED.

MR. WINSTON CHURCHILL TELLS HIS STORY.

SIX DAYS OF ADVENTURE AND MISERY.

The 'Morning Post" have most courteously supplied us with the following story from their special war correspondent, Mr. Winston Churchill, relating how he escaped from Pretoria and found his way to Delagoa Bay, which he subsequently left by sea for Durban.

LORENÇO MARQUEZ, Dec. 21 (10 p.m.).

On the afternoon of the 12th the Transvaal Government's Secretary for War informed me that there was little chance of my release. I therefore resolved to escape.

The same night I left the State Schools Prison at Pretoria by climbing the wall when the sentries' backs were turned momentarily.

I walked through the streets of the town without any disguise, meeting many burghers, but I was not challenged.

In the crowd I got through the piquets of the Town Guard and struck the Delagoa Bay Railroad.

I walked along it, evading the watchers at the bridges and culverts.

The out 11.10 goods train from Pretoria arrived, and before it had reached full speed I boarded with great difficulty, and hid myself under coal sacks.

I jumped from the train before dawn, and sheltered during the day in a small wood in company with a huge vulture, which displayed a lively interest in me.

I walked on at dusk.

There were no more trains that night. The danger of meeting the guards of the railway line continued, but I was obliged to follow it, as I had no compass or map.

I had to make wide detours to avoid the bridges, stations, and huts, and in the dark I frequently fell into small watercourses.

My progress was very slow, and chocolate is not a satisfying food.

The outlook was gloomy, but I persevered with God's help for five days.

The food I had to have was very precarious.

I was lying up at daylight and walking on at night time, and meanwhile my escape had been discovered and my description telegraphed everywhere.

All the trains were searched.

Every one was on the watch for me.

Four wrong people were arrested.

But on the sixth day I managed to board a train beyond Middelburg, whence there is a direct service to Delagoa.

I was concealed in a railway truck under great sacks.

I had a small store of good water with me. I remained hidden, chancing discovery.

The Boers searched the train at Komati Poort, but did not search deep enough, so after sixty hours of misery I came safely here.

I am very weak, but I am free.

I have lost many pounds in weight, but I am lighter in heart, and I avail myself of this moment, in the condition in which I find myself—which is a witness to my earnestness—to urge an unflinching and uncompromising prosecution of the war.

CHIEVELEY CAMP, Dec. 26 (10.30 a.m.).

Mr. Winston Churchill is once more in the British camp.—Central News.

the manager of a colliery. Howard and another British colleague, Mr Dewsnap, sheltered Churchill and hid him in their mine while they planned how to get him to safe territory. In the meantime, the Boers had appealed for Churchill's recapture as a wanted fugitive, with a price on his head of £25 – to be captured either dead or alive.

Churchill was eventually hidden amongst woolsacks on a train heading to Portuguese East Africa and arrived in safe territory on 21 December, marking an end to his successful escape. Never one to rest on his laurels, however, Churchill was soon back in action in South Africa and witnessed not only the Battle of Spion Kop, almost exactly a month later on 23 January 1900, but also the final relief of the besieged British-held Ladysmith in February and the occupation of Pretoria.

Churchill's published account of his experiences as a fugitive were avidly absorbed by British readers, and contributed to his increasing status as a celebrity hero. He would arrive back in the United Kingdom in July 1900 to receive a hero's welcome, with his new-found popularity proving instrumental to his proper entrance into the political arena.

APR

Churchill's subsequent accounts of his escape brought him fame, yet he was careful not to implicate those in South Africa who had assisted him.

12 | *London to Ladysmith via Pretoria*, 1900

In a letter to his mother in October 1897, Churchill quoted Dr Johnson's famous epithet: 'No man but a blockhead ever wrote, except for money.' In fact Winston emulated his father, Randolph Churchill, who had enjoyed great success as a journalist, using his fame and position to support his secondary source of income by sending home reports for the press while on ministerial duties overseas.

Winston knew the value of his own name as well as the worth of the war correspondent, claiming that the reason war correspondents should anticipate big salaries was that while they experienced all the numerous dangers associated with war, they took only a tiny percentage of the associated glory. When sending reports back from the fighting on the North-West Frontier of India in 1897 he was outraged when his mother 'sold' the

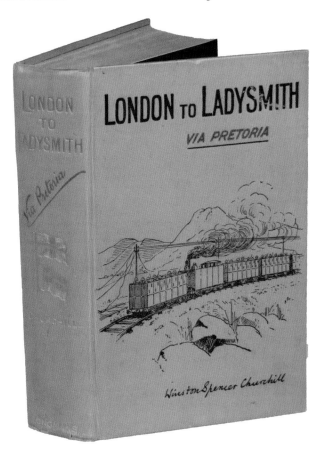

Writing was, for Churchill, a ready source of income throughout his life.

reports (effectively letters from the front) to the *Daily Telegraph* for just £5 apiece when he felt sure they merited twice that sum and threatened to return any cheques paying less than that. To add insult to injury they were published under the by-line of 'a young officer' and not under the name of Winston Churchill.

In fact, although additional money was almost essential for an Army officer with copious social obligations, the main driver of his journalistic work became to gain personal publicity and an enhanced reputation among the electorate which would grant him the political advantage that he desired. For this reason the vast majority of his early journalism was written for UK consumption and, in his younger years, he was contemptuous of American reporters, writing to his brother Jack during his first stay in New York in November 1895 en route to Cuba, that US journalism was simply 'vulgarity divested of truth'. That opinion changed with later visits to the USA, where newspapers and magazines provided him with a generous income for his writings.

Churchill first realised his journalistic skills and the huge monetary benefits he could gain from writing for the press when he went to Cuba in 1895 to cover the fighting between the local rebels and the occupying Spanish forces. He agreed terms with the *Daily Graphic*, which paid him 5 guineas a letter. He was later to conclude that his journalism in Cuba had paid him a multiple of the salary he earned as a soldier, putting his life on the line, and decided to forsake the Army for his new well-paid profession.

In fact he found a happier course, which he was to pursue for the rest of his early military career, of combining journalism and soldiering. He served on the North-West Frontier, in Sudan and later in South Africa as a war correspondent and, except for the last of these campaigns, continued to hold a commission in, and actively fought with, the British Army, allowing him to send back front-line reports for the avid British readership.

His experiences, especially at the great charge at Omdurman, in his escape from captivity in South Africa and in the later stages of the South African campaign, including the relief of Ladysmith, brought him massive fees and, more especially, kudos and fame. The name Winston Churchill was one that certainly attracted a wide readership, but also became associated in the popular press with adventure, heroics and bravado,

Churchill in Durban after his escape.

characteristics which attached themselves to his persona his whole life. His letters from Cuba had been tempered to ensure he avoided upsetting his Spanish hosts, whose policy he disapproved of, and later reports often fell foul of the higher command of the Army, who were offended by his often forthright and hyper-critical public utterances.

Even in the 1930s, when out of public office and needing (not least to support his luxurious tastes) a sizable income, he was unflinching in the public expression of his opinions, even to the extent of provoking the Foreign Office, which, like the government of the day, was keen to avoid upsetting Hitler and the Nazis, to claim that Churchill's opinions 'were not those of England'.

He had earlier shown his unrestrained, even intemperate tendencies when, during the General Strike of 1926, he took on, edited and wrote for the government-sponsored newssheet, *The British Gazette*. His efforts attracted well over two million readers, but, at the same time, offended great sections of the unions generally, who saw his stridency as particularly anti-worker and anti-socialist, a view that held sway with many working-class people and organisations for decades afterwards.

He effectively gave up his journalistic career in 1939 on the outbreak of war and his assumption of the office of First Lord of the Admiralty, putting an end to the all too often sententious output of his writing career in the 'wilderness years', when, out of office, he felt free to express, publicise and sell his opinions widely and without fear of retribution.

From his earliest years as a journalist, he had marketed his writings not only as submissions to newspapers and journals, but in a number of best-selling books. *London to Ladysmith via Pretoria*, the example given here, was published in 1900 and gave Churchill's impressions of the Boer War.

The contracts for later books were a source of suspicion from the tax collectors of the Inland Revenue, even while he was in office as Prime Minister. With the end of the war and with the help of a very capable agent, he wrote and globally serialised his memoirs, which made him the equivalent of a multi-millionaire and also made him an even more popular and well-paid speaker, with no need any longer to feed 'Grub Street'.

PHR

The State Model School in Pretoria, where Churchill was held before his escape.

13 | Butterfly House, Chartwell

Churchill was a man not only of many accomplishments, but also one who tended to devote considerable effort to whatever pastime he took up.

At school he involved himself in a wide variety of activities, including breeding silkworms and even playing the cello. He was a member of the Harrow School Volunteer Rifle Corps and in April 1892 won the Public Schools fencing (foil) championship at Aldershot. He did his first drawings at school and wrote profusely, both for the school magazine (under the *nom de plume* 'Junior Junior'), including several letters protesting about issues of life at school, which gave him a large following. He penned many long essays on historical subjects, several of which gave pre-echoes of later events, not least a deadly cavalry charge, a war in Russia, and speculation as to how he might one day save the nation from invasion and disaster.

At the Royal Military College Sandhurst he took up polo, a sport which he pursued

A Clouded Yellow butterfly photographed at Chartwell, a rare migratory species that has occasional bumper years in the UK.

until his final ride in January 1927 at the age of fifty-two, even though he had to strap his upper right arm to his body, following a dislocation of his right shoulder, which troubled him all his days. Horses became a focus of his life, be it riding them or owning them and he participated in many horse-races while he was in the Army.

When he reached India with the Army he took up a passion of his schooldays once more, collecting butterflies, of which the country around about boasted many 'rare and beautiful species'. After the Second World War, with the help of professional butterfly-farm owner, L. W. Newman, he built a butterfly house at Chartwell and would spend hours there observing his flying insects. It was in India that he first indulged what was also to become a passion, gardening; within a month of his arrival he started growing over 250 roses of different varieties. It was a passion that he was to apply in

Churchill's butterfly house has been recreated in Chartwell's disused game larder, but gives an impression of its original appearance.

earnest when he bought his country retreat of Chartwell, where he landscaped the gardens and surrounding areas. At Chartwell too he took up the practice of bricklaying and built several walls around the property, all of which are still standing today. He also oversaw the construction of a swimming pool and a fishpond, where he kept rare golden orfe.

Churchill, as was fitting for his class, often rode with fox-hunts and was a keen shot, enjoying the hospitality of his wealthy friends' estates, especially in Scotland, where, at Balmoral with Edward, Prince of Wales, he tried deerstalking for the very first time; he also took up salmon fishing there. (In 1929 he excelled in another style of fishing by hooking a 168-pound [76-kg] marlin off Catalina Island.)

In 1907 he used the opportunity of his role as Under-Secretary of State at the Colonial Office to go on safari in Kenya, and, typical of Churchill, engineered a

Churchill turned his skilled hand to many different hobbies and pastimes.

contract with *Strand Magazine* to sell several articles about his travels that helped him off-set the costs of his trip and also became the core of his subsequent best-selling book *My African Journey*. People in the twenty-first century often have difficulty relating to Churchill, who was decidedly a product of the nineteenth and nowhere is that better illustrated than in the fact that, for sport on this safari, he shot and killed a white rhino.

He played golf occasionally, though because of his dislocated shoulder, was never good at it or tennis (his wife's favourite pastime), which he tried for a time. He famously used the occasion of a round of golf with Prime Minister Herbert Asquith in 1911 to cajole him into offering him the job of First Lord of the Admiralty. He tried his hand at bridge, but instead soon became a lifelong fan of bezique (after he gave up mah-jong), poker and gin rummy.

Churchill was always a swimmer, even jumping into the Mediterranean against doctors' orders in August 1942, having only just recovered from a bout of pneumonia on the way back from his first visit to Stalin in Moscow. He loved to sing – mainly in the bath and was a devotee of old music-hall numbers, Gilbert and Sullivan and the Harrow songs – and dance, once embarrassing his Chief of the Imperial General Staff, General Alan Brooke, by twirling him around the dance floor at Chequers at 2 a.m.

Both Churchill and his wife Clementine gambled, in his case rather obsessively, which frequently left him having to find ways of making money to cover his losses, usually as a journalist, author and lecturer. He was a frequent visitor to the casinos of southern France for most of his life, at one point, according to his great-grandson, losing £100,000 in one night at a French casino. Happily, the proprietor wrote the debt off, saying it had been a privilege to have Churchill in his establishment.

PHR

14 | General Election Poster, October 1900

During the summer of 1899, Churchill was approached by Conservative Party representatives from the town of Oldham in Greater Manchester, who asked him to stand as a candidate in a forthcoming by-election in their two-member constituency.

Although he was in no way a local man and had no connection to that area of the country, Churchill's candidacy was appealing for one big reason: his father's political reputation was formidable and if even a little of Randolph had been inherited by Winston it would stand him in good stead. Churchill was keen to forge a political name for himself and had already proven himself at this early age to be something of an expert in self-promotion through his military adventures.

Despite Churchill exuding an air of confidence in his own abilities, the election on 6 July went in favour of the Liberals and he was defeated by some 1,500 votes. It seems that the Conservative government's recent Clerical Tithes Bill, which increased local taxes to subsidise the Anglican Church, had not gone down well with Oldham's largely nonconformist electorate. But, despite this setback, Churchill was determined to try again and remained convinced that the people of Oldham would welcome him as their representative if he could canvass enough support.

Churchill photographed in 1900
as the Conservative MP for Oldham.

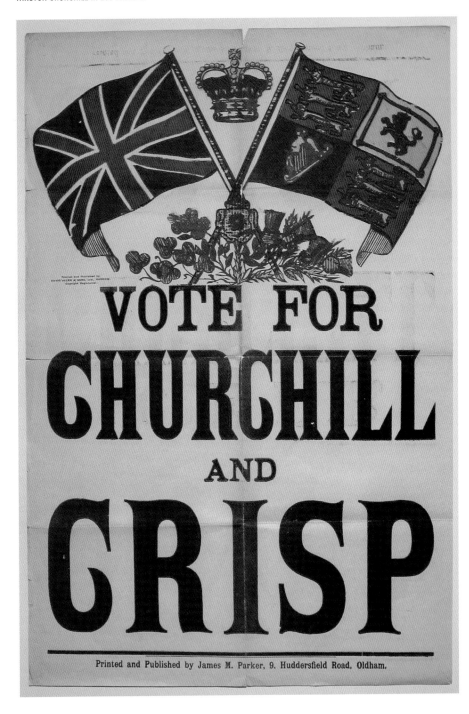

Churchill's new-found fame and fortune led to him standing for Parliament.

The answer to Churchill's problem was the press coverage of his Boer War experiences in late 1899, which made him a celebrity. When he returned home to Britain the following year to much public acclaim, the reputational boost certainly improved his standing in the imminent General Election, scheduled for 1 October 1900.

Keen to capitalise on his existing links with Oldham, he went to the town to drum up votes on 25 July 1900, almost exactly a year following his initial electoral defeat. But this time, Churchill was greeted by great cheering crowds and a brass band. Giving a speech in the local town hall, he related the story of how he had escaped from the Boers, stressing the important involvement of a mining engineer, one Dan Dewsnap, who had helped to hide Churchill during his time on the run. Dewsnap happened to come from Oldham, and Churchill's gratitude to this 'local hero' predictably went down very well with his audience. As the election was being held while the Boer War was still ongoing, Churchill could take full advantage of public patriotism for the conflict.

The result of the Oldham election was a close call, with the Liberals once again heading the poll, but Churchill was successfully elected as Oldham's second MP. It would mark the beginning of his exceptionally long career as a Member of Parliament, although Churchill would always be something of a remote parliamentary representative for his various constituencies, much preferring to be near the centre of power in London.

APR

15 | Letter from Major Pond, 2 November 1900

Churchill's *Morning Post* despatches from South Africa proved immensely popular among readers and were published in book form to great success.

Resigning his commission and returning to Britain in July 1900, Churchill found himself to have become something of a celebrity and in October published a further book on his South

An early portrait of Churchill, dating from around 1900, the time of his first lecture tour.

WINSTON SPENCER
CHURCHILL'S
AMERICAN TOUR
1900 ———— 1901

CONDUCTED BY
J. B. POND
EVERETT HOUSE 218 FOURTH
AVENUE NEW YORK

80

NEW YORK, **Nov. 2nd,** 1900

Mrs. Cornwallis West,
35a Great Cumberland Place,
London, W.

My Dear Madam:-

I want to congratulate you on the success of your
son,- a man who has attained a success at twenty-six which
most men would count brilliant at fifty.

Have you any idea how green your memory is here
in New York City ? I would suggest that you accompany your
son on the voyage and witness his reception here. It
seems to me it would be a very proud day for you, and your
friends here would appreciate it, and I need not add that it
would doubly enhance the value of the lecture.

Yours Very Truly,

J. B. Pond

African experiences, titled *Ian Hamilton's March*. That same month, he stood successfully in the General Election as a Conservative candidate in Oldham. As Members of Parliament were not salaried until 1911, it became a matter of some urgency for Churchill to boost his income before taking up his seat in February the following year, and a lecture tour to promote his new book was the obvious answer.

The tour would begin in Britain on 26 October 1900, taking in thirty locations across the country; the first happened to be his old school at Harrow where his talk was reported to have been 'received with loud applause'. Making revisions to his script as he progressed from town to town, Churchill projected photographic slides to illustrate particular points. Encouraged by his success, he decided to continue the tour overseas and embarked on 1 December for North America.

The agent responsible for promoting Churchill's first lecture tour of the United States was Major James Pond. A former abolitionist and supporter of the Underground Railroad who had also served as a Union officer during the American Civil War, Pond was a

Churchill decided on a lecture tour to capitalise on his fame as a war hero.

fascinating character in his own right who had been awarded the Medal of Honor for his 'extraordinary heroism'. During the 1870s, Pond had taken up a new role as lecture manager for writers including Mark Twain and Arthur Conan Doyle, and was now keen to represent Churchill.

In a letter of 2 November 1900, Pond attempted to persuade Churchill's mother to accompany her son to New York, the city of her birth. Jennie Churchill, now the recently remarried Mrs George Cornwallis-West, was clearly still regarded as a famous enough name to help generate interest in her son's tour. Pond described Churchill himself as 'a man who has attained a success at twenty-six which most men would count brilliant at sixty'.

Unfortunately for Churchill, the American lecture tour was not quite as successful as he had hoped. He encountered a degree of public opposition to the British involvement in South Africa, which generated some bad reviews in the American press and rather dented his

reputation as a popular speaker, although the tour did provide an opportunity for him to meet the elite of American society including Mark Twain, President William McKinley and future president Theodore Roosevelt.

Although initially grateful to Pond for promoting him in America, Churchill soon fell out with his manager, after having to speak to several near-empty houses; consequently, he would refer to him as 'a vulgar Yankee impresario'. While disappointed with this two-month-long American leg of the tour, Churchill remained buoyant over his earnings from the United Kingdom lectures and would resume touring through Europe in the spring of 1901, taking in Paris, Madrid and Gibraltar. Impressed by his overall earnings in such a relatively short space of time, Churchill would return to lecturing as a source of income on many future occasions.

APR

James B. Pond (1838–1903). Unlike Churchill, some of Pond's clients earned large sums from lecture tours he organised: Mark Twain and the explorer Henry Stanley, for example.

16 | *Why I Am A Free Trader,* April 1903

On the night of 10/11 May 1941 the chamber of the House of Commons was completely destroyed by a German incendiary bomb. In the debate held in October 1943 to decide the design of a new chamber, Churchill was a keen advocate of an oblong chamber, suggesting that this shape would prevent the chamber appearing too empty at any one time, encouraging adversarial debate while making 'crossing the floor', where a member leaves one party to join its opponents, an easier option. He reminded members that he had personal experience of that particular scenario.

Articles and pamphlets such as the one shown here were an important way for politicians to broadcast their opinions on important matters.

1904 saw Churchill switch his political allegiance to the Liberals.

Churchill had first taken up his seat in the House on 14 February 1901 as Conservative MP for Oldham in Lancashire. He sat in the 'Tory' benches, but espoused his father Randolph's concept of the 'Tory democrat' – essentially a 'fourth party' in Randolph's case, supporting more radical social policies and being openly critical of the Conservative leadership as well as the Liberal government. A lifelong apologist for Lord Randolph, Winston shared his father's rebellious streak, and, though he regularly defended his party, he also believed that principles should be put above blind party allegiance. In 1903–4 he found himself distanced from the government on various policies, but especially the treatment of the Boers in South Africa – against whom he had fought and whose political rights he now supported – and free trade. The government adhered to a protectionist trade policy, while Churchill and others felt that economic prosperity could only come about if tariffs were dropped and countries operated a free-trade regime. He spoke regularly in support of this idea and his published articles, such as the example shown here, were widely circulated.

This eventually led to his dramatic 'crossing the floor' of the House of Commons, to sit on the Liberal benches on 31 May 1904. The Conservative Prime Minister, Arthur Balfour, lost a major Commons vote in July 1905, but refused to resign, leading to one of the most vituperative invectives of Churchill's whole political career – most of it just typical Churchillian extravagance of oratory. On 4 December 1905 Balfour finally stood down and Sir Henry Campbell-Bannerman, leader of the Liberal Party, was asked to form a new, minority government.

Churchill was offered a senior post as Financial Secretary to the Treasury, but turned it down in favour of a lesser role of Under-Secretary of State for the Colonies, though because the Secretary of State, the Earl of Elgin, sat in the House of Lords, Churchill actually accreted a sizable level of responsibility. The party went on, in 1906, to win a landslide victory at the polls, a victory that Churchill described as a vindication of his father's life.

Though the policy of free trade lay at the heart of his reasons for 'ratting', as he called it, he wholeheartedly espoused the social policies of the Liberal Party and, with Lloyd George, who was to become Prime Minister in 1916, spent the next twenty years pushing through government policies that were to be the foundation of what we now know as the 'welfare state'. Policies we might think of as being tenets of the late twentieth century such as a living wage, labour exchanges, workers' unemployment insurance, reform of the prisons, rejection of capital punishment, regulation of industry and even introducing daylight saving time, were all measures the two supported which eventually became established rights.

He wavered on the right of votes for women (but supported the policy after the First World War), and, in a manner that was typical of Churchill's gallantry towards a former enemy, helped South Africa gain independence and dominion status (like Canada and Australia) in 1910.

Socially he had made himself a pariah in certain circles. His invective against Balfour and his slightly inept attempt to back Lord Milner against accusations of illegal treatment of Chinese labourers,

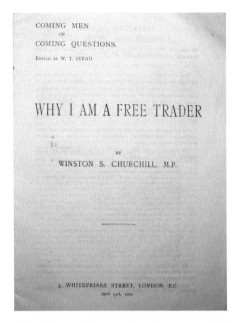

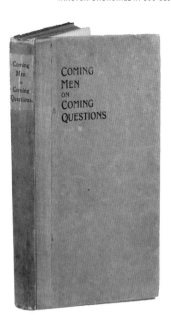

COMING MEN
ON
COMING QUESTIONS.

EDITED BY W. T. STEAD.

WHY I AM A FREE TRADER

BY

WINSTON S. CHURCHILL, M.P.

3, WHITEFRIARS STREET, LONDON, E.C.

April 13th, 1905.

Churchill's reputation as an important young politician is reflected in the inclusion of his free trade article in the book *Coming Men on Coming Questions,* edited by William T. Stead in 1905.

attracted odium from the King himself, who thought him a 'born cad' and 'simply scandalous', while others termed him a 'turncoat' and an 'arriviste'. The Hurlingham Polo Club rescinded his membership, while he felt obliged to resign from the Conservative Carlton Club. He simply went on to establish his own 'Other Club', in 1906, which would meet at regular intervals at the Savoy Hotel and counted among its membership not only close friends, but also political opponents. The Club still exists and meets regularly at the Savoy today. Churchill, who was never one to shy away from controversy in his political career, took the view that politicians should be judged on the level of animosity that they generated among their opposition.

One of the changes for which he was best known in this period and which established a system that was to remain central to the governance of Great Britain was the reform of the House of Lords,

which, in 1907, he disparaged for its ability to obstruct an elected government's policies at will. The measures introduced by Churchill and Lloyd George reduced the size of the house, and curbed its powers, changes which reverberate even today.

By 1924, appalled at the Liberal and Labour parties' mutual support, he had gradually moved back to the Conservative fold and won the constituency of Epping, east of London, as an independent constitutionalist with Conservative backing in the General Election that October. It was, in its different boundaries and titles, to be his constituency and the Conservatives his party for the rest of his political career. Soon after the election victory, Prime Minister Stanley Baldwin, who had been keen to have Churchill back onside, appointed him as Chancellor of the Exchequer.

PHR

17 | *Lord Randolph Churchill* Biography, 1906

Churchill's father, Lord Randolph, died in 1895 at the early age of forty-five when his son Winston was barely twenty years old.

Despite having been a strict parent, Randolph was in many ways an inspiration to his son, who was determined to follow a political career in his father's footsteps. During his final years in office, Randolph had become isolated within the Cabinet and lost much support, leading to his resignation in 1886 and his last speech in the House of to Winston's own growing reputation as a writer and politician. The general portrayal of Randolph was one of a sometimes extravagant man who enjoyed playing the game of politics. Yet many still believed him to have been a more cynical politician; as Theodore Roosevelt famously put it, Churchill's biography was a 'clever, forceful, rather cheap and vulgar life of that clever, forceful, rather cheap and vulgar egoist, his father'.

Churchill was, however, praised by many for having portrayed his father, as Oliver Cromwell demanded of his

---

One of Churchill's key literary works reveals much about his father's influence on him.

Commons in 1894. Yet Churchill resolved to vindicate his memory and pursued the same political aims as his father, at least to begin with. He adopted much of Randolph's philosophy and exhibited a similar kind of independence with regard to party politics; both men also served as Chancellor of the Exchequer, during which office they courted controversy.

One of the most obvious indications of how much Churchill admired his father is evidenced by the biography that he wrote of him, *Lord Randolph Churchill*, which was published in January 1906. The book received considerable attention, with readers eager to find out how the author would deal with his father's more controversial moments. It was also a very popular book due portraitist, 'warts and all', including his various faults and errors of judgement. The book was also admired for being based on personal correspondence and previously confidential papers which had been made available to Churchill by friends and colleagues.

However, more recent critics have pointed out that the biography is too heavily based on Randolph's political thoughts and decision-making rather than exploring his psychology and personality. Yet this perhaps reflects the time at which the book was written, with in-depth biographical studies being a more recent phenomenon. There have also been accusations that the author modified some of the evidence at his disposal in order to improve his father's reputation, yet it is

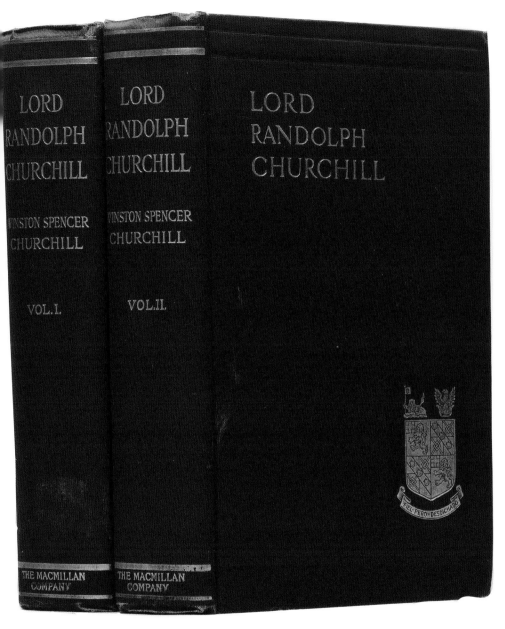

Churchill's biography of his father was first published in two volumes in 1906.

worth remembering that Churchill had to be careful about any commentary on his father's contemporaries, since many were still alive and active in the political world. Overall, it would be fair to say that the biography does indeed show Winston's family bias more than anything else and this, in retrospect, is one of the most interesting things about it.

The biography would not be the last time that Churchill revisited his father's life. In 1947, he wrote an essay entitled

Lord Randolph Churchill,
photographed in the
prime of his life.

The Dream in which he imagined a meeting with his long-deceased father and described to him the tumultuous events of the first half of the twentieth century.

On another occasion, while sharing a meal with guests, Churchill was asked the popular dinner party question of which historical figure he would want to join them. Without any hesitation, he chose his father.

APR

18 | The Temple of Diana, Blenheim Palace

While Churchill's mother would act as his main supporter in the early years of his political career, Jennie's role was soon eclipsed by Winston's wife Clementine, whom he married on 12 September 1908.

The couple had first met some four years before at a ball organised by the Earl and Countess of Crewe, yet had only begun courting after a dinner engagement in the spring of 1908. Churchill proposed to her in the Temple of Diana summer house, located in the grounds of his ancestral home of Blenheim Palace. Clementine (or Clemmie, as he

affectionately called her) would remain at Churchill's side until his death, giving him her full support despite the strains and stresses of being married to such an ebullient, active and important politician.

During the First World War, Clementine organised special YMCA canteens for munitions workers, in support of her husband's role as Minister for Munitions. Then, soon after the conflict, in 1922, she went on the electoral campaign trail on his behalf while he was incapacitated in hospital having his appendix removed.

The Second World War brought even greater challenges for the wife of the

Built by Sir William Chambers in 1772–3, the Temple of Diana served as a summer house in the grounds of Blenheim Palace.

Churchill's wife would become his strongest supporter throughout their long partnership.

Prime Minister. Clementine remained Churchill's regular companion during his many travels, whether inspecting bomb damage, military units or factory workers, and took on roles in numerous wartime charities. Among the most notable of these initiatives was the Red Cross Aid to Russia Fund, for which she raised a considerable amount of money and as a result was invited to tour the Soviet Union as a personal guest of Stalin. Her visit to Russia coincided with VE-Day, robbing her of the opportunity to be at Churchill's side during the nation's celebration of victory.

She also proved to be a popular companion to Churchill on their trips to North America and became a favourite of the American people, handling journalists effectively and being greatly admired for her public speaking, despite having been forced to conquer her natural shyness. Through her husband's work Clementine was ultimately involved in many aspects of the war, and her approachability and general appeal did much to foster Anglo-American relations.

Clementine's devotion and loyalty to Churchill were never in question. She certainly did not hesitate to defend her husband against public criticism, yet would be quick to point out mistakes to him in private when she felt that he had let himself down. Churchill was by all accounts rarely an easy man to work or live with, and Clementine's influence undoubtedly helped his relationships with staff and colleagues receiving the sharp end of rebuttals or sarcasm. While Churchill did not always take his wife's advice, he trusted her implicitly and recognised that she was his most robust supporter throughout their long and happy partnership.

APR

Clementine Hozier, photographed to mark the occasion of her engagement to Churchill in 1908.

19 | St Margaret's Church, Westminster

After a very short engagement, Churchill and Clementine Hozier were married at St Margaret's Church in Westminster, the church of the Houses of Parliament, on 12 September 1908.

At the end of Churchill's 1930 autobiography, *My Early Life*, he sums up his sentiments on his marriage with the simple words: 'I married and lived happily ever after.' That clearly does not capture the inevitable ups and downs of married life, but it certainly characterises the true devotion he held for his wife. It was a marriage that held firm till his death in 1965 and which was utterly imbued with love and affection, as his correspondence with Clementine bears witness.

Their correspondence also indicates just how difficult Churchill must have been to live with. At its simplest is the fact that he and 'Clemmie' would often write to each other when in the same house, mainly as

Clementine's only means of getting her point across. His letters, especially those with frank accounts of the risks he took while serving on the Western Front in 1915–16, show he spared her few details.

But these are also the couple who wrote to each other as 'cat' (her) and 'pug' (him), ending their letters with sweet drawings of their animal IDs. But Clementine was neither love-sick nor gullible: she was alive to Churchill's failings, even before they wed, not least his constant tendency to be late. (He proposed to her in the Temple of Diana at Blenheim, after the Duke had ushered him there when he had forgotten a planned assignation with Clemmie at which he was due to ask her hand in marriage.) But when Clementine wrote to Winston, shortly after their engagement, on 11 August 1908, '*Je t'aime passionnément*' ['I love you passionately'], she too was airing a very real devotion, despite all the challenges it faced.

St Margaret's, the parish church for the Palace of Westminster.

Churchill experienced the inevitable ups and downs of married life.

Most prominent of the challenges that Churchill gave his wife was his attitude to money, with the pair suffering from relative (within their class) penury from their first days of marriage, made worse by Churchill's extravagances, expensive tastes, self-indulgence and gambling addiction. The last in particular was a serious concern for Clementine, trying to manage a house (bought without first consulting her and which was forever a financial liability), a household (with Churchill's lifelong tendency to employ ever more staff), family commitments and, a corollary to his station in life, an expensive social round.

It is little surprise that, in the mid-1930s, when Churchill was out of government and was struggling financially, that Clementine went off cruising on a yacht with a wealthy friend, with whom she seems to have had a flirtation. Alone (albeit with a sizable staff), Churchill was helpless and clearly missed his beloved wife. She had proved herself a steadfast supporter when he was out of office, making sure that those in power knew he would be back. She campaigned for him in elections and was his comfort when he was at his lowest ebbs. When she died in December 1977, she had arranged for her ashes to be strewn on his grave, so that they would be together for eternity.

PHR

The impressive main aisle and chancel of St Margaret's, where Winston and Clementine were wed.

20 | Suffragette Pepper Holders

As Churchill entered politics at the beginning of the twentieth century, women's suffrage was already an increasingly important issue. The idea of women being given the vote had been opposed by much popular opinion in Victorian Britain, with Churchill himself commenting in 1897 that the political views of women should be represented by their husband's vote. Indeed, many British women (including his own mother) would have agreed with him in that era, when politics was commonly viewed as a somewhat rowdy male pastime.

But as government involvement in everyday life increased from the turn of the century, public opinion began to change and Churchill's views similarly adapted as he developed a more sophisticated political attitude. He was also certainly influenced by Clementine, an ardent supporter of women's suffrage. From the beginning of his career in

This poster, dating from 1909, advertises the weekly Suffragette newspaper *Votes for Women*.

Parliament, Churchill therefore supported the principle (albeit in a rather lukewarm manner) and voted for it as early as 1904.

Yet his attitude wavered somewhat over the next decade, as militant suffragettes began to cause social discontent in order to make their voices heard, disrupting parliamentary debates and a number of Churchill's own speeches. Women's suffrage soon became a matter for widespread debate, the argument even finding its way into novelty household items like this pair of Edwardian silver pepper holders featured here (whose placards display the promise that they could 'make things hot for you'). Churchill therefore resisted certain measures intended to introduce women's suffrage, although this appears to have been in response to the militant element, rather than any overall belief that the principle was unjust.

Many others, including Prime Minister Herbert Asquith, were ardently opposed

---

Churchill supported the principle of women's suffrage, yet was cautious over its introduction.

---

to the whole concept of giving women the vote.

It was, however, this perceived opposition to women's suffrage which led to Churchill being attacked on 14 November 1909, when arriving at Bristol railway station to attend a local speaking engagement. Theresa Garnett broke through a police cordon on the platform and struck at Churchill with a dog whip, cutting his face. Churchill seized her and, after a struggle, she was taken into police custody. Garnett had been a militant suffragette for some time, having already been arrested on several occasions earlier that year for disorderly conduct within the Palace of Westminster. Along with other activists, she had chained herself to one of the statues in the central lobby of Parliament.

Churchill did not press charges for the assault, which would have landed Garnett a more severe punishment than the month's imprisonment she was given for disturbing the peace. While in prison, she went on hunger strike and was force-fed,

tried to set her cell on fire, and finished her prison sentence in hospital. Although still supporting the women's vote, she dropped militancy and ended up caring for wounded soldiers on the Western Front, for which she was commended for her 'gallant and distinguished service'.

Indeed, the crucial role played by women during the war strengthened the support of Churchill and others for women's suffrage, which was finally introduced in February 1918 for most women aged over thirty. Yet he remained cautious, opposing the extension of the franchise in subsequent years to younger women in case it might increase the Labour vote. He also expressed concerns over universal suffrage in the 1930s, seeing a link between extensions of the franchise in Europe and the rise of dictatorships. Yet these concerns were more strategically motivated than anything else, and certainly indicative of his Victorian upbringing.

APR

21 | Astrakhan Coat

In the Victorian era London's East End had often been characterised by destitution, over-crowding and crime. The late nineteenth century had also seen a dramatic influx of migrants to the capital, which caused even more societal unrest as different cultures clashed. Many newcomers had originated from eastern Europe, from where both religious and political persecution had encouraged them to flee.

Gang clashes and incidents involving socialist revolutionaries became increasingly common in the East End at the turn of the century, and worrying violence erupted on a number of occasions. For Churchill, in post as Home Secretary from 15 February 1910, the East End was a danger zone which needed to be watched carefully. A specific concern was gun crime, at a time when British police were not normally issued with firearms.

Since the beginning of 1909, one particular gang of revolutionaries from Russian Latvia had been responsible for a series of crimes in London, which were widely covered by the press, and the criminals as a result had become something of a sensation. An armed robbery in Tottenham on 23 January 1910 led to a dramatic police chase in which shots were fired, leading to two fatalities and twenty-seven people being injured. Then a plan to rob a jeweller's shop in Houndsditch by tunnelling through from an adjacent property was thwarted on 16 December 1910, leading to a street battle in which three unarmed policemen were killed before the gang fled.

A manhunt began for the criminals, in the face of public outrage that such events could be allowed to happen. After a few days the police learned that two members of the Latvian gang were hiding at 100 Sidney Street nearby and the force moved in on the morning of 3 January 1911 to lay siege to the property.

Churchill's time as Home Secretary gave him a notable opportunity to involve himself in police operations at ground level.

Armed police surrounded the house and a gunfight commenced, the criminals refusing to surrender. A stalemate was soon apparent, and calls for military reinforcements were made which reached the Home Secretary while he was enjoying his morning bath. Churchill would admit that he could never resist his strong sense of curiosity and desire to be at the centre of any action and, once dressed, he therefore rushed to the Home Office to size up the situation before leaving for Sidney Street itself. Hastening to the front of the cordon, Churchill was conspicuous in his astrakhan-collared coat, as illustrated here and now preserved at the Churchill War Rooms, plus top hat. While not taking actual command of the police,

Churchill, pictured in the middle of the photograph and seen wearing his astrakhan coat and top hat, on the scene of the Sidney Street siege.

he was clearly the figure of authority on the scene that everybody looked to for ways to resolve the situation.

Never one to shirk from giving an opinion, Churchill encouraged calls for artillery guns to support a storming of the residence, as well as metal bulletproof shielding to allow the police to approach the house safely. But before any of these plans could be put into full operation, a fire unexpectedly broke out on the upper floor of the building and began to spread. The London Fire Brigade arrived but Churchill stepped in, with the support of the police, to stop them extinguishing the flames, in the hope that it would force the gang members to give themselves up. However, the fire spread before any surrender was possible, and the two criminals were later found burned to

death inside. Five firemen were also hurt during the incident, one of them dying from his injuries six months later.

Afterwards, Churchill was mocked for his attendance at the siege in so public a manner. Accusations were made that he was 'grandstanding' in a moment of self-publicity, and his presence at Sidney Street was indeed memorably recorded in both newspaper photographs and newsreel film footage, in which he can be seen at the front of the cordon, gesturing excitedly at those around him. Forced to clarify his position, he wrote to *The Times* to explain that he was careful not to over-rule the police authorities on the scene. His real reason for being there was a simple desire to be where the action was, to witness the situation first-hand and to satisfy the same impulse which years later would encourage him to want to watch the D-Day landings. Churchill himself later regretted attending the siege.

The aftermath of the siege saw increased demands for more stringent laws regarding immigration, with Churchill personally proposing a harsh Aliens (Prevention of Crime) Bill directed against 'unassimilated foreigners'. In the event, his bill failed to receive the necessary support. Churchill's radicalism was now directed in a much more right-wing manner, perhaps as a direct reaction against the social disorder that he was tasked with addressing.

The most important outcome of the siege was that the Metropolitan Police were given access to better firearms in future. But Churchill would forever be associated with the incident, despite his tangential influence on its result; the striking image of the top-hatted gentleman in the astrakhan coat would live on in images of the event.

APR

22 | HMS *Enchantress*

Churchill was appointed as the new First Lord of the Admiralty (the title then given to Britain's Navy Minister) on 24 October 1911. As the political head of the Royal Navy, he was now in direct control of the Admiralty and served as the government's senior adviser on all naval affairs.

Within a matter of days, he had made his key concerns known through a Cabinet memorandum which called

yacht was bought by the Royal Navy to be used exclusively by the First Lord of the Admiralty and fellow Admiralty Board members. At 320 feet long and displacing 3,470 tons, she could travel at 18 knots and carried three 3-pounder guns, plus a complement of 196 officers and ratings.

During the almost three years that he served as peacetime First Lord, Churchill spent a total of eight months travelling in the *Enchantress*. He wasted no time

---

Churchill's role as First Lord of the Admiralty brought with it certain benefits, including his own ship which would serve as a home away from home.

---

for the establishment of a Naval Staff in preparation for a likely European conflict. For his next two and a half years in the post, Churchill made such warlike preparations his overwhelming priority and visited hundreds of naval stations, dockyards and ships both around the British Isles and in the Mediterranean, coming to understand naval tactics and gunnery skills while seeking to ensure that the nation stayed ahead of Germany's ever-advancing naval construction. These itinerant duties were made possible through his regular use of the official Admiralty yacht, HMS *Enchantress*.

HMS *Enchantress* was built by Harland and Wolff, the leading shipbuilders based in Belfast who would later construct the famous trio of White Star passenger liners *Olympic*, *Titanic* and *Britannic*. Launched in November 1903, the steam-powered

in adopting the ship as his new office, arriving on board on 5 November 1911 for his first voyage. On this occasion he set off from Cowes on the Isle of Wight, in order to inspect the dockyard and submarine depot at Portsmouth; three days later, Churchill and HMS *Enchantress* joined the naval vessels escorting the King and Queen out of Portsmouth harbour on their embarkation for India. Some MPs would come to question the not insignificant costs of keeping such an Admiralty vessel, yet Churchill was quick to refute such arguments by stressing the ship's importance in ensuring he could stay in touch with all corners of the naval empire.

By 1913 the impressive accommodation on board HMS *Enchantress* had led to the vessel becoming Churchill's second home, and he encouraged friends, family and

HMS *Enchantress*, originally launched at Belfast on 7 November 1903 and constructed at a cost of £131,000.

colleagues to come aboard the ship at any opportunity. Clementine would join her husband on voyages whenever possible, while Prime Minister Herbert Asquith and his family were also frequent visitors. A Mediterranean voyage in the summer of that year saw the ship travel to Malta where Lord Kitchener came aboard to discuss matters of defence.

As a European war became increasingly likely over the summer of 1914, many of the crew of the *Enchantress* were transferred to more active roles and the yacht converted into a floating field hospital for officers. She would be re-commissioned in 1919 after the war but finally scrapped at Dover in June 1935. Teak from the yacht was extensively recycled, and can still be identified having been re-purposed into items of furniture. Churchill would always remember his time on the yacht with definite affection.

APR

23 | *Punch* Cartoon, 1913

In a 1931 article he wrote for the *Strand Magazine* entitled 'Cartoons and Cartoonists' Churchill recollects how a photographer had suddenly appeared while he was walking on Southport beach in 1910 and snapped him wearing a hat that had been randomly packed in his luggage and which was far too small for his head. This one picture led to his being identified in the public imagination as having a penchant for odd hats and also to cartoonists regularly picturing him in various items of headgear. He acknowledged the value of having a distinctive characteristic to aid

link him with today. *Punch* was ahead of the game, with its May 1913 cartoon of him lounging half asleep on board HMS *Enchantress*, smoking his famous cigar, with Prime Minister Herbert Asquith seated next to him. Both men were supposedly inspecting naval facilities in the Mediterranean at the time.

The V-signs, the bulldog and the bow tie all became fodder for cartoonists in the Second World War, when Churchill and his image were the biggest focus of public attention. While Churchill exploited photography and posters for building his public persona, cartoonists, in many

---

As a leading politician, Churchill was a regular feature in satirical cartoons.

---

public recognition but utterly dismissed the idea that he had unusual tastes in hats. Yet Churchill, ever alive to the value of publicity, decided to exploit the public interest and on at least one occasion bought a new hat on purpose to fulfil the need of his cartoonists.

Churchill was a natural subject for cartoonists throughout his political career and he generally enjoyed their attention and the publicity it gave him. He appreciated the PR value of the cartoonist, arguing that politicians would even feel offended when their portrayals stopped appearing in newspapers and magazines.

The cartoonists' obsession with Churchill's hats lasted for a few decades, before the hat was supplanted by the cigar as the one item above all, that we

ways, established his image more than anybody else. Sidney Strube's 8 June 1940 *Daily Express* cartoon of Churchill as a stern bulldog in a steel helmet marked 'Go to it' and staring across the English Channel from the south coast, and 'Poy's 1941 cartoon of him as a friendly cigar-smoking, bow-tie-wearing bulldog, set the image in the public mind of Churchill as the fearsome guard dog, raring to fight any opponent, or, as in a July 1943 cartoon, biting the tail of the German dachshund. Ironically, though Churchill owned numerous dogs throughout his life, he only kept one bulldog (briefly and against school rules, while he was at Harrow).

Churchill's rapid rise to a position of power – Under-Secretary of State for the

This *Punch* cartoon from May 1913 was titled 'Under His Master's Eye'. While the two relax aboard HMS *Enchantress*, Churchill asks if there is any news from home, to which Asquith replies, 'How can there be with you here?'

Colonies – only six years after entering Parliament, ensured that he would feature prominently in the news organs of the day, and, inevitably, in caricatures and cartoons, and it is at this point that the portrayal moves from respectful caricaturist portraits to cartoons, highlighting particular characteristics.

Harold Nicolson remarked that 'There is always a time-lag between the date when the features of a politician become generally recognizable and recognized and the date when they assume what might be called standard caricatural form.' It wasn't until 1920 and the arrival on the scene of the New Zealander, David (later Sir David) Low, that the caricature of Churchill began to take off.

Ironically, given that Low was to become Churchill's favourite cartoonist, the most famous of his early Churchill cartoons is heavily critical, showing Churchill standing on top of 'decayed cats', each noted as failures of his career (Sidney Street, the Dardanelles, Antwerp and Russian intervention).

From his first encounter with Churchill at a dinner in 1922 Low saw him as 'an upholder of democracy … when he was leading it. Impatient with it when he was not,' and he was critical of Churchill's obsessive campaigns, initially against

Bolshevism and then against Indian self-government.

In his cartoons he depicts Churchill as a rhinoceros, 'tough of hide, short of sight' and later annoyed Churchill intensely with his cartoon of him as 'mahatma windhi', leading to Churchill dismissing Low as a 'radical' and 'mischievous'. Churchill was subsequently satirised in cartoons as a proto-Mussolini, whom Churchill initially admired, and as an armed tribal African war deity, carrying a spear and a pen, for his call for Britain to re-arm in the 1930s.

The public clamour in 1939 for Churchill to be brought back into government was vigorously supported by the press cartoonists, the most evocative being *Punch*'s 12 July 1939 cartoon of him as Drake playing bowls and awaiting the Spanish Armada. Four days after Churchill became Prime Minister in May 1940 the *Evening Standard* published a cartoon by Low that was to become possibly the most famous of all of Churchill – and certainly one of Churchill's favourites – 'All behind you Winston', showing a tough Churchill rolling up his sleeves and leading his coalition Cabinet to the fight.

During the war, most cartoons of Churchill were sympathetic and relatively uncritical, with eminent cartoonists such as Leslie Illingworth and Philip Zec joining Low in showing Churchill as tough, resolute and forever smoking a cigar.

However, after Churchill's defeat at the 1945 election Low produced a cartoon showing him on a plinth marked 'the leader of humanity', telling his alter ego, 'the party leader', that 'they will forget you, but they will remember me'.

But that was not the end of the cartoonists' treatment of Churchill. Illingworth, who had drawn many sympathetic cartoons of Churchill deeply upset him in February 1954 with his cartoon captioned: 'Man goeth forth unto his work and to his labour till the evening' and showed Churchill visibly affected by a recent partial paralysis.

Strube by contrast paid tribute to Churchill's achievements in his *Daily Express* cartoon of 29 November 1953, entitled 'A man in his time plays many parts', while in the next year, when pressure was growing for Churchill to stand down at last, Low made his final tribute to Churchill in his February 1954 cartoon 'the grand old evergreen'.

PHR

24 | First Lord of the Admiralty's Telephone

It was President Roosevelt's habit during the Second World War to address correspondence to Churchill as 'Former Naval Person'. However, although he twice served as First Lord of the Admiralty (1911–15 and 1939–40), Churchill never served in the Navy. He had honorary ranks in the Army (as colonel of his original regiment, the 4th Queen's Own Hussars) and Air Force (as Air Commodore of No. 615 Squadron), but no such honorary rank in the Royal Navy. Indeed, his usual 'naval' uniform was that of an Elder Brother of Trinity House, the body responsible for British lighthouses and other navigational markers and also a maritime charity, where he was sworn in, in 1913.

Churchill was appointed First Lord of the Admiralty at the age of thirty-six, his third major government role. Much of his reputation in this post rests on his success in getting

the fleet better prepared for war in 1914, mainly by ensuring that new ships would generally use modern oil-fired engines rather than inefficient coal burning designs (Churchill secured Great Britain's oil supply from the Middle East with a deal concluded in the summer of 1914).

Throughout his initial term as First Lord of the Admiralty, Churchill would have used the telephone illustrated here. It sat on the First Lord's desk at the Admiralty building in Whitehall, and would be used by Churchill and his successors, Arthur Balfour, Sir Edward Carson and Sir Eric Geddes.

One of the accusations levelled against Churchill in the higher echelons of the Navy (and it was a trait he retained, to the annoyance of many, throughout the Second World War) was that he had a bad habit of talking with officers below flag rank and acting on their advice, without consulting their seniors. The Navy was also the victim both of his wit and his tendency sometimes to let his verbosity run away with itself, as when, in 1913, he was criticised by one admiral for scuttling naval tradition by converting ships to oil-fired engines, and allegedly responded by dismissing naval tradition as no more

hundreds of thousands of British, French, Indian, Australian, New Zealand – and Turkish – lives. As a result Churchill was effectively forced out of office in late 1915 and his political career evaporated. The subsequent enquiry largely exonerated him, but the dirt stuck.

In his second term of office as First Lord in 1939–40 he could so easily have seen his career taking a similar nosedive

---

Churchill's terms of office as First Lord of the Admiralty were full of controversy.

---

than 'rum, sodomy and the lash'. The folk punk group The Pogues ensured his words were not forgotten by using the phrase as the title of a 1985 album.

It was in his capacity as chief overseer of the Navy that Churchill embarked on his slightly madcap mission to try and defend Antwerp against the rapid German advance in October 1914. The mission itself, involving the use of Churchill's recently created land-based naval force, the Royal Naval Division, was doomed to failure, though it did buy valuable time in holding back the German offensive into France. It was also another occasion of Churchill 'grandstanding', insisting on effectively personally taking over command of the defence force on the spot.

The next year, 1915, Churchill pressed forward with his grand plan for opening a new front against Turkey through a naval attack against the strategically significant Dardanelles strait. Though it had wide support in the various branches of the military, Churchill was generally blamed for the failure of the operation, which expanded into a ground campaign on the Gallipoli peninsula that cost

to his post-Dardanelles experience, as he shared responsibility for the costly failure of Britain's attempt to ward off a German invasion of Norway in April–May 1940. Instead, famously, blame rested at the door of the prime minister of the day, Neville Chamberlain, facilitating Churchill's accession, at last, to the premiership.

As the operation to invade France, Operation Overlord, approached in June 1944, Churchill made plans to go over on D-Day itself, on board HMS *Belfast*, which was to fire the first shots against the beaches targeted by British forces. Attempts at the highest level to dissuade him – the Chief of the General Staff, the Supreme Commander of the operation, General Eisenhower, even King George VI himself – were unsuccessful. Finally, a second letter from the King, entreating him not to go, made him change his mind, though he went just six days later, when it was still supremely dangerous. He was taken across on board the destroyer HMS *Kelvin*, and he was wearing the uniform of Trinity House.

PHR

25 | Colt .45-inch Automatic Pistol

C hurchill had been made a scapegoat for the failure of the Dardanelles campaign, and it was clear that any continued involvement in directing the war would no longer be possible on his part. Feeling let down by Asquith and others in the government, he decided to fight in the front line. Resigning from his Cabinet position in the coalition government, he decided to return to military service and so resumed his commission as an officer in the British Army, embarking for France and Belgium in November 1915 in order to make his mark there.

To gain experience of the trenches, Churchill was initially attached to the Grenadier Guards before being promoted

---

Churchill decided to continue fighting the First World War in the most direct way possible.

---

to lieutenant-colonel in command of the 6th Battalion, Royal Scots Fusiliers, in January 1916. He deliberately avoided the comparatively safe option of a staff position away from the front and instead spent over three months in the front line.

Churchill's Colt .45 pistol featured his name engraved along the side.

him by Clementine, including hampers of food from Fortnum & Mason and ample supplies of alcohol. He would go so far as to fill letters to his wife with detailed lists of culinary requirements, ensuring that his diet did not suffer unnecessarily by having to rely on basic Army rations.

When his battalion commandeered a hospice run by the Sisters of Zion, Churchill successfully persuaded the nuns to cook up soup and other meals for himself and his fellow officers. His personal hygiene was catered for, too, by a portable tin bath and hot water tank which travelled along with him.

Throughout his time in the trenches, Churchill carried a Colt .45-inch automatic pistol. He had originally purchased it in London in 1915 and it is reputed to have remained one of his favourite guns, as he kept it for many years afterwards. The pistol certainly bears signs of frequent use, and is likely to be the same one that Churchill would later employ in the Second World War for target practice. He had his name engraved on this weapon.

Churchill took great delight in directing his men in the core duties of

He was fortunate that his service on the Western Front occurred at a time when no major battles were being fought in the British sector. Yet shell bombardments were a daily occurrence, along with the constant threat from rifle and machine-gun fire.

Despite the regular dangers Churchill faced at the front, he did not appear to be overly bothered about personal safety and by all accounts completely ignored the discomfort of life in the trenches. Admittedly, for him the basic nature of trench life was ameliorated somewhat by the comforts of home that were sent to

trench construction while looking after their health and safety, yet could not help but make impractical suggestions to 'improve' their situation, such as ordering artillery bombardments for no obvious advantage but which provoked the Germans to retaliate in kind. While he propounded strict orders in the trenches, he could also be generous and full of humour, allowing fellow officers to use his tin bath and keeping everybody entertained during mess times.

He had already suggested new inventions to fight the war, such as more sophisticated armoured vehicles capable of dealing with trenches and rough ground, and had formed a Landships Committee to investigate the idea while still at the Admiralty in February 1915. But his new-found experience of serving in the trenches allowed Churchill to push such ideas (which led to the first tanks) with greater clout.

Churchill used his time on the Western Front as an opportunity to lead by example, as he often undertook reconnaissance into no-man's land under the cover of darkness. He experienced several narrow escapes, with one in

Churchill photographed in Armentières, France, on 11 February 1916, having just been appointed to command of the 6th Battalion, Royal Scots Fusiliers.

particular having a profound effect on his attitude to death. On 24 November he had been called to meet a staff car behind the lines which would take him to a meeting with his corps commander. But after an hour's walk in dangerous conditions, he reached the location only to find that the car had turned back due to shelling. Churchill trudged angrily back to the trenches, cursing his commander, only to find his dugout in ruins – it had received a direct hit by a shell, killing one of the three officers who were inside at the time. The fatality might easily have been Churchill himself.

Despite the excitement of life in the trenches, Churchill still aspired to return to politics. In London on leave during March 1916, he took the opportunity to make a speech in Parliament which, although badly received, reminded people of his continued presence. The official investigation undertaken by the Dardanelles Commission would allow him to give his side of the story behind the Gallipoli debacle, while the amalgamation of his battalion with another and subsequent loss of his command allowed him to re-evaluate his military future. Churchill decided to return to civilian life.

APR

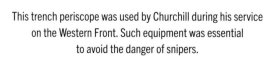

This trench periscope was used by Churchill during his service on the Western Front. Such equipment was essential to avoid the danger of snipers.

26 | Churchill's Collapsible Easel

Despite a brief dalliance with sketching whilst at school, Churchill only began to consider painting as a serious pastime in 1915 at the age of forty. His sister-in-law Lady Gwendeline Churchill (affectionately known as 'Goonie') was already an enthusiastic amateur, and during a visit to Winston's Hoe Farm country house near Godalming suggested that he take up such a hobby to help dispel the melancholy from which he was suffering as a result of the Gallipoli failure.

Lady Gwendeline offered him her young sons' watercolour paints and advice on how to get started, but within days Churchill had gone out and purchased his own easel, oil paints, palette and brushes. He was clearly taking his new hobby very seriously.

To further his skills, he invited Hazel Lavery to visit a few days later; the wife of the distinguished artist Sir John Lavery, Hazel was a talented painter in her own right, and both Laverys tutored Churchill in his new-found hobby. Friend and colleague Edward Marsh would describe Churchill's 'new enthusiasm' as 'a distraction and a sedative that brought a measure of ease to his frustrated spirit'.

Churchill with his collapsible easel,
which allowed him to paint outside.

First taken up as a means to combat his melancholy,
painting became Churchill's main method for relaxation.

Churchill would continue to pursue his love of painting for the rest of his life, whenever opportunity permitted. Early 1916 saw him set up an easel at his Laurence Farm billets on the Western Front, even as shells exploded above the nearby village of Ploegsteert, intent on capturing a view of the farm with its many shell holes and signs of battle damage. Rather than ruminating over the troubled political situation or the immediate danger to his own life, Churchill could direct his energy into a more creative and rewarding pursuit.

Despite having only taken up the brush a few years earlier, he wrote two articles for the *Strand Magazine* in 1921 and 1922 which extolled the pleasures to be gained from painting – he was never one to miss an opportunity to make money from writing. His articles proved popular among readers and no doubt encouraged him to develop his own skills further. Travelling to all corners of the world for either official political business or personal pleasure, Churchill would seize any opportunity to set up his easel, whether in breaks between peace conferences or in the middle of lecture tours.

An opportunity to expand his hobby further presented itself in 1924, when Churchill moved into his new home of Chartwell in Kent. Here, he was able to create a large artist's studio. Constructed in the gardens, away from the main house, the studio allowed Churchill to paint without fear of interruption and so became a favourite refuge, particularly during his so-called 'wilderness years' of the 1930s. A wooden grid system was installed on the walls, allowing the artist

Churchill paints another landscape. He particularly enjoyed painting outdoors when opportunity permitted.

to display many of the paintings that he would execute over the following years. Although he continued to prefer to paint outdoors in order to take advantage of the light, with landscapes therefore among his favourite subjects, he also painted still-life compositions of bottles, fruit and glassware. Friends and family would recall Churchill's enthusiasm when setting eyes on an interesting bottle or jar that might form the basis for a new painting.

Some critics dismiss Churchill's drawing and composition skills, yet most admire his use of colour; he favoured bright tones in a style that could be seen to represent attempts to dispel the misery he often felt as a result of being idle. Churchill himself always insisted that he painted purely for his own pleasure and, despite welcoming compliments about his work, was keen to avoid being regarded as too ambitious in his hobby.

Churchill continued to seek and accept constructive criticism throughout his life, befriending established painters such as Walter Sickert and studying the works of others, including Turner, Pissarro and Singer Sargent. Many notable artists accepted invitations to visit Churchill in his studio at Chartwell, while the Anglo-French painter Paul Maze would join him on a number of painting trips. The only time that Churchill neglected his hobby was during the Second World War, when the pressures of leadership meant that he simply did not have the leisure to devote to such pleasures. He did, however, find the opportunity to produce one painting at Marrakesh in January 1943.

Perhaps inevitably, Churchill's post-war reputation as a world leader would serve to boost his repute as a painter. He submitted two paintings to the Royal Academy Summer Show in 1947 under the pseudonym of David Winter and was successful in having his work exhibited (though it has since been suggested that his real identity was, in fact, known). The Royal Academy went on to recognise him as an Honorary Academician Extraordinary in 1948, and other galleries and critics heaped praise upon him for his enthusiasm as a painter.

Yet the importance of painting in Churchill's life remained chiefly as a means to keep his mind active during moments when he might otherwise be struck down by the gloominess which always threatened to reappear.

APR

27 | Dardanelles Report, March 1917

For many centuries the Dardanelles, the narrow strip of water in north-western Turkey dividing Europe from Asia, has been of great strategic significance.

When the Ottoman Empire entered the First World War in 1914 in support of Germany, the Dardanelles was effectively closed in order to prevent access to the Sea of Marmara and thereby protect the Turkish capital of Constantinople from naval bombardment and to block the passage of ships to and from Britain's ally Russia across the Black Sea. As the fighting on the Western Front turned into a stalemate by the end of 1914, the

hold back the invaders and the campaign was finally abandoned in January 1916. It had been a complete failure on almost every level, with total casualties on the two sides reaching a figure of over half a million.

As one of the chief instigators of the Dardanelles campaign, and having served as one of the key members of the committee which had overseen its direction, Churchill was perceived by many to be personally responsible for the campaign's failure and subsequently received much of the blame. Criticism towards him had already begun early on during the Dardanelles affair, and

---

Churchill's reputation received a major blow from his involvement in the Dardanelles campaign.

---

opening of a new front via an attack on the Dardanelles presented itself as an attractive new strategy for the British and French.

Many in Britain, including Churchill, felt that removing Turkey from the war would weaken Germany. As First Lord of the Admiralty, Churchill pushed for an attack by ships alone in order to force the Dardanelles, yet such a plan relied on a gross underestimation of the strength of the Turkish defences. British and French ships began an unsuccessful naval assault on 19 February 1915, which was followed by military landings on the Gallipoli peninsula on 25 April. Despite a fresh assault in August, the Turks managed to

reached a point in May 1915 when he was effectively sacked as First Lord of the Admiralty by Prime Minister Asquith. Churchill's removal was a condition imposed by the Conservatives before they would help Asquith form a new coalition government, while Churchill's increasing disagreements with the First Sea Lord (the professional head of the Navy), Admiral Lord Fisher, had already created a tense atmosphere hardly conducive to winning the campaign. Churchill would, however, remain in the coalition Cabinet, in the more junior but still influential position of Chancellor of the Duchy of Lancaster.

But with his relationship with Asquith fast deteriorating, Churchill felt that

DARDANELLES COMMISSION.

FIRST REPORT.

[Excisions in this Report, which have been made for diplomatic, naval, or military reasons, are shewn by asterisks, thus   *   *   *   *   *.

Any words that have been inserted are shewn in square brackets, thus [   ]]

Presented to Parliament by Command of His Majesty.

LONDON:
PUBLISHED BY HIS MAJESTY'S STATIONERY OFFICE.

To be purchased through any Bookseller or directly from
H.M. STATIONERY OFFICE at the following addresses:
IMPERIAL HOUSE, KINGSWAY, LONDON, W.C., and 28, ABINGDON STREET, LONDON, S.W.;
37, PETER STREET, MANCHESTER; 1, ST. ANDREW'S CRESCENT, CARDIFF;
23, FORTH STREET, EDINBURGH;
or from E. PONSONBY, LTD., 116, GRAFTON STREET, DUBLIN;
or from the Agencies in the British Colonies and Dependencies,
the United States of America and other Foreign Countries of
T. FISHER UNWIN, LTD., LONDON, W.C.

1917.
Price 6d. Net.

[Cd. 8490.]

The First Report of the Dardanelles Commission provided the initial official findings of the investigation into why the campaign had failed.

In this Punch cartoon from May 1916, Churchill's political downfall has led to him turning to writing instead of politics – 'After all, some say the pen is mightier than the sword.'

the Prime Minister was making him a scapegoat for the Dardanelles failure. Regarding himself as increasingly sidelined and failing to secure the release of government papers that he believed would vindicate his position, Churchill resigned again in November 1915. He decided to take out his frustrations on the enemy in person, resuming his Army commission as an infantry officer in the trenches of the Western Front.

A Commission of Inquiry into the Dardanelles affair was finally appointed on 18 July 1916, following Churchill's return to London for parliamentary duty. He gave evidence to the committee in September that year and encouraged others to step forward to support his position. While the final report would not be published until 1919, the preliminary findings were released in a *First Report* of March 1917.

The Commission's findings presented few surprises, as they concluded that the campaign had been poorly planned and executed, with a gross underestimation of the problems involved. Supply shortages, and personality clashes between those in command, only served to exacerbate existing problems. Perhaps more than anything else, a lack of communication between the decision makers and military experts was highlighted.

As far as Churchill himself was held individually liable, he escaped fairly lightly. He was criticised for having advocated the initial attack by ships alone without also sharing the views of his naval advisers. But otherwise a broader criticism of the Dardanelles Committee leadership meant that Churchill was at least partially vindicated of blame. He was, however, still commonly regarded by critics as somebody who was quick to present his own uninformed opinions on a subject, especially in matters of military strategy. His supporters, on the other hand, pointed to Churchill's ability to cut through unnecessary bureaucracy and show initiative in the absence of any leadership from the joint naval and military planning staff.

The findings of the Dardanelles Committee did not prevent the affair from tarnishing Churchill's reputation, with such close personal association with a military disaster continuing at least until the next major global conflict with which Britain was involved. Churchill's link with the Dardanelles and Gallipoli failures continued to dog him throughout the 1920s and 1930s, being the subject of regular heckling received both in Parliament and on the campaign trail. But he attempted to put the failure behind him, even claiming on one occasion to glory in it. Never one to wallow in the past, Churchill's tendency was rather to look to the future and the next big challenge.

APR

28 | Ministry of Munitions Identity Pass

Churchill's reputation was partially salvaged as a result of the report of the Dardanelles Commission, first released in March 1917, which saw him escape many of the most serious charges held against him. The new Prime Minister David Lloyd George was therefore more inclined to give Churchill another opportunity in office, partly due to this exoneration but perhaps more to do with the pressure Churchill was putting on the government's current war policy. It would be better to enlist the troublesome Churchill rather than to exile him.

Yet Churchill's appointment as Minister of Munitions in July 1917 proved controversial, with protests even from within the coalition government itself.

when he moved to the War Office. In 1917 he threw himself into the job at hand with characteristic enthusiasm and energy.

He embarked on an efficiency drive, simplifying bureaucracy in the ministry and working to boost the productivity of munitions workers. He made particular efforts to reduce strikes, initially by supporting the workers by raising wages, but eventually by threatening to conscript them into the armed forces. Churchill managed to win over many former critics, although he still could not resist interfering in the affairs of others, using his armaments remit to justify influencing war strategy at every opportunity. He was a particularly ardent supporter for greater mechanisation, calling for bigger guns, more aircraft and wider use of the new

---

Churchill's drive for efficiency boosted the reputation and importance of his ministry.

The Secretary for War and First Lord of the Admiralty both threatened to resign, due to perceived 'meddling' by Churchill in their respective spheres, while the press had a field day questioning Churchill's suitability. Ultimately, though, differences had to be set aside in order to maintain the coalition.

The Ministry of Munitions was a relatively new government department that had been created in 1915 in order to oversee the creation and supply of munitions for the war effort. Churchill would remain in this post for the rest of the war, only giving it up in January 1919

tanks, although was rather ahead of his time in pushing for tank warfare when they were still largely untested in battle.

He also used his position to visit the Western Front on a regular basis, serving to bolster his reputation as somebody with a genuine interest in how the war was being fought and an understanding of what was needed to win it. Churchill's popularity with the high command improved so much that Lloyd George came to accuse him of 'echoing the sentiments of GHQ'. But his wider responsibility as a member of the Cabinet was not totally forgotten. As the Minister

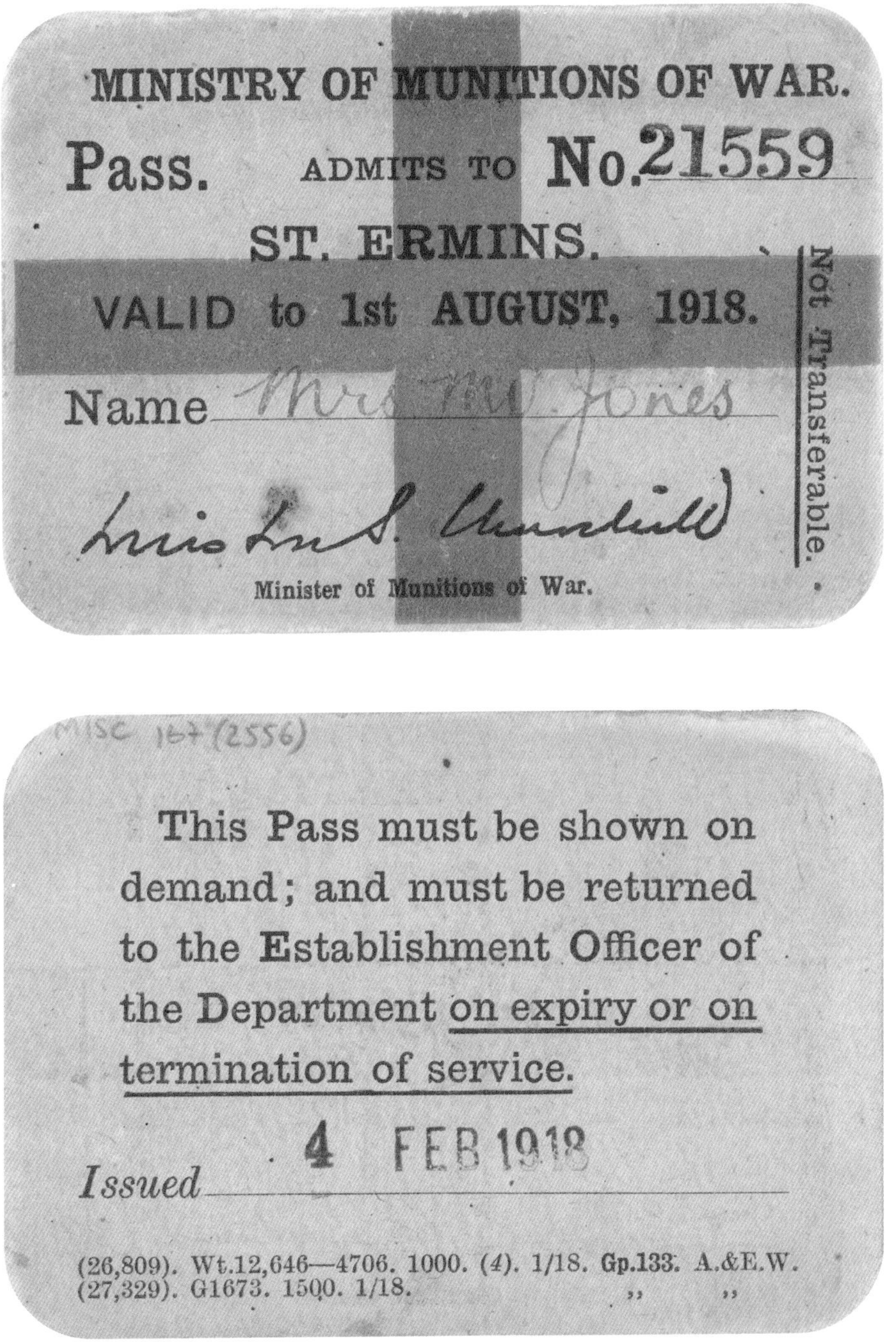

MINISTRY OF MUNITIONS OF WAR.

Pass. ADMITS TO No.21559

ST. ERMINS.

VALID to 1st AUGUST, 1918.

Name *Mrs. M. Jones*

Winston S. Churchill

Minister of Munitions of War.

Not Transferable.

MISC 167 (2556)

This Pass must be shown on demand; and must be returned to the Establishment Officer of the Department on expiry or on termination of service.

Issued **4 FEB 1918**

(26,809). Wt.12,646—4706. 1000. (4). 1/18. Gp.133. A.&E.W.
(27,329). G1673. 1500. 1/18.   ,,   ,,

This typical Ministry of Munitions pass, signed in facsimile by Churchill,
allows access to St Ermin's Hotel in London which was used by the Ministry.

This 1916 poster encourages women to enrol as munitions workers as part of Britain's civilian war effort.

of Munitions, Churchill's facsimile signature adorned every identification pass issued to munitions workers in the nation's many factories, who undoubtedly felt a personal connection – however slight – to their 'boss'. It was perhaps his responsibility for female munitions workers in particular that influenced Churchill's support of the Representation of the People Act, passed in February 1918, which gave most British women the right to vote for the first time.

APR

29 | Beauvais Agreement, April 1918

I n the twenty-first century we may find it hard to believe that, not many years ago, an academic debate raged as to which of Churchill and Lloyd George should be considered the greater statesman. Even in recent times one academic concluded that Lloyd George's many social and political reforms gave

of the Board of Trade in 1908, when Lloyd George became Chancellor of the Exchequer. In 1910 Churchill became Home Secretary and, in this capacity in particular, supported Lloyd George in his reforming zeal, not least in passing the National Insurance Act in 1911, which helped protect working people against

---

Churchill experienced both friendship and rivalry with another great statesman of the twentieth century.

---

grounds for considering him one of the great reforming prime ministers, while Churchill 'did not leave a lasting legacy, apart from winning the [Second World] war'.

In 1904 Churchill famously 'ratted' and joined the Liberal Party – Lloyd George had been a Liberal member of Parliament since 1890 – and was quickly given political office as Under-Secretary of State for the Colonies, before succeeding Lloyd George as President

loss of income as a result of sickness or unemployment and put in place the fundamentals of the future 'welfare state'.

The two men were not just political allies, but also close friends – Churchill had strongly defended that 'brave honest little man' when his colleague was threatened with claims of corruption in 1912 – but that did not stop Lloyd George from urging Prime Minister Herbert Asquith in 1915 to remove Churchill from the office

Churchill walks alongside Lloyd George
as they make their way to the House of Commons
for Lloyd George's budget speech, on 27 April 1910.

BEAUVAIS, le 3 Avril 1918.

Le GénéralFOCH est chargé par les Gouvernements Britannique , Français et Américain de coordonner l'action des
Armées Alliées sur le front occidental; il lui est conféré
à cet effet tous les pouvoirs nécessaires en vue d'une réali-
sation effective. Dans ce but, les Gouvernements Britannique,
Français et Américain confient au Général FOCH la direction
stratégique des opérations militaires.

Les Commandants en Chef des Armées Britannique,Française
et Américaine exercent dans sa plénitude la conduite tactique
de leur Armée. Chaque Commandant en Chef aura le droit d'en
appeler à son Gouvernement, si dans son opinion, son Armée
se trouve mise en danger par toute instruction reçue du Général FOCH.

The Beauvais Agreement, dated 3 April 1918 and with signatories including Lloyd George,
marked an important turning point in the First World War.

of First Lord of the Admiralty, when he was largely blamed for the failure of the Dardanelles campaign.

This alternation between friendship/ alliance and rivalry bordering on personal dislike, characterised their relationship right up to Lloyd George's death in March 1945. They worked together on achieving a resolution to the long-grumbling problem of Ireland and home rule and on the Versailles Peace Treaty in 1919. This last was a subject of great importance to Lloyd George, as a man who, despite leading Great Britain in war from 1916 to 1918 and being credited with Britain's victory in that war, loathed war and repeatedly worked to sustain peace.

Although little remembered today, the Beauvais Agreement shown here, signed by Lloyd George in April 1918 and undoubtedly including input from Churchill as Minister for Munitions, laid the ground for victory by placing the Allied forces on the Western Front under the unified command of the French General Ferdinand Foch.

His antipathy to war led Lloyd George to meet Hitler in 1936 in an effort to avoid a possible conflict, but also led to his vocal approval of Hitler, a hyper-critical attitude to the incompetence, as he saw it, of the British government – of which he had not been a part since 1922 – and to his openly expressed defeatist belief that Britain was facing a catastrophe in 1940. When Churchill became prime minister in May 1940, and wanted to keep this now enemy from causing trouble, he invited Lloyd George to join his War Cabinet. His former friend peevishly refused the invitation three times, citing the presence of Chamberlain in the War Cabinet as an obstacle to his own participation, while also taking a shot at Churchill and his predecessors for either overlooking him or making only half-hearted efforts to enlist his support. He suffered the deluded belief that Churchill would fail and the country would then rally round the victor of 1918.

In May 1941 the relationship between the two men reached a nadir, when Churchill likened Lloyd George to Marshal Pétain, the former hero of France in the First World War, who had become head of the collaborationist regime of Vichy France. Nevertheless, Churchill maintained a life-long admiration for Lloyd George, even considering him a dominant influence by describing their relationship as that of 'master and servant'.

In his tribute to Lloyd George on his death in 1945, Churchill generously, but judiciously, declared that when the history of the first quarter of the twentieth century was written it would be revealed that the nation's fortunes were shaped by Lloyd George more than anybody else. He very deliberately focussed on Lloyd George's successes in the First World War and the early 1920s, carefully avoiding any mention of the less praiseworthy part he played in the Second World War. To the end Churchill maintained the public image of two mutually admiring statesmen working together, neatly avoiding any indication of the deep-seated private and personal rivalry – more on Lloyd George's part than on Churchill's – between the two men.

Churchill, widely commemorated by statuary, was recognised with a statue in London's Parliament Square, facing the House of Commons, which was erected in 1973, just eight years after his death. A statue of Lloyd George was only finally erected – behind that of Churchill – in 2007, some sixty-two years after his death.

PHR

30 | Bust at Mishkenot Sha'ananim, Jerusalem

Antisemitism has a millennia-old history, with Great Britain having its own shameful record of discrimination towards Jewish people.

Throughout the Victorian era and early twentieth century in which Churchill grew up, it was unusual for those in higher society in Britain to have Jewish friends and to break with this convention could lead to social ostracism. Churchill claimed that his personal sympathy for for Zionism by the Prime Minister, Lloyd George, and was also intended to encourage support for the British war effort among Jewish people in neutral countries, and the USA and revolutionary Russia. While not a signatory to the declaration, Churchill also backed the idea. Then, in 1918, he went further, persuading not only the British Parliament to ratify the establishment of a Jewish homeland in Palestine, but later also the League of Nations, thus giving it

---

Churchill was a keen supporter of the creation of a Jewish homeland.

---

the re-establishment of a Jewish nation in Palestine ('Zionism') began when he met a group of Jews in Manchester in 1910 and, as with his father before him, he counted many Jewish people among his close friends; the result was that both men were considered in certain powerful circles to be atypical and to be treated with suspicion. Even in May 1940, when Churchill was a candidate to become prime minister, his friendship with Jewish people was one of the reasons that he did not attract the universal approval in political circles that we sometimes assume must have been the case.

On 2 November 1917, the then British Foreign Secretary, Arthur Balfour, wrote to the leader of the Anglo-Jewish community, Baron Rothschild, to express his backing for the establishment in Palestine of a homeland for Jewish people. It was a personal expression of respect international recognition by letting Jews in Palestine know that they were there 'as of right and not on sufferance'.

Although aware of the rich heritage of the Arab world, Churchill believed that Arab nations had gone into decline and declared that an infusion of Jewish people would help boost the economies of the Middle East. In this regard, Churchill's beliefs were certainly influenced by the racial stereotyping which was common throughout Britain and most other countries at that time. This support was at least in part contingent on the Jewish people raising their own money for investment and development, however; the British Treasury was certainly unprepared to take on such an extra burden.

Churchill would remain firm in his support for Zionism throughout his life, only wavering at times due to the degree

SIR WINSTON CHURCHILL
(1874-1965)

סר ויסטון צ'רצ'יל (1965 – 1874)

سير ونستون تشرشل (١٩٦٥ – ١٨٧٤)

"There is no limit to the ingenuity of man if it is properly and vigorously
applied under conditions of peace and justice."
Upon recommending British recognition of the State of Israel,
26 January 1949

Oscar Nemon's bronze bust of Churchill, overlooking Jerusalem's Old City.

of acrimony and eventual violent hostility shown by Arabs to the 'invasion' of their lands by the Jewish people. His attitude was also sorely challenged at times by the violence that Jewish terrorists (as they were branded at the time) enacted against the British forces administering the mandate of Palestine, not least after the assassination of Lord Moyne (the British government's Minister-Resident for the Middle East) in November 1944 and then following the bombing of the King David Hotel in July 1946, which housed the British administration in Palestine.

Perhaps Churchill's support of Zionism can best be understood in the context of his beliefs and fears regarding 'Bolshevism' and the wellbeing of the British Empire. Like so many others of that time he accepted the racist stereotype of Jews encouraging revolutionary tendencies, most notably through the Communism that he felt was constantly threatening the security of Europe. He therefore decried what he believed to be a Jewish influence behind the revolutionary terror in Hungary under Béla Kun's rule as well as in parts of Germany after the First World War. Yet he was also generous towards 'peaceful' Jews and believed that the creation of a Jewish homeland in Palestine would provide the pacifist stability required to counter the negative elements elsewhere. In this sense, Churchill's support of Zionism was

perhaps more reliant on what it offered Britain. He also no doubt found the idea of a restored homeland naively appealing to his romantic nature.

Churchill's advocacy of Zionism means that, to this day, he still has a considerable number of Jewish admirers. This bronze bust of Churchill, created by the sculptor Oscar Nemon, was dedicated in Yael's Garden at Mishkenot Sha'ananim in 2012, overlooking Jerusalem's Old City. Born in Croatia, Nemon spent much of his early life in Vienna but chose to settle in Britain after 1938, to avoid Nazi rule. He became famous for his sculptures of numerous high-profile figures, but was best-known for his many public statues of Churchill.

PHR

Churchill visits Tel Aviv in March 1921,
in his role as Secretary of State for the Colonies.

31 | Red Cross Aid to Russia Fund Poster

In May 1919 Churchill publicly described Bolshevism as a 'pestilence' rather than a creed. Many feared that the contagion of Bolshevism would spread to other countries and indeed Germany was already experiencing exactly that problem first hand. The government was divided over a proposal to send troops to Russia to aid the 'White Russians', who were resisting the Bolshevik forces and proposed using the defeated German Army to fight the Bolsheviks, but the idea gained no traction. Churchill was at the heart of that debate because in

struggle (other nationalities participating included the Americans with 11,000 troops, the French 15,000 and Japan, with its own ambitions, 70,000). That decision led to Churchill, as Secretary of State for War, being wrongly seen for decades afterwards as the principal proponent of this strategy. When it quickly became clear that these forces could not win, he wholeheartedly supported and implemented by September 1919 the evacuation of the British forces. Slightly garnishing the truth later in life, he claimed in 1955 that, had he been better supported, it might have been wiser to

---

Churchill was implacably opposed to the ideology of Communism, or 'Bolshevism' as he called it.

January 1919 Lloyd George had appointed him both to the War Office (the Army Ministry) and as Secretary of State for Air.

Previously, shortly after the signing of the Brest-Litovsk peace treaty of March 1918 between Germany and the new Bolshevik government in Russia, Churchill actually proposed offering the Bolsheviks protection against counter-revolution, in return for their re-joining the war against Germany. The offer was never formally made, but, just a year later, his views had changed. He totally opposed Bolshevism, but initially also opposed the strategy of sending troops to support anti-Bolshevik forces in Russia. He finally acceded, agreeing to send a small contingent of 7,500 soldiers to support the

have eradicated the idea of Bolshevism before it had the chance to establish itself properly.

In the 1920s, Churchill and others feared that Communism was becoming a popular political philosophy, especially among the British intelligentsia and workers. Churchill never visited the USSR in the inter-war years, though he remained vehemently opposed to Communism. But Churchill was always a pragmatist, generally a realist and frequently a political seer. From the late 1930s the main focus of his campaigning was for Britain to re-arm and prepare to oppose Hitler. This gradually evolved into direct opposition to appeasement and, as a corollary to this, his advocacy for a 'Grand

Launched in 1941, Clementine's Aid to Russia Fund raised money to send
clothes and medicine to the Russian population.

Alliance' involving France, the USA and the Soviet Union.

In 1938, appalled by Britain's abandonment of Czechoslovakia, political wisdom took precedence over political ideology and he supported courting the Soviets in an effort to isolate Germany. In 1937 he had likened Communism and Fascism to the poles of the earth: they had minor differences, but both were basically alike (and bleak).

His political realism can be seen in his pronouncement that same year that, if he had to choose between Communism and Nazism/Fascism, he would choose Communism, adding that he hoped never to live in a world ruled by either political philosophy. But his fundamental opposition to Communism remained, as evidenced by a conversation he had in 1943 with the Soviet ambassador to the UK, Ivan Maisky, in which he made no bones about his view, saying that Communism should be fought against in the same manner as the fight against Nazism.

Despite his inveterate opposition to Communism, he had long seen the strategic value of, at the very least, maintaining a friendship with the USSR. In 1934 he declared himself a 'friend of the Soviet Union', pressed for it to be admitted to the League of Nations and, in 1937, told Maisky of the absolute need for a 'strong Russia' to protect peace. At this time Prime Minister Chamberlain was vacillating, seeking an accommodation with Hitler. Churchill, by contrast, argued strongly the political necessity of allying with Moscow, if Britain were to have any chance of surviving a possible war with Germany.

When the USSR and Germany signed their non-aggression pact on 23/24 August 1939 on the eve of war, Churchill kept his channels to the Soviets open, meeting regularly with Ambassador Maisky. While never quite going back on the criticisms he had made of Soviet communism, Churchill began to regard it as a lesser evil than Nazism and a clear way to attack Germany from both sides. He even went so far as to condone Stalin's later operations against Finland and the Baltic States, describing Soviet claims as 'natural and normal'.

From June 1941, with the German invasion of its territory, the Soviet Union became a fully-fledged partner in the struggle against Nazi Germany and its allies. Churchill was well aware of how much the Western Allies relied on Soviet resistance to the Nazi advances and on the sacrifices the Soviets were making, and therefore sent what armaments, food and other supplies he could, via the Arctic convoys, with their heavy costs in British and American lives.

Churchill's wife, Clementine, was patron of the Red Cross 'Aid to Russia' fund, the largest charity of the Second World War, and she visited the USSR to signify the Western Allies' acknowledgement of its sacrifice.

Stalin had been demanding from early on for Britain and the USA to open a 'second front' in Europe. However, this was simply not a realistic option before 1944 and Churchill made quite clear to Stalin that, from 1939 to 1941, Britain had heroically fought alone against Nazism and planned to open a 'second front' through North Africa and Italy.

The alliance with the Soviet Union survived to the end of the Second World War, but not after the Soviet creation of the 'eastern bloc' incorporating the Soviet-controlled zone in Germany. Never afraid to speak out, but led by political insight and foresight, Churchill made brutally clear in his famous 'Iron Curtain' speech, which he delivered in March 1946 at Fulton Missouri, that the Soviets now represented a real threat to Western democracy and freedom and even to its territories. He was roundly condemned at first by President Truman and by the media on both sides of the Atlantic for rocking the boat and risking upsetting the great wartime ally. But, within months, the wisdom of his words became recognised and the reality of what was to become the Cold War sank in.

PHR

32 | Proclamation of Martial Law in Dublin, 1916

In 1876 a high society scandal erupted, in which the Prince of Wales was effectively blackmailed by Randolph Churchill in an effort to protect his family's name. The consequence of this was that Prime Minister Benjamin Disraeli appointed Randolph's father, the Duke of Marlborough, to the position of Viceroy of Ireland with the condition that he took Randolph with him as his private secretary.

The Churchill family, including two-year-old Winston, decamped to Ireland

and impractical'. His ardent support of Ulster Unionism and his withering views on Irish self-government made him a controversial figure.

By 1912, however, Winston had softened his opposition to Irish Nationalism and was beginning to accept the possibility of Home Rule to some degree. Believing in Dominion status for Ireland under British authority, he supported the Home Rule Bill that year, while, as his father had before him, still staunchly defending the rights of Ulster Unionists. In a speech in a Belfast park – for his

---

Churchill's political career saw him directly involved in attempts to resolve the Irish Question.

---

for three years until the scandal subsided. Jennie Churchill's two sisters met and married Irishmen as a result, and Winston therefore had two Irish cousins, Claire Sheridan and Shane Leslie.

Randolph began to involve himself in Irish politics, dominated by arguments from Irish Nationalists who called for Home Rule to be introduced, with a smaller Republican group lobbying for full independence. He soon became a fierce defender of the Unionist demands for Ireland to remain part of the United Kingdom and, as a result, the Churchill name was closely associated in Ireland with that political viewpoint. Indeed, on joining the Liberal Party in 1904, Winston declared that he believed a separate Irish parliament both 'dangerous

safety the venue was moved from Ulster Hall, where his father in 1886 had defended Unionist demands with the words 'Ulster will fight, and Ulster will be right' – he supported the creation of a Dublin Parliament and was heckled and violently jostled by Unionists who totally opposed any such compromise to their cause.

Such was Churchill's reputation in Ireland that he was accused of fomenting a possible Irish civil war in 1914 when, as part of the response to the increasingly bellicose stance of Sir Edward Carson's Ulster Volunteers, a paramilitary force founded to block Home Rule, he organised the deployment of Royal Navy ships off the coast of Ulster. The Home Rule Bill was signed into law in September

G. R.

PROCLAMATION.

WHEREAS, in the City of Dublin and County of Dublin certain evilly disposed persons and associations, with the intent to subvert the supremacy of the Crown in Ireland, have committed divers acts of violence, and have with deadly weapons attacked the Forces of the Crown, and have resisted by armed force the lawful Authority of His Majesty's Police and Military Forces. AND whereas by reason thereof several of His Majesty's liege Subjects have been killed and many others severely injured, and much damage to property has been caused.

AND, whereas, such armed resistance to His Majesty's authority still continues. NOW, I, Ivor Churchill, Baron Wimborne, Lord Lieutenant-General and General Governor of Ireland, by virtue of all the powers me thereunto enabling DO HEREBY PROCLAIM that from and after the date of this Proclamation, and for the period of One Month thereafter (unless otherwise ordered) the CITY OF DUBLIN and COUNTY OF DUBLIN are under and subject to

MARTIAL LAW

AND I do hereby call on all Loyal and well affected Subjects of the Crown to aid in upholding and maintaining the peace of this Realm and the supremacy and authority of the Crown. AND I warn all peaceable and law-abiding Subjects within such area of the danger of frequenting, or being in any place in or in the vicinity of which His Majesty's Forces are engaged in the suppression of disorder.

AND I do hereby enjoin upon such Subjects the duty and necessity, so far as practicable, of remaining within their own homes so long as these dangerous conditions prevail.

And I do hereby declare that all persons found carrying Arms without lawful authority are liable to be dealt with by virtue of this Proclamation.

Given at Dublin this 25th day of April, 1916.

WIMBORNE

GOD SAVE THE KING.

1914, but its provisions were placed on hold as a result of the outbreak of the First World War. Feelings on the issues in Ireland continued to bristle, however, reaching new heights in the republican rising in Dublin in 1916. Martial law had to be introduced in Dublin to curb the uprising, with posters such as the one illustrated here appearing around the city that Easter.

Churchill had no further involvement in Irish affairs until the end of the First World War, when Prime Minister Lloyd George appointed him Minister for War and Air, which included responsibility for the return home of the fighting troops. It was in this capacity that blame has been heaped upon him for the deployment in 1920 of the infamous 'Black and Tans', an auxiliary police force intended to bolster the British Army presence in Ireland. Comprising unemployed and largely undisciplined ex-soldiers, these men had often been brutalised by their war experiences and were now placed on the streets of Ireland. Although Churchill was responsible for their recruitment, he was not solely to blame for their conduct – although one might suggest that his selection criteria should have been more stringent. While Lloyd George had encouraged the creation of the force, it was General Sir Hugh Tudor who oversaw their militarisation.

Although not being directly responsible for their actions, Churchill chose not to speak out against the reprisal murders carried out by the 'Black and Tans'. He did make an attempt to improve their reputation, however, by creating an Auxiliary Division of officers for the Royal Irish Constabulary, although this led to little improvement. Both the Black and Tans and Auxiliaries wore a uniform combining British Army khaki ('tan') and Royal Irish Constabulary green (a very dark colour, almost black).

The partition of Ireland in May 1921 began the process of splitting the country into what would eventually become the southern Irish Free State and Northern Ireland. Churchill was closely involved in the negotiations and astonishingly, considering their rival stances, maintained a good relationship with the leading Republican Michael Collins. Despite their strongly opposing views, each man respected the other. When the post of Chief Secretary for Ireland was abolished that year, responsibility for overseeing the transition of power to the new Irish government fell to Churchill as the then-Secretary of State for the Colonies.

However, Éamon de Valera, the president of the new Irish Parliament (the Dáil), opposed the Anglo-Irish Treaty, which would have meant that Ireland continued as a Dominion of the United Kingdom by swearing allegiance to the British crown. A near year-long civil war in Ireland followed. Churchill's plans for the British Army to violently suppress the Irish Republican Army in Dublin were thwarted by the man he deputed to manage the operation, General Macready, who saw this as a recipe for sectarian violence and refused the job, which then fell to the Irish government.

Southern Ireland formally left the United Kingdom in December 1922, but Great Britain retained access to and rights over three Irish ports – Berehaven, Queenstown (Cobh) and Lough Swilly – until in May 1938 Prime Minister Neville Chamberlain unilaterally ceded Britain's rights to these during trade negotiations. Churchill deplored the loss of these strategic ports, which he saw as a major risk in the event of de Valera declaring Ireland neutral in a future war with Germany. It was a concern for which Churchill was widely derided and dismissed, yet his fears were eventually realised, with the concession being blamed by a later Admiralty study for the loss of 380 Allied ships and over 5,000 lives.

Churchill's relationship with Ireland was at all times determined by his loyalty to Britain and its Empire, and his enduringly unpopular reputation in Ireland reflects these political priorities, which he stuck to throughout his life.

PHR

33 | *Agal* (Headrope) Worn by T. E. Lawrence

O n the death of T. E. Lawrence – most often referred to as Lawrence of Arabia – in 1935, as a result of a motorcycle accident, Churchill wrote an extensive obituary in tribute to a man for whom he had almost unalloyed admiration. He began the piece by describing not simply their first meeting, but what Lawrence had achieved in the Middle East in the First World War and the importance of the Arab Revolt in realising victory in that part of the world.

He invited Lawrence to lunch in 1919, after a friend had described his exploits as 'epic'.

In that first meeting Churchill, as Minister for War, felt professionally obliged to upbraid Lawrence for the 'discourtesy' he had shown to the King in turning down the DSO and Order of the Bath at the very ceremony at which they were to be bestowed. He was, however, clearly massively impressed with Lawrence's intellect and by his absolute dedication to the Arab cause. Lawrence used the occasion of his meeting with the King – which Churchill later discovered was a private meeting at which the King had suddenly offered him the decorations – to highlight the Arab plight and their sense of betrayal following the French expulsion of Emir Faisal from Syria, which the French saw as their fiefdom, under the Sykes–

Churchill expressed huge admiration for the man who is now known as Lawrence of Arabia.

Picot agreement, which the British had accepted before the end of the war. His refusal – actually a polite request to the King – of the honours was simply typical of his selfless attitude, which never wanted reward or recognition.

Churchill realised the truth of the incident by the time of their next meeting at the Versailles Peace Conference in 1919. Lawrence was there endeavouring to fight the Arab cause (accompanied by Faisal), to the point of arguing vehemently and directly with the French President, Clemenceau. Churchill believed that it was a lost cause, the harsh French experience on the Western Front making them insistent on their share of the spoils.

Lawrence felt that his promises to Emir Faisal and the Arabs, effectively offered in the name of the British government, had been completely betrayed and he left the conference crushed. In early 1921 Churchill, as Colonial Secretary, formed a new department within the Colonial Office, in an attempt to bring order to the Middle East and, more in hope than expectation, asked Lawrence to join as a member of the team of specialists established to assist in the task. Much to Churchill's surprise, Lawrence quickly agreed to join the team and went to the Cairo Conference that Churchill had convened to attempt to sort out the problems of the region.

Churchill, T. E. Lawrence and Emir Abdullah walk in the gardens of Government House, Jerusalem, on 28 March 1921. Following the Cairo conference, Churchill and Lawrence had informed Abdullah that Palestine was to remain a British Mandate.

Prominent among the measures that Churchill introduced was the establishment of the Kingdom of Iraq, with Faisal as King, and the appointment of Emir Abdullah to head the government of Trans-Jordan. This was, as Churchill saw it, an attempt to fix the situation and as such raised Lawrence's esteem of Churchill to one of lifelong admiration, for having, in large part, redeemed the promises Lawrence had made to the Arabs during the war.

When, some years later, Lawrence produced a privately printed limited edition of his great work *Seven Pillars of Wisdom* – for which Churchill was full of praise – he invited subscribers to purchase copies for £35 (equivalent to over £1,700 today). Churchill offered to buy a copy, but, when the copy arrived, it came with a personal inscription from Lawrence, thanking him for the lasting and 'honest settlement' that he had brought to the Arab world and refusing any payment for the book.

In 1934 the film director, producer and writer Alexander Korda secured the rights to film Lawrence's own abridgement of *Seven Pillars of Wisdom* and signed up not only Leslie Howard in the starring role, but also Churchill to advise and coach the lead actor. Churchill had been hired as a consultant with Korda's London Film Productions Ltd in 1934 and, in 1937, he began work on revising the Lawrence script, sending Korda long letters advising on accuracy of geography and personalities. Despite his stress on the need for accuracy, as with many of Churchill's portrayals of great individuals, there is a strong element of myth-building in his portrayal of Lawrence, most of which took decades to dispel. Sadly, the interruption caused by the outbreak of war in 1939 meant that no film about Lawrence was made until David Lean brought his story to the screen in 1962 with *Lawrence of Arabia*.

PHR

T. E. Lawrence about to take off for a flight with Sir Herbert Samuel, the first High Commissioner for Palestine, to Al-Azraq in Transjordan, April 1921.

34 | Chartwell

In the summer of 1921, feeling financially flush after a recent inheritance and wishing to have the trappings fitting Winston's station in life as Colonial Secretary, the Churchills considered the purchase of a property sufficiently large for their needs, which would mean a minimum of twelve bedrooms to accommodate both their family and servants. Churchill took Clementine to look over a very run-down property he had found in Kent called Chartwell, a house large enough for a family of nine children and a domestic staff of thirteen and set in seventy acres of land, managed by a workforce of twenty. Clementine was smitten with the house,

though wary of the commitment the land and farming it would present.

It is not known if Churchill bid for the house at the subsequent auction, but it did not sell and the Churchills, beset by family tragedies – the death of his mother, Jennie, followed soon afterwards by the death from septicaemia of their fourth child, the three-year-old Marigold – had other concerns. But he revived his interest the following year and took his children to see this rather dilapidated residence, which they simply adored on sight and tried to persuade their father to buy, not knowing, as he then revealed, that he had already bought it for £5,000. Typical of the headstrong, somewhat self-centred

Churchill he had bought the house without first consulting his wife.

Although Clemmie did her utmost to make Chartwell into a welcoming and comfortable family home, she never had the same affection for it as Churchill most certainly did. This must have been in no small part because of the seemingly constant and ever-escalating outlays in which the house involved them: repairing

about Chartwell, which he considered his vital refuge, a mere forty-minute drive from the cauldron of political life. It was the place he largely retreated to when out of office from 1929 to 1939, though the word 'retreat' has to be taken with a note of caution.

The Churchills' visitors' book shows they frequently entertained guests in the decades that he lived there – his scientific

---

In 1921 Churchill bought the house that would serve as his family home for the rest of his life.

---

extensive dry rot and serious structural faults, as well as replacing the decrepit roof and making physical alterations to the building to suit the Churchills' specific needs. The ultimate costs incurred exceeded £23,000 (in modern-day terms, over £1 million) and they were only able to move in to the partially renovated house in 1924, after several acrimonious legal disputes with the builders.

Churchill's secretary, Grace Hamblin, claimed that Churchill would rhapsodise

adviser Professor Lindemann (later Lord Cherwell) went eighty-six times, Field Marshal Montgomery forty-six times and his close friend, advisor and later a minister in his wartime administration, the maverick Brendon Bracken, thirty-one times. But the visitors' book does not show the names of many of those who came in the second half of the 1930s, when Churchill was increasingly harassing the government to invest far more heavily than it considered necessary

Churchill modelled much of Chartwell's gardens himself, including the impressive lakes.

The gardens feature this sculpture of Churchill and Clementine, by Oscar Nemon.

in rearmament, to face the potential and increasing threat posed by Hitler's Germany. Churchill used discreet visits by members of the upper ranks of the Civil Service, not least the Foreign Office – 'whistle blowers', as we would now call them, and anti-Nazis – to keep himself as fully briefed as possible on what was happening in Germany and on the British government's response.

During the Second World War his staff tried to keep him away from Chartwell, fearing that the German air force might target it deliberately, but after the war, once more out of government after the Conservative defeat at the 1945 election, Chartwell again became his haven. Not only did he entertain there – richly: in just the two-month period of April and May 1949 it is recorded that 454 bottles of champagne were drunk, as well as 311 bottles of wine, 58 bottles of brandy, 56 bottles of whisky, 58 bottles of sherry and 69 bottles of port – it is also where he would write his famous history *The Second World War* and finished his great oeuvre *A History of the English-Speaking*

Peoples. The house still has the original rostrum that he habitually stood at to dictate his many books, with the serried ranks of highly qualified researchers around him to transcribe, fact-check and re-write.

Periodically during their life there the Churchills, faced with mounting debts and financial commitments, made worse by the spendthrift Churchill and his serious gambling habit, would go on an economy drive. Several times they considered selling the house to raise funds until, finally, in late 1945, his rich friends clubbed together and raised £50,000 – at least £2 million in modern terms – to buy the house and allow him to stay there till his death, when it would become the property of the National Trust. And so it is today one of the National Trust's most visited properties, allowing the public a unique insight into Churchill's life, as he peered across the beautiful tranquillity of the Weald of Kent, swam in the pool he built, and painted in his studio.

PHR

35 | Churchill's Budget Box

In November 1924, Prime Minister Stanley Baldwin appointed Churchill as Chancellor of the Exchequer. The post of Chancellor, the second most powerful in the British political hierarchy after Prime Minister, was the highest office achieved by Winston's father, Lord Randolph.

Many in the Conservative Party were appalled at the appointment, given that century. It became a tradition in the later twentieth century for the Chancellor to carry his budget plans in the case and to wave the box before the cameras in Downing Street on what used to be the once a year 'budget day'. It was retired to the National Archives, its current owner, in the late 2000s and placed on display in the Churchill War Rooms.

Churchill's period of office as Chan-

Churchill's service as Chancellor of the Exchequer controversially included moving the country back onto the Gold Standard.

Winston had 'ratted' from the party to the Liberals in 1904 and had only recently 're-ratted' (his term) to the Conservatives. As Chancellor he continued to pursue policies best described as liberal Conservativism, something that earned him few friends in his party and his appointment has remained a stain on his character for many Conservatives till modern times.

The budget box is the original 'despatch' box that once belonged to William Ewart Gladstone, four-time Chancellor and four-time Prime Minister in the second half of the nineteenth

cellor (1924–9) is widely considered to have been unsuccessful, largely based on his decision to move the UK economy back on to the Gold Standard in his first budget in April 1925. While the Bank of England supported the strategy, many, including the famous economist John Maynard Keynes, foresaw problems, which actually came to pass in the form of inflation and unemployment, which are widely believed to have led to the General Strike of 1926. During the General Strike, although relatively sympathetic to the miners' cause (the root of the strike),

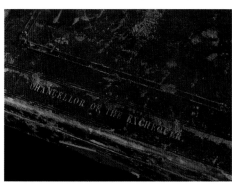

The tradition of carrying a red despatch box to Parliament to announce a new budget dates back to 1860.

Churchill edited a newspaper entitled the *British Gazette*, which was critical of the strikers and was not the balanced newssheet it purported to be.

While Churchill is famed for his vociferous campaigns for the country to invest heavily in rearmament in the second half of the 1930s, it is often forgotten that throughout his term of office as Chancellor, he drove through a policy of reducing expenditure on the armed forces, especially the Royal Navy. In keeping with government policy of the day, he espoused the belief that there was no risk of war for another ten years and that the country could therefore afford to reduce its defence commitment. He spent a large part of the 1930s and his period of office as First Lord of the Admiralty in 1939–40 arguing for the reversal of those very policies he had earlier supported.

Churchill lost his position in 1929, when the Conservative government was beaten at the General Election by Ramsay MacDonald's Labour Party, which began a ten-year period of Churchill being out of office, which came to be called his 'wilderness years'.

PHR

The budget box shown here and used by Churchill as Chancellor originally belonged to Gladstone.

36 | *The British Gazette, 5 May 1926*

One of the most challenging moments for Churchill during his time as Chancellor of the Exchequer would prove to be the General Strike, which began on 4 May 1926 and would last for just over a week. Some 1.7 million workers, mainly from the transport and heavy industry sectors, went out on strike to force the government to step in to protect workers' pay. Many of Britain's key public services and industries ground to a halt, through strike action coordinated by the Trades Union Congress (TUC).

The conditions leading to the General Strike had been simmering away for the previous year or so. One of the most significant factors which had caused

damage to the British economy had been the country's return to the Gold Standard in April 1925. In a move instigated by Churchill himself as Chancellor, the value of sterling was tied to gold in an attempt to boost the nation's prestige. Yet this resulted in an over-valuation of the British currency, making the country's exports too expensive while interest rates increased, both proving detrimental to British businesses. Business owners responded to the crisis by expecting their employees to work longer hours and for lower wages in many cases. The mining industry in particular was already facing a sharp crisis in the face of renewed competition from Germany, which had led British owners to lock out some 1.2

The General Strike of 1926 saw Churchill return to his journalistic roots.

million workers in an attempt to resolve a pay dispute.

Serious concern was expressed by the government that the strike might encourage socialist revolutionary activity. Churchill tried to follow his own course through the crisis, by sympathising with the miners and calling for a government subsidy to cover their wages. Yet the idea of a General Strike was anathema to him; as Chancellor of the Exchequer, his job was to 'balance the books' and a swift resolution to any labour dispute was therefore of the greatest importance to him. He also responded in angry terms to what he saw as a straightforward trade dispute being turned into a potential workers' revolution.

The government's immediate response to the General Strike was to recruit volunteers, largely from the middle classes, in order to maintain essential services during the crisis. But as Prime Minister Stanley Baldwin described it, fears continued that a long strike might serve as 'the road to anarchy'. A particular government concern was that striking printers might paralyse the nation's press or use their power to dictate and influence newspaper coverage of the strike, and so plans were put in place to print a government newspaper which might deliver accurate reporting and 'prevent alarming news from being spread about'. And what better individual to lead such a project than the member of the Cabinet who was both an experienced journalist and politician? Churchill's energy was therefore channelled into the *British Gazette*, as the official paper was named, although any veneer of impartiality was discarded at the outset with Churchill comparing the *Gazette*'s relationship to

the General Strike as to that between a fire engine and a fire.

Occupying the offices of the *Morning Post*, Churchill embraced the opportunity with characteristic enthusiasm, eagerly taking on the role of both editor and press magnate. Requisitioning newsprint and improvising at every turn with a ramshackle staff, he imposed his own views on everything and everybody, dictating leading articles and ensuring that the publication pushed his own viewpoint as far as possible. The general tone of the *Gazette* was that the General Strike was a challenge to the government, but one which could only be resolved by an unconditional surrender by the TUC.

In pushing the government's agenda, Churchill gave prominence to 'positive' stories illustrating how normal life was carrying on despite the strikes, while he ignored or downplayed instances such as shortages of food, violence towards civil transport still operating despite the union action, or looting which had been violently put down by the police. Such selective reporting led to frustrations on both sides, yet despite this the *British Gazette* proved immensely popular. Each issue was more widely distributed than the last, and the newspaper finally achieved a circulation of well over two million readers.

The General Strike ended on 12 May with what was effectively a complete surrender by the TUC in the face of the uncompromising government stance. Workers were forced to return to their jobs in order to survive, still struggling on low wages and working long hours, while unemployment throughout the country became rife. The coal mining industry in particular never fully recovered.

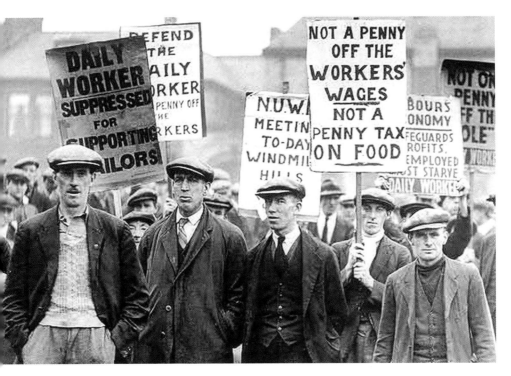

The General Strike of 1926 involved some 1.7 million workers.

Despite Churchill's numerous attempts to resolve the pay dispute in favour of coal miners, making life difficult for the mine owners in the process, opposition from his own Cabinet as well as business owners foiled such efforts at benevolence. Churchill's involvement with the General Strike is therefore remembered more for his belligerent attitude as editor of the *British Gazette,* prevailing against a potential socialist uprising, rather than his magnanimity towards workers' conditions.

APR

37 | *The Brooklyn Daily Eagle*, 24 October 1929

Baldwin's Conservative government was defeated in the polls of May 1929, reducing Churchill to the opposition benches once more.

While many in Britain regarded him as a political 'has-been', holding on to unfashionable views supporting rearmament and opposing Indian home rule, it was a somewhat different situation in North America. There, Churchill's political profile remained high, with a buoyant reputation dating from his first high-profile lecture tour of 1900. It therefore seemed a logical choice for him to make the trip across the Atlantic once more, partly as an opportunity to boost his confidence at a time when his political influence was on the wane, but also as a straightforward means to make much-needed money. A combined holiday and lecture tour was planned in order to take advantage of the respect and generosity which he enjoyed in North America.

Beginning in Canada during the summer of 1929, Churchill's trip was characterised by lavish dinners, drinks receptions and meetings in which he socialised with the rich, famous and influential. His speeches throughout the Canadian parts of his trip emphasised the strong ties which bound the British Empire together, while in the United States he pronounced on the importance of the unbreakable link between the English-speaking nations.

Churchill visited the country's west coast for the first time, being hosted by the famously rich newspaper magnate William Randolph Hearst at his Californian estate of San Simeon. Another millionaire friend, Charles Schwab, provided a private railroad car for the personal use of Churchill and his retinue, while Hearst introduced them to Hollywood and many of the great film stars of the day. Charlie Chaplin in particular proved popular and the actor

A lecture tour of North America at the time of the Wall Street Crash saw Churchill experience both sides of life.

would enjoy an ongoing friendship with the Churchill family in later years, visiting Chartwell when opportunities permitted.

Though Churchill's American tour began with luxury and extravagance, it ended with financial ruin. He arrived in New York on 24 October, which has become known as 'Black Thursday', marking the first signs of the Wall Street Crash that was to come days later. Share prices on the New York Stock Exchange collapsed, leading to a worldwide economic depression and everything that entailed, causing some investors to lose entire fortunes overnight.

Churchill himself had invested large sums in the American stock market when the nation was experiencing its economic boom, yet now the market collapse wiped out any financial gains he had made. The disastrous situation was demonstrated in the most immediate way as Churchill was gazing out of his New York hotel window one morning, only to witness a ruined stockbroker throwing himself out of a skyscraper window some fifteen storeys up to commit suicide.

Sailing home on 30 October, Churchill's mood was likely one of worry and concern over his future. The stock market disaster meant that he was now forced to be increasingly dependent on profits earned from writing and public speaking. In order to maintain his lavish lifestyle, he would need to spend much of the next decade trying to recoup these losses.

APR

William Randolph Hearst, the immensely wealthy newspaper magnate, who befriended Churchill during his trips to the United States.

107

38 | Lindemann Telegram, 30 December 1931

By the final months of 1931, Churchill was no longer a leading player in government and needed a new purpose to keep himself busy. His personal financial situation needed attention, too, since his investments had suffered dramatically as a result of the Wall Street Crash. Writing books and articles for publication therefore remained a vital source for

On the evening of 13 December, Churchill had been invited to the home of the financier and statesman Bernard Baruch. He took a taxi from his hotel to Fifth Avenue, but, when preparing to cross the road at a corner after he dismissed the cab, looked left but not right, forgetting the American rules of the road. A car struck Churchill and left him in a crumpled heap at the roadside, still

---

Churchill enjoyed many successful visits to North America,
yet one of the most eventful saw him suffer a serious accident.

---

regular income, although it was his public speaking overseas which tended to provide the most lucrative opportunities.

Churchill therefore decided to return to the nation which had first given him such a warm reception some thirty years before, and begin another extensive lecture tour of North America. He left Britain, accompanied by Clementine and their daughter Diana, on 5 December, already contracted to deliver forty lectures at a guaranteed minimum fee of £10,000. The *Daily Mail* was also paying him some £8,000 for a series of articles on the United States. Together, by the standards of that era, his earnings from the trip would be huge.

After arriving in New York on 11 December, Churchill delivered his first lecture the following day at Worcester, Massachusetts, to great success. But an unexpected accident was to ruin his well-made plans.

conscious but in great pain. He was taken immediately to Lennox Hill Hospital with a fractured nose and ribs, plus a deep cut to his forehead. Churchill's recovery was complicated when he developed pleurisy, yet a week later he was well enough to return to his hotel, the Waldorf Astoria, for a fortnight of recuperation. The patient would prove far from idle, as he persuaded his doctor to prescribe alcohol to aid his recovery – which was a particular feat at the time of Prohibition.

With characteristic resilience Churchill sought to turn the episode to his advantage and used it as the basis for one of his written pieces for the *Daily Mail*. To this end, Churchill wrote to one of his closest friends, the Oxford University physicist Professor Frederick Lindemann, to calculate the precise force of the impact he sustained during the accident. In a telegram sent in reply on 30 December, 'The Prof' (as Churchill liked to call him)

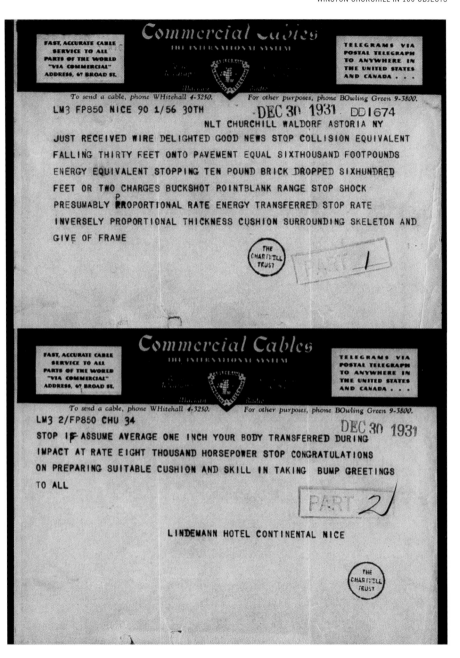

Commercial Cables
THE INTERNATIONAL SYSTEM

FAST, ACCURATE CABLE
SERVICE TO ALL
PARTS OF THE WORLD
"VIA COMMERCIAL"
ADDRESS, 67 BROAD ST.

TELEGRAMS VIA
POSTAL TELEGRAPH
TO ANYWHERE IN
THE UNITED STATES
AND CANADA . . .

To send a cable, phone WHitehall 4-3250.   For other purposes, phone BOwling Green 9-3800.

LM3 FP850 NICE 90 1/56 30TH   DEC 30 1931   DD1674
                    NLT CHURCHILL WALDORF ASTORIA NY
JUST RECEIVED WIRE DELIGHTED GOOD NEWS STOP COLLISION EQUIVALENT
FALLING THIRTY FEET ONTO PAVEMENT EQUAL SIXTHOUSAND FOOTPOUNDS
ENERGY EQUIVALENT STOPPING TEN POUND BRICK DROPPED SIXHUNDRED
FEET OR TWO CHARGES BUCKSHOT POINTBLANK RANGE STOP SHOCK
PRESUMABLY PROPORTIONAL RATE ENERGY TRANSFERRED STOP RATE
INVERSELY PROPORTIONAL THICKNESS CUSHION SURROUNDING SKELETON AND
GIVE OF FRAME

THE
CHARTWELL
TRUST

PART 1

Commercial Cables
THE INTERNATIONAL SYSTEM

FAST, ACCURATE CABLE
SERVICE TO ALL
PARTS OF THE WORLD
"VIA COMMERCIAL"
ADDRESS, 67 BROAD ST.

TELEGRAMS VIA
POSTAL TELEGRAPH
TO ANYWHERE IN
THE UNITED STATES
AND CANADA . . .

To send a cable, phone WHitehall 4-3250.   For other purposes, phone BOwling Green 9-3800.

LM3 2/FP850 CHU 34   DEC 30 1931
STOP IF ASSUME AVERAGE ONE INCH YOUR BODY TRANSFERRED DURING
IMPACT AT RATE EIGHT THOUSAND HORSEPOWER STOP CONGRATULATIONS
ON PREPARING SUITABLE CUSHION AND SKILL IN TAKING BUMP GREETINGS
TO ALL

PART 2

LINDEMANN HOTEL CONTINENTAL NICE

THE
CHARTWELL
TRUST

This telegram from Lindemann was delivered to Churchill
while he was recuperating at the Waldorf Astoria hotel in New York.

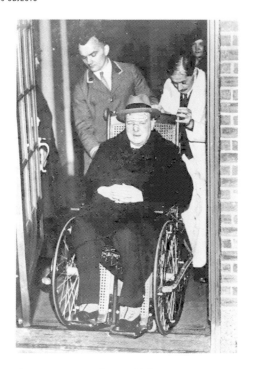

Churchill leaves the Lennox Hill Hospital in New York,
following his accident.

estimated the force from the car as being
equivalent to a ten-pound brick dropped
from 600 feet, or two charges of buckshot
fired at point-blank range. As an old
friend, Lindemann could not resist teasing
Churchill about how the mitigating
effect of his weight had proved beneficial
by serving as a suitable cushion for the
bump.

Never one to sit on his laurels for too
long, Churchill's determination to resume
the lecture tour remained and from
28 January 1932 (following a short holiday
in the Bahamas) he travelled almost every
day for three weeks, delivering lectures in
nineteen American cities. His articles had
proven immensely successful too, having
been circulated widely and generating a
great deal of public sympathy towards his
health. While still in the United States he
received an enormous number of letters
and telegrams from concerned well-

wishers, and on his return home to the
United Kingdom in March, some 140 of
his closest friends celebrated his escape
from near death by clubbing together to
buy him a luxury Daimler limousine as a
'welcome back' present.

Despite the setback of his accident,
Churchill's American trip of 1931–2 was
immensely successful. It instilled a sense
of hope and confidence in his audiences at
a time when the United States was deep in
recession. It had also reminded Churchill
of his own popularity as a public speaker,
at a time when his political reputation at
home was suffering somewhat.

This sense of optimism above all was
what people in the USA continued to
associate with Churchill, and which
became such an important part of his
character for them during the years ahead.

—APR—

39 | Gandhi's Glasses

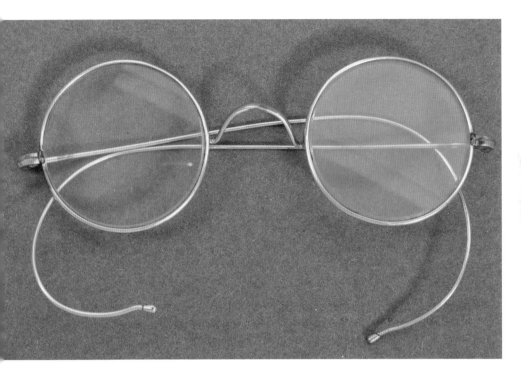

Churchill's father, Randolph, was born in 1849 and died in 1895. His son Winston was born in 1874. Both grew up in, and were nurtured in, the values of Victorian Britain and, in Winston's case, these influenced his thinking and attitudes for the rest of his days.

In Victoria's reign the concept of the 'Empire' was central to British life. Often described as the 'jewel' in that Empire was India. And, throughout his time, Churchill firmly held to the belief that the Empire was a power for good and that India not only benefited greatly from being part of it, but also much needed its support to flourish.

Mohandas (Mahatma) Gandhi was one of the most important figures associated with calls for Indian independence – and famous for wearing distinctive circular spectacles. This particular pair was sold at auction in 2020 for £260,000. Gandhi was also known for giving away old pairs of glasses to those in greater need.

Churchill served in India early in his military career and was certainly cognisant and appreciative of the bravery and sacrifice of the Indians fighting with the British. His dismissal of India in his twenties as 'this tedious land' and his praise for Britain's achievements in ruling 'these primitive but agreeable races' are the words of a bored subaltern and an arch-Imperialist. While these intemperate outbursts cannot be condoned in themselves, they need to be understood in the context of their times. More than anything else, Churchill retained a firm belief in the importance of the British Empire and much of his thinking stemmed from that.

It was therefore in complete opposition to Churchill's views that Mohandas (Mahatma) Gandhi began to call for Indian independence towards the end of the First World War. Having been a

by imprisoning Gandhi and many other Congress leaders. Violent demonstrations by nationalists resulted in the deaths of over 1,000 Indians.

Throughout the war Gandhi was imprisoned on a regular basis and in February 1943 began one of his longest hunger strikes, lasting some 21 days. He was already well-known for such acts of protest in previous years, and Churchill was quick to accuse Gandhi of cheating during his fast by taking glucose, a charge that was without foundation.

Churchill maintained that India was essential to the British Empire.

---

civil rights activist in South Africa for many years, Gandhi returned to India, the country of his birth, in 1915 and five years later became leader of the Indian National Congress, turning it into the principal party of the national independence movement. As his political voice grew louder, so Churchill's response grew harsher, with him dismissing Gandhi in February 1931 as 'a seditious Middle Temple lawyer, now posing as a fakir … striding half-naked up the steps of the Vice-regal palace'. Churchill's attempts to isolate Gandhi gained some support amongst Imperialists, but the vitriol with which he insulted Gandhi also led to many taking the side of independence.

The Second World War saw over 2.5 million Indian men volunteer to serve as soldiers with the British Indian Army and support Great Britain's resistance to Nazi Germany and Japan. Yet Gandhi was a pacifist who opposed the use of Indian forces to support Britain's struggle, arguing that India could not be involved in a war fought to achieve democratic freedom, at a time when freedom was being denied to India itself. He refused to support the war effort in any way, and the British government responded harshly

Churchill, with his focus firmly on prosecuting the war and defeating the Nazis and Japan, inevitably had a deep dislike of Gandhi. He even suspected Gandhi of being supportive of the Japanese. It was indeed the case that Gandhi had earlier, naively, written to Hitler to expound the values of non-violent resistance and universal friendship.

Churchill was implicated in other events occurring in India during the war. Greatly reduced imports due to the Japanese invasion of Malaya, combined with bad weather and poor colonial administration, led to a serious famine in the province of Bengal in 1943.

Blame for the tragedy that killed some three million people is frequently placed at Churchill's door, with accusations that he deliberately withheld food aid, at a time when such support was feasible, because of his hatred of Indian nationalism. In fact Churchill replaced the ineffective viceroy of India at that juncture with the more competent Field Marshal Archibald Wavell, who was encouraged to do all he could to alleviate the situation, and eventually did. Massive additional supplies were sent from Australia despite

President Roosevelt refusing to provide aid due to the Japanese submarine-infested waters off Bengal being a serious risk to shipping.

Independence finally came in 1947, an outcome that Gandhi, somewhat idealistically, hoped would be peacefully achieved. But the partition along religious lines that created Pakistan and India was to lead to the deaths of over a million people. Churchill, as much as any British Prime Minister, had been guilty of not preparing the country for independence; the Labour government that succeeded Churchill's Conservatives in 1945 inherited that position. It bowed to pressures, be they global, from India itself, from the USA – which had demanded Indian independence throughout the war, or from within the Labour Party, to bring about Indian independence at the earliest possible time. But this was done without a realistic appraisal of India's lack of preparedness, the country's internecine internal divisions and the inevitable struggle that would follow.

PHR

40 | Poster for the Film *Shoulder Arms*

In April 1918 Churchill proposed that former US President Teddy Roosevelt be sent as plenipotentiary to Russia to attempt to persuade Lenin to bring the Russians back into the First World War on the side of the Allies, but the proposal was never taken up.

Churchill had a deep admiration for Teddy Roosevelt, whom he met for the first time during his trip to the USA in 1900. Unfortunately, the admiration was far from mutual, with Roosevelt describing Churchill as 'not an attractive fellow' and 'a rather cheap character' with

December 1900, at which Twain pitched a few awkward questions, which Churchill fielded confidently.

Twain was then persuaded to act as host for Churchill's first speech in the USA, which he gave at the Waldorf Astoria on 16 December 1900, and which he was delivering to a fairly hostile audience. He professed himself 'thrilled' to be introduced by Mark Twain, one of his boyhood idols, but Twain's introduction berated the UK and the USA for their colonial policies, and his praise of the speaker was solely for his Anglo-

---

Churchill's fame as a politician and writer brought him into contact with notable celebrities of the day.

---

a 'lack of sobriety, lack of permanent principle and an inordinate thirst for that cheap form of admiration which is given to notoriety'. When Roosevelt represented the USA at the funeral of Edward VII in 1910, he refused to meet Churchill.

Another of Churchill's great heroes, Mark Twain, was also not greatly enamoured of him. He met Churchill when Winston was visiting the USA in 1900 for his long lecture series on the subject of his part in the Boer War. Britain's actions in the war had not been popular in the USA and Twain (real name Samuel Clemens), was a keen campaigner against empire-builders (including what he saw as a burgeoning US empire). They first met at a press conference that Churchill held in New York City on 9

American heritage. They later argued about the war, although in Churchill's eventual, somewhat sanitised account of the meeting, he did not believe this to have caused displeasure. Churchill remained a lifelong admirer of Twain, even joining the Mark Twain Society in 1929, which subsequently awarded him their Gold Medal.

Churchill, who had a love of the theatre since his childhood, relished his relationships with actors of the screen and the stage. In the 1930s he was employed – and handsomely paid – by Sir Alexander Korda, the noted film director and producer, writing film scripts and advising on others.

One of his favourite films, which he is said to have watched seventeen times

Churchill was invited to a private screening of Chaplin's *Shoulder Arms* in 1929.

during the Second World War, was *Lady Hamilton* (known in the USA as *That Hamilton Woman*), starring Laurence Olivier and one of Churchill's great screen idols, Vivien Leigh. Churchill later presented Leigh with one of his paintings, 'Roses in a Glass Vase' which he gave to her when she visited him at Chartwell in 1951. It is said that their friendship led to Leigh and Olivier taking up painting.

Eight years earlier Churchill's total opposition to the Powell and Pressburger film, *The Life and Death of Colonel Blimp*, had prevented Olivier (who was serving in the Royal Navy) from taking a star role. Churchill felt the story, which centred on a good German, was not good for the war effort. No such restrictions were imposed when Churchill personally persuaded Olivier to direct and star in a film of Shakespeare's *Henry V*.

Churchill met many celebrities during his life, but actor Richard Burton's account of his encounter with Churchill was one of the oddest. Burton was of Welsh working-class origin and so, by background, inevitably opposed to Churchill; despite elements of admiration and even fear of him, he openly admitted to a serious loathing. Churchill once caused him especial annoyance when, seated in the front row of the theatre for Burton's performance of Hamlet, he continuously and audibly muttered the lines of Hamlet's great soliloquy a few words ahead of Burton's own rendition.

One encounter with the director and actor Orson Welles was on the Venice Lido, where a nodding greeting from Churchill was observed by the Russian whom Welles was courting for finance for his next film. On meeting the next day, Welles thanked Churchill, as the Russian was massively impressed at Welles's acquaintance.

The actor whom Churchill most admired and whom he first met on a visit to Hollywood in September 1929, where he was taken by Randolph Hearst, was Charlie Chaplin. Chaplin was an excellent host, showing Churchill and his party over the set of the film he was making, *City Lights*, and providing a private screening of his 1918 film *Shoulder Arms*. Although Churchill was an assiduous night owl and frequently worked his staff till 3 a.m., he did spend a lot of his evenings, especially at Chartwell, which was equipped with a professional film projector, watching films. Chaplin's films were among his favourites. On the same trip he met P. G. Wodehouse, and the movie stars Pola Negri and Harold Lloyd.

Churchill warmed quickly to Chaplin, despite his strong pro-socialist views, as Chaplin did to the Conservative Churchill. They met again at Chartwell in February 1931 and September 1932 and cemented a friendship that lasted the rest of Churchill's life, with Chaplin even contributing to the gift of a Daimler car, following Churchill's accident in New York in 1932. The two men met for a final time at the Savoy Grill in London on 25 April 1956, after Churchill had retired, giving Churchill one final chance to voice his deep admiration for Chaplin's art.

PHR

Churchill and Chaplin pictured together in London, in 1931.

41 | Churchill's Standing Desk

Churchill made his first public speech on 3 November 1894, when he and some friends banded together to break down barriers that women of a 'social purity campaign' had erected around what they saw as a centre of debauchery within the Empire Theatre of Varieties in London's Leicester Square. A more salubrious occasion on 26 July 1897, an assembly of a hundred or so members of the Conservative-supporting Primrose League at Claverton

Down on the outskirts of Bath, offered Churchill the opportunity to make his first reported official speech. It was, as recent biographer Andrew Roberts describes it, 'a classic statement of pugnacious late Victorian imperialism', which excited a keen response from his audience and convinced Churchill of his latent talent.

Churchill was well aware from very early in his life of the potential power of oratory. In an unpublished 1897 essay entitled 'The Scaffolding of Rhetoric', which he wrote at the age of

---

Throughout his life, Churchill would be known
for his powerful and memorable speeches.

---

twenty-two while not yet a politician but still a professional soldier, he described how anyone with the precious gift of oratory holds the power to incite passions and to produce in an individual, or even a crowd, conviction and belief. Looking at how Churchill used words, particularly in his oratory, in the Second World War to share his convictions and convince others to believe them too, it is remarkable how he had discovered the means of doing this over forty years earlier.

President John F. Kennedy, in presenting Churchill with an honorary American citizenship in 1963, quoted the famous American wartime London correspondent, Ed Murrow (himself

quoting the 1940 words of the journalist Beverley Nichols), who summarised Churchill's oratory with the words: 'He mobilized the English language and sent it into battle.' There can be no better description of how Churchill used the power of language and of oratory to reach the hearts and minds of people and to rouse them to stand up and fight for their beliefs and for their freedom. Churchill's wartime speeches are justifiably seen as some of the finest examples of their kind, and at the core of Churchill's reputation as the ultimate leader in adversity. It is this, more than anything, that causes so many modern statesmen and women to admire, to envy, and to try to emulate him; it

It was in the grounds of Claverton Manor, near Bath, that Churchill gave his first proper political speech.

also makes his words widely quotable – often in inappropriate contexts for the power they have to support a campaign – decades after their airing.

When, in 1953, the Committee of the Nobel Prize decided to give Churchill the Nobel Prize for Literature, it was given, uniquely, not just for his writings, but also, in the words of the citation, 'for brilliant oratory in defending exalted human values'. It is no accident that in 2017, over seventy years after the war ended, a film about Churchill's first days as prime minister (*Darkest Hour*) could win an Oscar for its star Gary Oldman: the very power of Churchill's oratory, as the film portrays, not only trumped the arguments of the naysayers and appeasers around him in 1940 but, decades later, roused audiences to their feet.

Churchill had many enemies in the House of Commons, not least for 'ratting' on the Conservative Party and crossing to the Liberals in 1904 and then 're-ratting' back to the Tories twenty years later, but also because he was considered emotional, mercurial, bombastic, and lacking judgement. But when he spoke in the Chamber, the house would fill, with many attending just to hear the wordsmithery of the man generally considered one of the most powerful speakers of the era.

It was not always thus and, when he fluffed the lines of a speech he was giving in the Chamber in April 1904 (parliamentarians, then as now, were not allowed to read prepared speeches and Churchill generally memorised his beforehand), he was derided, not least because of the echoes it gave of a similar incident in his father's declining years. After that, he revised his speeches till they were perfect in every detail, while his secretaries would type them out in what came to be called 'psalm form', akin, in appearance, to free verse, helping him to place emphasis and intonation at exactly the right points. Many of his best-known speeches were composed in the study at Chartwell, where he dictated them to his secretary while standing; the standing desk shown here was a piece of furniture gifted to Churchill by his family at Christmas 1949.

He spoke bravely, never more so than when he warned the world of the Soviet threat in his 1946 'Iron Curtain' speech, for which the US media and the US President initially strongly rebuked him. He used words to put his enemies (and often friends) in their place, but sometimes allowed himself to be carried by his own verbiage, bringing odium and lasting criticism, such as when he compared the Labour Party in the 1945 election to the Nazi Gestapo.

Churchill was well aware of the power his speeches possessed and enjoyed playing with words, even inventing terms, such as 'summits' for meetings between national leaders, and phrases that are now an essential of the English language ('when you are going through hell, keep going'). In this regard, some of his words and sayings are almost as widely quoted as those of Shakespeare.

PHR

42 | *The Yellow Spot,* 1936

Antisemitism was widespread in Britain in the 1930s and beyond and allowed many people of standing to condone Hitler and his clearly expressed antipathy to the Jews. Churchill had visited Germany in 1932 and narrowly missed meeting Hitler, having offended him by complaining to Hitler's friend Ernst 'Putzi' Hanfstaengel about Hitler's antisemitism.

Churchill's subsequent awareness of Hitler's antisemitic policies being found academic posts in the UK for a number of German Jewish scientists, who went on to contribute to the Allied war effort, not least in the development of the atomic bomb. Churchill's personal efforts to find a placement for a German Jewish student at Bristol University, of which he was Chancellor, fell on deaf ears, though.

Churchill became increasingly aware through the second half of the 1930s of the worsening repression of Jews in Germany, with the wider introduction

---

Churchill did much to highlight the Nazi persecution and murder of Jewish people.

---

converted into harsh everyday reality undoubtedly added to his existing concerns over Britain's real need to re-arm in the face of Germany's increasing militarism. He also displayed remarkable prescience as early as April 1933 when he spoke of the danger of the abhorrent conditions in Germany, which threatened to be extended to other countries including Poland, with further persecution of Jews being begun there. What to most parliamentarians sounded like typical Churchillian hyperbole was to prove painfully true.

Churchill welcomed the German Jewish exiled scientist Albert Einstein to his Chartwell home in early 1933 and Einstein sought Churchill's help in getting Jewish scientists out of Germany. Churchill immediately pressed his scientific adviser Professor Frederick Lindemann to do what he could. Lindemann successfully

of more extreme antisemitic legislation making such persecution more obvious to those outside the country. After receiving a copy of Victor Gollancz's publication *The Yellow Spot: The Extermination of the Jews in Germany* in 1936 from the leading Labour Party theorist Harold Laski, Churchill used this to reinforce his existing campaign to re-arm, and thus to halt the rapid advance of the Nazis. The next year he gave an emotional and powerful speech in the House of Commons, as it was about to pass legislation limiting the number of Jews allowed to emigrate to Palestine, urging Parliament not to close that door and thereby allow ever greater repression of the Jews in Germany. The increasingly vicious persecution, imprisonment and torture of Jews during and after the pogrom of 9/10 November 1938 ('*Kristallnacht*') were widely publicised

THE YELLOW SPOT: The Extermination of the JEWS in Germany

WITH AN INTRODUCTION BY THE BISHOP OF DURHAM

THE FIRST COMPLETE DOCUMENTARY STUDY

The Yellow Spot, published in 1936, was among the first books to offer evidence for the wide-scale persecutions of Jewish people living in Germany.

in Britain, but all of Churchill's efforts and his scathing condemnation of the government's 'line of least resistance', highlighting the fate of Jews in Germany, failed to elicit support – on both sides of the House – for rearmament or an increase in the number of Jews allowed to emigrate to Palestine.

In June 1940, as Prime Minister, he overruled his C-in-C Middle East to allow nearly 2,000 Jews who had been forcibly expelled from Germany to go to Palestine to stay there, as he did again in 1942. In early 1944 he enabled over 6,000 Jews fleeing from eastern Europe to enter Palestine via Turkey with immediate effect and in June 1944 persuaded Marshal Tito to allow the transit of Jewish refugees from Hungary to safety in Italy.

From June 1942 details of the extermination of Jews across Nazi-occupied Europe were widely broadcast by the BBC and a united Allied declaration condemning the Nazi crimes made graphically plain the fate of those 'hundreds of thousands' who perished in 'mass executions'. Churchill alone insisted that the declaration make clear that those responsible for these crimes (he also insisted, against US advice, that the word 'alleged' be omitted) would be hunted down after the war and brought to trial.

Following on from this he tried, but failed, to have air raids conducted over Berlin in direct reprisal for the murder of Poles and Jewish people, but he did manage to have the anti-Jewish laws still in place in Algeria after the Allied expulsion of the Vichy French repealed. He also persuaded the Spanish government to re-open its borders with France to enable several hundred Jewish refugees to flee there, and then, opposed by Roosevelt, created a safe haven for them in North Africa.

Churchill wrote to Harold Laski in June 1943 to highlight his awareness of the persecution of Jewish people within the occupied countries of Europe and how he constantly thought about what could be done, both during the war and afterwards, in order to alleviate their suffering. Numerous accounts exist of people who were suffering horribly under Nazi oppression gaining comfort, support and hope from listening to Churchill's words on the radio.

When early reports of the full scale of the horrors of Auschwitz and other extermination camps came out, Churchill became even more adamant that anyone connected with the killings should be hunted down and justice delivered. He knew, too, that the only real means of putting an end to the horrors would be a rapid Allied victory.

PHR

43 | Bust of the Duke of Windsor, by Clara Haas

Churchill was described by his wife Clementine as being one of the last true believers in the divine right of kings, and his support of Britain's royalty was unwavering throughout his lifetime. He lived through the reigns of six monarchs in all, and enjoyed close relationships with many.

January 1936 saw Edward, Prince of Wales, succeed his father as King. He had already embroiled himself in a number of romantic affairs, yet the British press had respectfully avoided drawing attention to what many considered as simple youthful errors of judgement. But during Edward VIII's first few months on the throne, his romantic links with Wallis Simpson, an American woman about to divorce her second husband, became public knowledge. It was not long before Edward declared that they intended to marry.

Prime Minister Stanley Baldwin and much of the establishment were firmly against the idea; it was an era in which marriage to a divorced woman was widely regarded as socially unacceptable, while the Church of England (of which Edward, as King, was head) disapproved of marriage after divorce if a former spouse was still alive. With Baldwin and the government prepared to resign over the matter, Edward had little option but to abdicate if he wanted to marry Mrs Simpson and avoid a constitutional crisis.

In a manner characteristic of his staunch support for the Royal Family, Churchill embroiled himself in the crisis by begging Baldwin to give the King more time to resolve the issue. But in doing this, he fatally misread the public mood, which suggested that most people either wanted the King to marry, or to abdicate – not to dither even further. Churchill had given in

Churchill and Edward, when still Prince of Wales, photographed at a lunch party at the House of Commons on 5 June 1919.

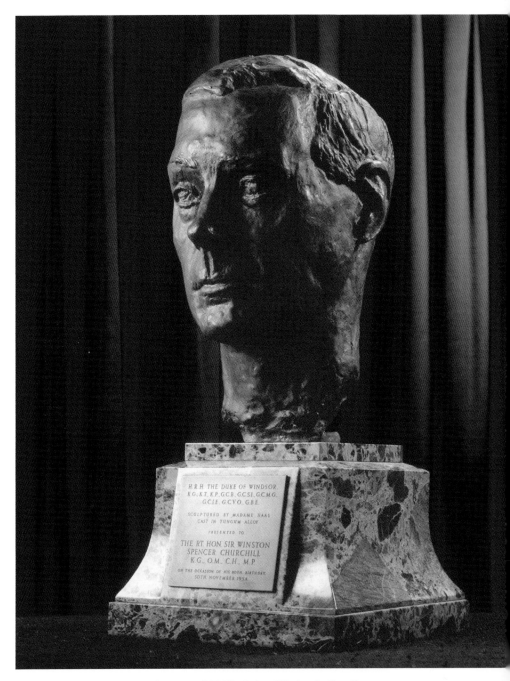

Sculpture of HRH The Duke of Windsor, by Clara Haas.

As an ardent supporter of the royal family, Churchill's loyalty was called into question during the abdication crisis.

---

too easily to his personal feelings. He was a man of intense emotion who never shied away from showing either pain or delight. It was not unknown, for instance, for Churchill to weep openly when listening to a particularly emotional piece of music. This character trait meant that any appeal to his romantic nature tended to elicit a positive response, and the abdication crisis perhaps provides the ultimate example of this.

Further attempts by Churchill in the House of Commons to postpone a decision on the matter were met with howls of derision, and for a time Churchill's reputation was almost in as much danger as that of Edward himself. In the end the King abdicated on 11 December to be succeeded by his younger brother, who became George VI.

Churchill's political isolation was now almost complete, yet the final years of the 1930s saw the situation turn in his favour, as the threat of war that he had been predicting for so long finally became a reality. His friendship with Edward, now the Duke of Windsor, would remain but in a necessarily more detached manner. Some of Edward's actions during the Second World War would prove questionable to Churchill, whose relationship with George VI only strengthened. Yet a gift presented to Churchill on the occasion of his eightieth birthday in November 1954 perhaps indicates the continued respect which he still held for the former sovereign. This sculpture of Edward by the American artist Clara Haas had been forged from tungum alloy (a type of brass) in 1936, and was displayed at Chartwell.

APR

44 | A Typical Lunch Bill

For somebody commonly regarded these days as a figure of stability and reliability, Churchill spent much of his life as a maverick, swimming in a sea of personal debt. This was partly a result of the lavish lifestyle that he enjoyed, but also due to a gambling obsession which followed him all his days.

Financial problems pursued Churchill from the very beginning, as he declared at the age of twenty-three in a letter to his brother how money was the single thing which worried him in life. By the

a ready means of raising significant amounts of money. Books and newspaper articles led to speaking tours, which were similarly trusted sources of income. The drawback was that his regular visits to North America and Europe, where he mixed with rich and influential people, meant that he was continually surrounded by opulence – which encouraged more spending to maintain such a lifestyle.

One of the main causes of Churchill's extravagance was alcohol, on which he spent huge amounts. A heavy drinker at the best of times, he was also very

---

One of the few things which almost defeated Churchill was his love of spending money.

---

time that he was married and with four children also dependent on his income, Churchill's annual holiday to the South of France saw him gamble so heavily that he lost on average the equivalent in today's money of some £40,000 per year. Throughout his life, he struggled to get a grip on his spending and, although Clementine expressed concern at this extravagance, she was unsuccessful in encouraging him to change his ways.

Born as he was into the world of the aristocracy, it was perhaps inevitable that Churchill would look to enjoy the finer things in life and expect a standard of living above that experienced by most ordinary people. Much of his personal income was sourced from his extensive writing career, which proved itself as

particular as to the quality of his alcohol, which made any bills from wine merchants or restaurants notably large. Churchill also found himself unable to resist any opportunity for gambling, whether in casinos or through private betting between friends. He once made a successful wager with Lord Rothermere that he could avoid drinking brandy for a whole year, and won £600. Such a love of betting also encouraged Churchill to gamble on the stock market. His fascination with new technology and innovation led to regular trading in shares and commodities, through investments in such things as oilfields, electricity, gas and rolling stock.

But this excessive spending would lead to a sudden sharp shock. One of the worst

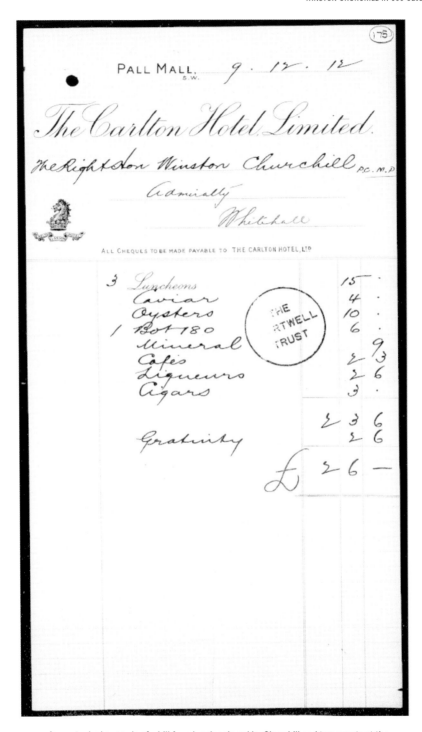

A very typical example of a bill for a lunch enjoyed by Churchill and two guests at the Carlton Hotel in London. Caviar and oysters were followed by liqueurs and cigars.

moments for Churchill proved to be the Wall Street Crash of 1929, in which he claimed to have lost about $50,000; the true amount is likely to have been far greater. He would spend the following decade feverishly writing and lecturing in order to make back at least some of what he had lost. He also never hesitated to borrow money, whether from friends and family, his publisher or bank, and relied on regular bail-outs to keep him from bankruptcy.

Decades before the political scandals we see today involving expense accounts and tax avoidance, Churchill proved particularly inventive at coming up with means of obtaining ready cash. When hit by a car in New York in 1931, he claimed a medical insurance payout for being left 'totally disabled', yet was able to make a fairly swift recovery. He also avoided paying tax on his book royalties, by selling the publishing rights and successfully arguing that any money he received was exempt from income tax.

This extravagant spending and ardent gambling meant that Churchill's money had run out by 1938. His borrowing had reached its limit and he was forced to put Chartwell and his London home on the market. But before losing everything, he experienced some remarkable good fortune. He was introduced to Sir Henry Strakosch, a rich admirer of Churchill's stance against Hitler and the threat from Nazism, who offered to pay off a good deal of his debts in a secret show of support. Churchill's appointment as Prime Minister in 1940 also contributed to a turn in his financial fortunes.

Churchill's improved status in due course brought with it numerous opportunities to improve his finances, whether by selling film rights to his various books, or through public speaking engagements. His reputation as the successful war leader brought with it many advantages. After the war, a group of friends bought Chartwell on behalf of the National Trust and rented the property back to the Churchill family for a nominal amount. In addition, the Nobel Prize for Literature awarded to Churchill in 1953 was accompanied by a tax-free sum of £12,000.

No longer in danger of bankruptcy, Churchill continued to spend to excess during the final decades of his life. He maintained an expensive staff who accompanied him on his regular travels, and continued to spend exorbitant amounts on luxury hotels and of course alcohol. He was a regular visitor to the casinos of Monte Carlo and spent much time with Aristotle Onassis, the billionaire shipping magnate. Indeed, by all accounts, Churchill's ability to spend money never wavered until his death.

APR

Churchill enjoys a glass of champagne, one of his favourite drinks.

45 | La Mamounia Hotel, Marrakesh

hurchill first visited Morocco over the winter months of 1935–6. Although ostensibly on holiday, he was finishing writing his epic two-volume biography of his ancestor, the first Duke of Marlborough.

he could sit and admire the beautiful panorama. The luxurious hotel was a popular destination for the world's rich and famous, and at the time of Churchill's visit it was already hosting former Prime Minister David Lloyd George and his family.

Morocco became one of Churchill's favourite places to holiday, with one hotel in particular being visited regularly.

After travelling to Tangier, the party moved on, because of bad weather, to Marrakesh where Churchill stayed at the La Mamounia hotel and occupied a fine bedroom sporting a large balcony where

But it was the view from his balcony that Churchill would take most delight in, praising it enthusiastically in a letter written home to Clementine shortly after his arrival in Morocco. The contrast

The Churchill suite, photographed in the present-day La Mamounia hotel in Marrakesh.

between the arid desert country and its mountainous backdrop fascinated him and he would spend the next few weeks enjoying the sun and using the opportunity to continue his hobby of painting, with the view of the mountains providing the perfect subject.

Displaying the bright colours so characteristic of Churchill's artistic style, the painting showed the green leaves of the orange and olive trees standing in front of the houses and fortifications of the old city of Marrakesh, with the snow-clad Atlas Mountains towering behind. The beautiful scene clearly remained strong in Churchill's memory, and explains his insistence on taking President Roosevelt for a 150-mile drive across the desert to Marrakesh in January 1943 in order to let him witness the sunset over the mountains. The party stayed in the Villa Taylor, an impressive home owned by a wealthy New York family in the city's upper-class residential area. Following their joint deliberations at the Casablanca conference, it would prove to be a brief escape for the two leaders before the hard slog of war would re-impose itself.

It is also illustrative of the friendship shared by the two men. As Winston's youngest daughter Mary Soames described the moment, 'The two friends sat side by side and watched the sun set in all its splendour on the distant snow-clad peaks: a moment of tranquillity amid the tumult and stress of the war.'

Once Roosevelt had left, Churchill seized the opportunity to paint the sunset once again, although this time from a different viewpoint – the tower of the villa occupied by the American Vice-Consul. This particular work proved to be the only painting which Churchill produced during the war, perhaps illustrating how special this particular view remained to his personal happiness.

Churchill enjoyed several further excursions to Marrakesh, both during and after the war, usually in an attempt to find sun and warmth in the winter months at home. In January 1944 he was there to recuperate after a bout of pneumonia, and chose to spend his afternoons in the foothills of the mountains. On one occasion, he decided to clamber down a rocky gorge and ended up trapped on top of a large boulder, necessitating a hasty rescue by his retainers. In the post-war years he returned regularly to La Mamounia to enjoy the view again.

APR

Churchill spent Christmas at La Mamounia in 1947.

46 | Door to No. 10 Downing Street

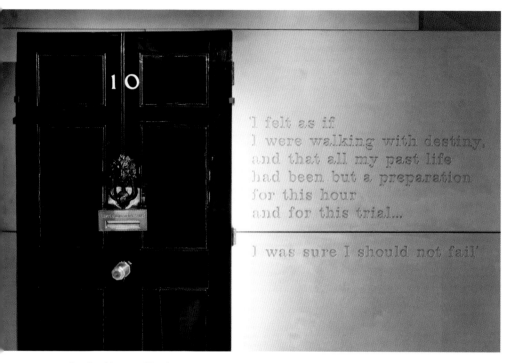

I felt as if
I were walking with destiny,
and that all my past life
had been but a preparation
for this hour
and for this trial...

I was sure I should not fail'

In the final lines of his book, *The Gathering Storm*, published in 1948 as the first part in his six-volume history entitled *The Second World War*, Churchill said of his appointment as Prime Minister on 10 May 1940 that he felt as though he was following his destiny, with everything he had done in his life to that point having been in preparation for this testing moment. In fact his ambitions and belief that he would one day take on the mantle of Prime Minister of Great Britain were present when, as a precocious sixteen-year-old, he confided to a friend at Harrow School, Murland Evans, that he would one day be the person who would save not only London and England but the Empire from disaster.

In November 1915, he was effectively forced to resign over the failure of the Dardanelles campaign, and suddenly saw his political career as finished. At one blow he was out of office, just as he nurtured real hopes of ousting and succeeding the prime minister, of the day, Herbert Asquith, against whom opposition was intensifying (in fact, leading to Asquith's replacement in December 1916 by Churchill's political ally, Lloyd George).

Churchill's most famous dictum, issued to the boys of Harrow when he visited as Prime Minister in October

Churchill finally assumed his best-known political role in 1940.

1941, 'never give in', was a perfect reflection of his own view on life, when he returned to high government office as Minister of Munitions in Lloyd George's administration in July 1917. The next decade saw his political career advance steadily, till he was appointed, by Prime Minister Baldwin to the second-highest role in government, as Chancellor of the Exchequer, a post that Churchill rather tongue-in-cheek claimed fulfilled his ambitions, though few believed it.

In 1929 the Conservatives lost the election and he was once more out of office. On their return to power, Baldwin again led the government, being replaced as Prime Minister by Neville Chamberlain in May 1937. Churchill had told his wife in 1929 that such a turn of events would lead him to consider emigrating to Canada, making his continued ambitions quite plain. Chamberlain, aware of Churchill's hopes, as much as he was of his tendency, once in office, to assume responsibilities far beyond his remit, kept Churchill out of government. In these, his 'wilderness years' as his biographer Martin Gilbert labelled them, he spent a large part of his time hammering the government for its failure to invest more heavily in

PM's CARD

● ENGAGEMENTS ●

SEPTEMBER, 1940.

SUN. 1	Thur. 12	Mon. 23
Mon. 2	Fri. 13	Tues. 24
Tues. 3	Sat. 14	Wed. 25
Wed. 4	SUN. 15	Thur. 26
Thur. 5	Mon. 16 12.30 Cabinet	Fri. 27
Fri. 6	Tues. 17	Sat. 28
Sat. 7	Wed. 18	SUN. 29
SUN. 8	Thur. 19	Mon. 30
Mon. 9	Fri. 20	
Tues. 10	Sat. 21	
Wed. 11 6. Broadcast	SUN. 22	

H.M. STATIONERY OFFICE

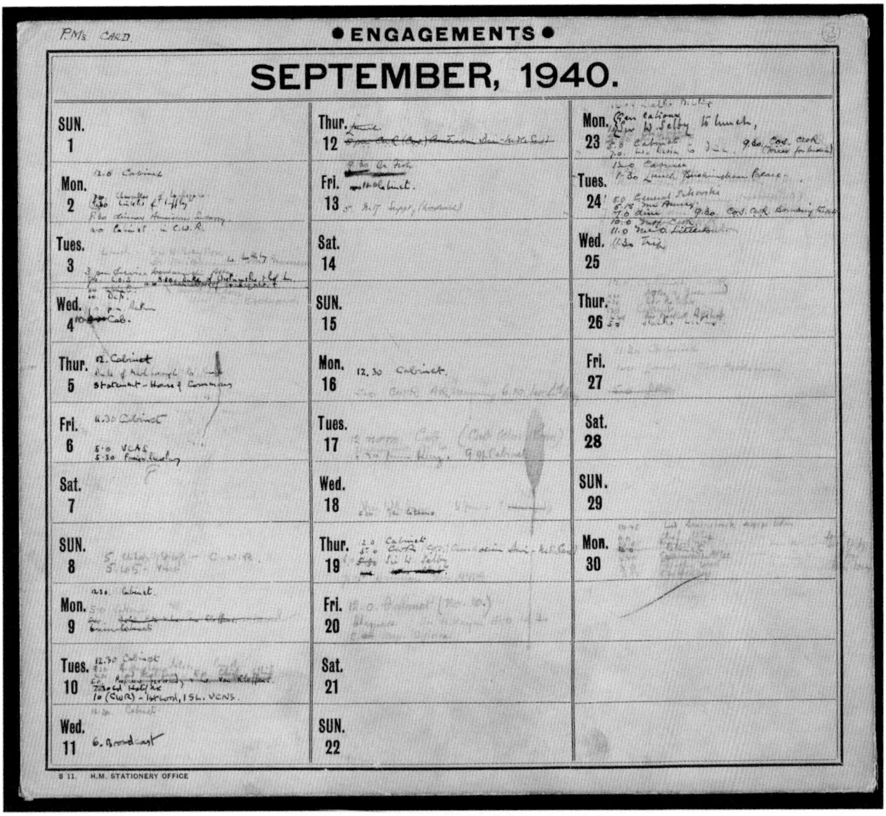

Churchill's engagements diary illustrates the busy life of a Prime Minister, with September 1940 being one of the most stressful times of his Premiership.

rearmament, to be ready to face down an increasingly strong Germany under the war-mongering leadership of Adolf Hitler. Churchill's outright opposition to the Prime Minister's policy of appeasement truly only began with Hitler's annexation of Czechoslovakia in 1938. But, when war was declared in September 1939, Chamberlain was pressured, especially by the media, to bring Churchill – the man who had warned of the likelihood of war – back into government.

Because of the ongoing failures of the Anglo-French campaign in Norway, it became clear by early May 1940 that Chamberlain was not the man to lead the country in a war. In the question of who was to succeed him, the general view – and certainly that of King George VI – was that Lord Halifax would be the obvious choice. Halifax himself demurred, not least because, sitting in the House

of Lords, he felt that he would not be able to direct operations from the House of Commons, reducing his role to that of a 'cypher', as he saw it. Though the Labour Party's presence in the House of Commons was relatively small, it was generally felt that any new government should be a 'national government', encompassing all parties. Though small in number, the Labour Party was strong enough to be the deciding factor and, as they refused to serve under Chamberlain, and Halifax refused the post of Prime Minister, their last-minute agreement to serve under Churchill carried the day. Thus was Churchill, the sworn enemy of 'socialism' (he generally referred to the Labour Party as 'socialists'), put into office with left-wing support.

PHR

47 | Churchill's Nightshirt

Churchill was once quoted as saying that while it was his rule in his younger days not to take strong drink before lunch, this had changed to never doing so before breakfast.

Churchill, an occasional literalist in what he said, practised what he claimed, but only just, in that his staff would traditionally add to his breakfast tray a glass of well-watered whisky (ten parts water to one part Johnnie Walker Black Label; his staff used to refer to it as 'mouthwash').

Champagne was his preferred lunch and dinner tipple (Pol Roger was his favourite from as early as 1909, but he would never turn down any quality champagne). He is quoted as saying that the pint bottle of champagne (about three-quarters of a standard bottle) – which was a regular size of French exports to the UK in the first part of the twentieth century – was enough for two people at lunchtime and one at dinner.

Cecil Beaton in his wartime diaries records how, while waiting at 10 Downing Street to take an official photo of the Prime Minister, he witnessed a servant taking a glass of vintage port to him – at about 11 a.m. Hine Cognac claim theirs was his favourite brand and a regular evening tipple and certainly his cellar was well stocked with Pol Roger, Hine and Black Label whisky – as well as some highly regarded white Burgundy that he had personally bottled with the writer Hilaire Belloc.

The distance between his own lifestyle and that of the common man is nowhere better illustrated than in his letter to his brother Jack, written while he was briefly living at Hoe Farm in Surrey (a large residence converted by the renowned architect, Sir Edward Lutyens) to which he retreated after being forced to resign as First Lord of the Admiralty in 1915. Here he referred to the essentials of the 'simple life' he was living as 'hot baths, cold champagne, new peas and old brandy'.

At night, as relaxation in later years, he would often watch films and had fixed projection facilities installed at both Chartwell and the Admiralty. He loved Hollywood 'weepies' – he was famously an utter sentimentalist, renowned for shedding tears at the least occasion – but he was very fond of the Marx Brothers, Charlie Chaplin, Disney cartoons and almost anything featuring Vivien Leigh. After the Second World War, when out of office, he would often use the period from about midnight to 3 a.m., to dictate to his covey of academically highly qualified researchers, who would transcribe what would become his *History of the Second World War*, fact-checking, correcting and occasionally re-writing.

Churchill's daily routine was unusual in many different ways.

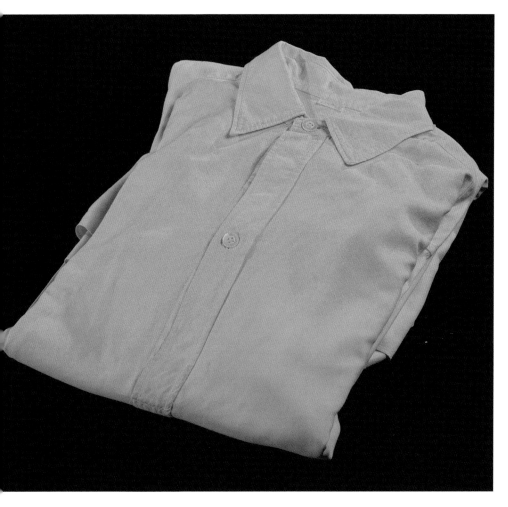

Churchill's nightshirt, worn not only at nighttime but also during his daytime 'naps', which he regularly took in order to give him the energy to work late into the night.

Churchill always slept well, claiming that he did so throughout the Second World War, despite all the crises that challenged him. Breakfast was almost always taken in bed. He once asked an American friend if he regularly had breakfast with his wife and, when told that he did indeed, almost always, Churchill explained that he never did and considered this arrangement an important factor to a continued happy marriage.

In order to ensure his safety during the war his staff often arranged for him to spend weekends in the country houses of friends, where whatever was grown, farmed, shot or fished on the estate would not be rationed, resulting at certain times of the year in his breakfasting on left-over grouse (often with a glass of Chablis).

Breakfast was routinely followed by a bath – the temperature and depth of the water being strictly regulated to meet his exact demands. He would dictate to secretaries from his bath (through a closed door), would smoke cigars there and occasionally wash himself.

This Remington 'noiseless' typewriter was specially imported from America for use in the Cabinet War Rooms. Churchill was insistent on quiet conditions to encourage work.

Afternoons were regularly punctuated by a second bath, which would be preceded by what many described as his 'naps', which, as he himself explained, actually involved undressing, going to bed and having a deep sleep for an hour. This, he claimed, allowed him to accomplish so much more and would enable him to stay up till 3.00 the next morning.

PHR

48 | Map Room Clock, Cabinet War Rooms

The 'V for Victory symbol united not just the British population for much of the Second World War, but encompassed the wider Allied cause, extending to the United States and occupied Europe too. Churchill made the two-fingered 'V' hand gesture particularly popular, encouraging its use as one of the defining images of wartime defiance. Yet although the symbol is synonymous with Churchill, being as much a part of his image as the cigar, bow tie and 'bulldog determination', he was not actually the creator of this famous sign.

Churchill would regularly give the 'V' sign in the same manner as the popular British insult, despite being aware of its double meaning.

Significantly, 'V' was a symbolic first letter not just in English, but also in French (*Victoire* meaning 'victory') and Dutch (*Vrijheid* meaning 'freedom'). As early as May 1939, a French newspaper had printed the headline '*V pour Victoire*' but it was not until January 1941 that a broadcast by Victor de Laveleye, in charge of Belgian French-language broadcasts on the BBC, suggested that Belgians should use the letter as a rallying emblem during their country's occupation. This idea proved popular, and within weeks the simple emblem was chalked on walls as graffiti throughout occupied territories, to show resistance to the Nazis.

Inspired by this success, the BBC pushed for a wider 'V for Victory' campaign to promote greater use of the symbol, even using the Morse code version of 'V' (three dots and a dash) as the call-sign for its broadcasts to occupied Europe, in musical form identical to the famous four-note opening phrase of Beethoven's Fifth Symphony.

In a speech on 19 July 1941, Churchill approved of the campaign and began to adopt the 'V' hand gesture himself on numerous occasions. Other Allied leaders similarly began to give the sign when giving addresses and being photographed. A member of staff in Churchill's underground War Rooms even highlighted the 'V' on their map room clock, as shown here, to reinforce the Victory message.

Normally the gesture would be made with the palm facing outwards, but often (due to holding a cigar in the same hand) Churchill would make the gesture with

While he was not the creator of the famous 'V for Victory' gesture, Churchill did much to promote it.

his palm towards him. He was allegedly unaware that this version was a common British insult, since such a rude sign was not regularly used by the aristocracy. But even after he became aware of the difference, he refused to stop using the gesture that way, seemingly as a deliberate decision to insult his German enemy. This alternate, and almost unwritten, double meaning behind the 'V' sign became more popular as the war went on, with many British people adopting it towards Hitler and Germany.

The popularity of the 'V' sign across Europe led to the Germans adopting it as their own, in recognition of their military successes. Large 'V' signs were displayed prominently in Paris, for instance, including on the Eiffel Tower during the Nazi occupation.

In its normal usage, however, the 'V' sign could be regarded as something approaching an unofficial Allied counterpart to the Nazi swastika, signifying victory against all that the swastika stood for. Its success as a strong symbol of Victory is confirmed by the association that Churchill continued to have with it, even in the postwar years and since his own death. Since the protests against the Vietnam War in the 1960s, however, the symbol is now largely intended to represent 'peace'.

APR

A 'V for Victory' wartime brooch which associates Churchill and his instantly recognisable image.

49 | British Restaurant Meal Ticket

In 1954, the year before he stood down as Prime Minister, Churchill looked back at his life as a writer and speaker and admitted that he had always earned his way by his pen and his tongue. He had delivered some 5 million words in speeches and wrote innumerable telegrams, memoranda and letters. Words were indeed his métier and, as Churchill pithily remarked, 'Words are the only thing that lasts forever.' It could have been

Feeding Centres'. This ready source for cheap wartime meals, as illustrated by the meal ticket shown here, proved a popular scheme to help a population suffering from rationing and homelessness caused by bombing.

In his oratory he had a strong preference for brevity and his speeches provided perfect illustrations of his claim that 'short words are the best' and that 'old words, when short, are the best of all'.

Churchill would be remembered for his impressive use of language in both his writings and speeches.

---

a case of Churchill once again presciently foreseeing his own place in history and culture: should a time ever come when his name was forgotten, it was safe to assume that his words would always be remembered, quoted and misquoted or re-hashed to suit a particular campaign.

It would be no exaggeration to say he had a passion for words and used them to great effect, as few before him and no one since has done. Churchill was very precise in his choice of words, with a rare understanding of the power of cadences, emphasis, alliteration, anaphora (repetition of the same words or phrases) and quite simply of sound. He also understood how language could give people a greater sense of dignity, re-naming the newly formed Local Defence Volunteers as 'The Home Guard', and coining the term 'British Restaurants' to replace the prosaic and dull 'Communal

Old, biblical and often arcane words often featured in his speeches, not simply because they said precisely what he wanted to say, but because he felt they had a ring and a resonance that went beyond meaning and it is the case that, even when the actual words of his speeches are not fully understood or appreciated, they can still have that spine-tingling result. He once asked a friend if she thought words could have effect, even if the meaning was not clear. She quoted back to him two lyrical lines from Keats's *Ode to A Nightingale*, which simply astonished him with the power of the sound of the words (and he promptly went away and learned much of Keats's work by heart, having never previously read him).

In his early wartime speeches in particular he knew that he needed to choose his words carefully if he was to inspire a split Cabinet and, after

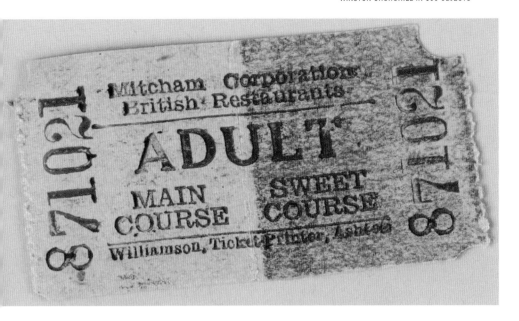

British Restaurants sold meals at a maximum price of 9d per ticket, which would then be exchanged for two courses. No ration coupons were required.

the Fall of France, a nation which was faced with the real fear of an imminent German invasion. Nowhere is his skill in choosing words as a means of turning and trumping any defeatist argument better illustrated, than in the thrilling and brilliant climax of his speech on 28 May 1940: if 'this long island story of ours is to end', he remarked, it would only be when everyone 'lies choking in his own blood upon the ground'.

In 1940 he knew that a popular self-belief and trust in victory were vital to Great Britain surviving the Nazi onslaught. The words and phrases he employed at that time are as well-known as any of the stirring words and speeches in Shakespeare. His magnificent 'we will fight on the beaches' speech, delivered in Parliament on 4 June 1940, stands as one of the truly most epic speeches ever delivered in English. The message of the speech was simple and sure: the British would fight to the death to defend their shores, their history and their freedom.

He referred frequently to the history of the British people, to their record of resistance to oppression and their indomitable spirit. These were core to convincing not just the enemy that any attack on Britain would be resisted and would ultimately be futile, but also to provide the backbone needed in the population to support this thesis. Almost as importantly and in a similar way, his words gave hope to those in Nazi-occupied territories, where people listened to his stirring exhortations on secret radios at risk to their lives.

However, occasionally his love of words, and more especially his liking for the sound of his own voice, would lead to trouble. After he referred to the Mediterranean theatre in 1942 as 'the soft underbelly of Europe', the phrase would come back to haunt him as the Italian campaign developed into some of the most brutal fighting of the war.

PHR

50 | Mrs Landemare's Recipe Book

I n common with most officers in the Army in the late nineteenth and early twentieth centuries – officers being, at that time, largely chosen from the privileged classes – when Churchill served in India, the Sudan and on the Western Front, he was amply supplied with food and alcohol (he claimed he took to drinking whisky in India to purify the water). Officers were sent, directly or by their families, hampers and large consignments of, usually luxury, comestibles and drink, from the best stores in London. Even when Churchill was sheltered in a mine by John Howard, to aid his escape from the Boers in South Africa in 1899, he was supplied with good stocks of food, whisky and even cigars.

Being from a wealthy (if forever indebted) background, he never went hungry, eating frequently in the best restaurants and enjoying the hospitality of rich sybaritic friends. In the Second World War, when his staff initially kept him from staying in the Prime Minister's official country residence of Chequers or his rural retreat, Chartwell, for fear of their being clear targets for German bombers, he spent many weekends at wealthy friends' country houses.

One in particular, Ditchley, belonged to the Anglo-American Conservative MP for Harborough in Leicestershire, Ronald Tree, and was situated not far from the home of Churchill's cousins, Blenheim Palace. He had dined well at Ditchley on a number of occasions before the war, enjoying the company of Tree as a fellow anti-appeaser and bon viveur, and was happy to make it his weekend residence. It was well-supplied with off-ration items, because the owners grew or hunted them. Hence, in the season, he could be

found waking up there to a breakfast of left-over grouse and could enjoy venison, duck and fish without restriction.

Chartwell itself encompassed a farm, which kept him supplied with dairy produce and meat throughout the war, which led to the embarrassment of his showing no sympathy for the common man when shown a plate of the rations of the time, until he was informed that it was

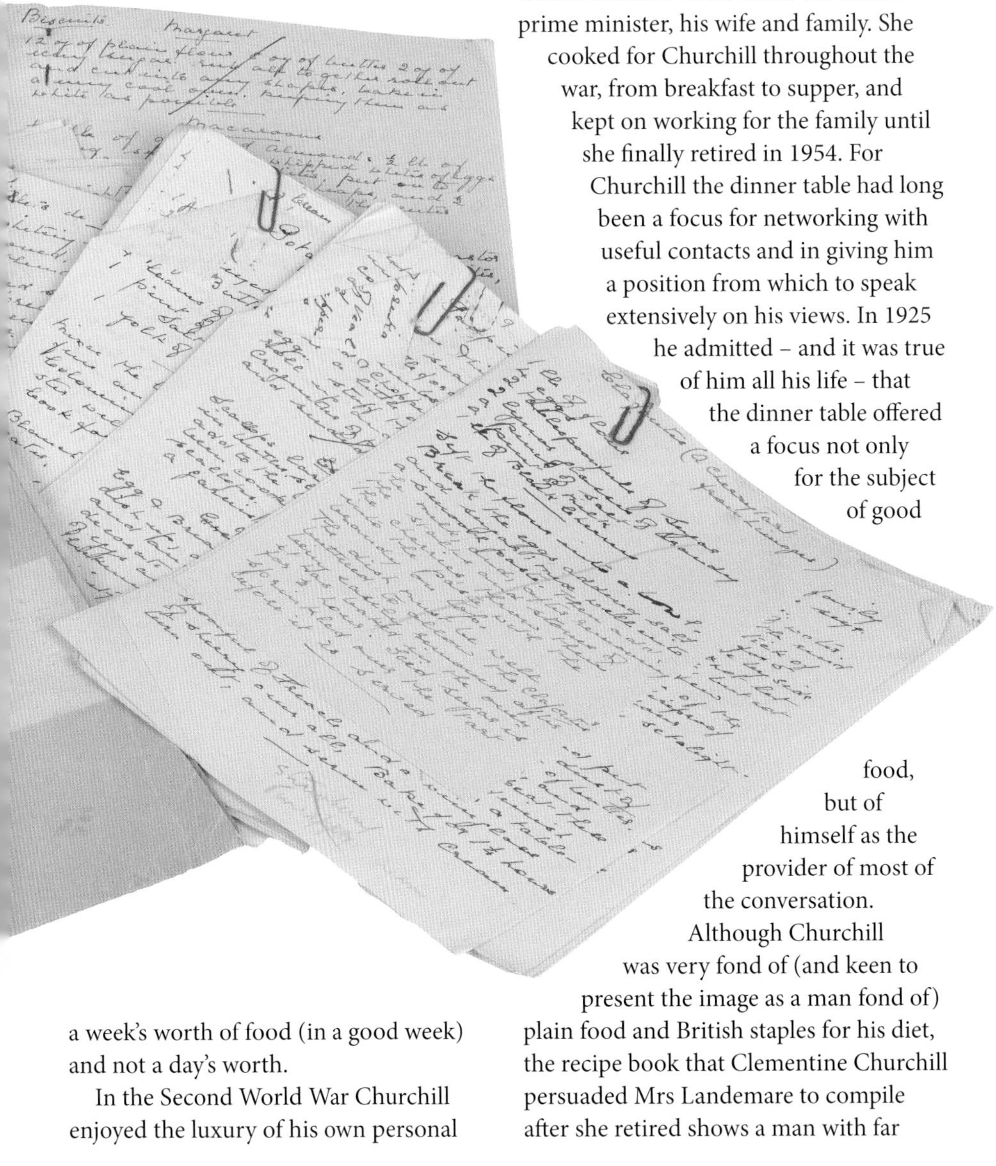

chef in the figure of Mrs Georgina Landemare, the widow of Paul Landemare, a Frenchman who had cooked in the Ritz and for many of the richest people in London. Georgina, an accomplished and highly successful chef who cooked for the highest levels of society, had worked for the Churchills among others in the 1930s and, in 1940 she decided that, as 'war service', she would continue to do so for the future prime minister, his wife and family. She cooked for Churchill throughout the war, from breakfast to supper, and kept on working for the family until she finally retired in 1954. For Churchill the dinner table had long been a focus for networking with useful contacts and in giving him a position from which to speak extensively on his views. In 1925 he admitted – and it was true of him all his life – that the dinner table offered a focus not only for the subject of good

food, but of himself as the provider of most of the conversation. Although Churchill was very fond of (and keen to present the image as a man fond of)

a week's worth of food (in a good week) and not a day's worth.

In the Second World War Churchill enjoyed the luxury of his own personal

plain food and British staples for his diet, the recipe book that Clementine Churchill persuaded Mrs Landemare to compile after she retired shows a man with far

Superior food and drink were both huge passions to Churchill throughout his life.

more eclectic and sophisticated tastes, for which Mrs Landemare, despite the restrictions of rationing, would lavishly cater.

On 6 March 1941 Churchill's dinner guest was King George VI, and Mrs Landemare on this occasion cooked fish patty, tournedos steak with mushrooms accompanied by braised celery and chipped potatoes, and followed by peaches and cheese. What might sound like plain and wholesome fare with a hint of the exotic, was, in wartime, a veritable feast of rarities.

Even the Prime Minister and his wife were subject to rationing, as were the Royal Family.

Perhaps his own enjoyment of relative comforts at the dinner table persuaded Churchill, in 1940, to support the introduction of 'British Restaurants'. These communal kitchens were soon serving over 600,000 meals a day, consisting of good but cheap food, with no ration coupons required. While ordinary people might not have enjoyed the haute cuisine available to Churchill, these restaurants helped ensure they were well fed and given a balanced diet.

PHR

Members of the public enjoying a meal in a British Restaurant, London, 1943.

51 | Siren Suit

Despite occasional efforts on his part to be seen as having something in common with ordinary working people Churchill had surprisingly little knowledge of everyday people's lives.

Evidence of his less than common tastes can be seen in his wardrobe. All of Churchill's clothes were tailor-made by the best London tailors and he was loyal to certain businesses, particularly in the St James's district of London. His favoured suppliers were all among the most respected and expensive in London: his shoes (including the zipper shoes he loved to wear) were usually crafted by Lobb or Palmer & Co., while his favourite monogram slippers were made to measure

wall, the aim being to show him unafraid, metaphorically and physically, of 'getting his hands dirty'. This was similar to a jump suit or one-piece set of overalls and was designed to be put on quickly – perhaps over night clothes – during an air raid. It was generally not superior in quality to either of those. In air force blue with a zipper up the front, this 'ready for action' suit was something he wore increasingly from the early 1930s and which became a signature part of his public image.

When he posed with General Eisenhower and a host of British generals in Algiers in January 1944, with each general wearing his uniform and a vast array of medal ribbons, Churchill was wearing his workaday siren suit, with his

---

Churchill's distinctive clothing was a key aspect of his character.

---

for him by N. Tuczek, at a cost of £14 in 1950, over £400 nowadays; his hats – of which he kept a variety – were mostly supplied by Chapman & Moore or Scott & Co. of Old Bond Street, Piccadilly; his suits and overcoats were made by Bernau & Sons of St James's or Henry Poole of Savile Row; his umbrellas and canes came from Thomas Brigg and Sons in St James's.

Even his underwear was tailor-made, including the famous pink silk vests that he wore for a very large part of his life to alleviate a sensitive-skin complaint.

In 1928 the press featured a picture of Churchill in the gardens at Chartwell wearing a 'siren suit' while building a

favourite dragon-motif dressing gown over it. Churchill was recovering from a bout of pneumonia and had only recently been allowed out of bed, so he had relaxed his normal observance of appropriate dress for the occasion.

Churchill was an aristocrat, the grandson of a duke, and his tastes in all things, but not least clothing, reflected his high-born origins and social standing. In that respect he expected to change into formal clothes for dinner and the plebeian siren suit would not have been

One of Churchill's red velvet siren suits, from the collection of the Imperial War Museum.

A pair of Churchill's much-loved (and expensive) made-to-measure slippers, displayed with a commemorative glass.

considered appropriate dress for any such occasion. Churchill found the solution to the effective social ban on his favourite bodywear by having it replicated in green and red velvet, commissioned from Turnbull & Asser, who were among the best and most expensive tailors in London. His family referred to this article of his clothing as his 'rompers', while modern tastes would immediately see in it a precursor to the 'onesie'.

Churchill was given various items of clothing by well-wishers during the war and his iconic polka-dotted bow ties, which he also had tailor-made by Turnbull & Asser, were a case in point. A close American friend and supporter, who supplied him with hundreds of top quality cigars during the war, at one point decided to give him a stock of his favourite bow ties, which he wore in tribute to his father,

Lord Randolph, for whom they had also been a valued part of his wardrobe.

A vital accompaniment to this wardrobe was his cane, which he regularly used when walking, not so much as a support, but as a social accoutrement. The King gave him as a wedding present a gold-topped Malacca cane, though, as with his hats, he had several to choose from. When he followed the army crossing the Rhine in March 1945 he allegedly prodded his cane into the ground – with the sole purpose of freeing himself up to urinate on German territory in the same way that General Patton had already publicly done. The common man would undoubtedly have admired their prime minister for that, if only the stunt had been publicised.

PHR

52 | Dr Seuss Cartoon, 1 October 1941

I n November 1895, Churchill was travelling to Cuba to cover the local insurrection and stopped off in New York en route, to meet his mother's friend (and former lover), Bourke Cockran, who entertained Churchill and his travel companion, Reggie Barnes, to several days of intense activity and social engagements.

The brash and over-confident twenty-year-old Churchill recorded his early impressions of America, believing that the country could boast a sense of freshness and good nature that might make older

of reparations. He was further troubled by America's insistence on a major expansion of its navy, something which Churchill saw as a real threat to Britain's long dominance as a naval power. In conversation with a fellow Conservative politician in 1928 he freely described America as arrogant, hostile and out to dominate world politics, complaining to his wife Clementine that America was gradually forcing Britain into the shade. He concealed his hostility to America during what one biographer describes as 'a short but . . . secret anti-American

---

Churchill's strong links with the United States were challenged by its isolationist stance prior to the Second World War.

---

nations envious of its successes. His second visit to the USA came some five years later, when, for the first time, he visited for purely profit-making reasons, embarking on a lecture tour before entering Parliament, a vocation that at that time paid no salary.

Churchill's affection for America generally grew as time passed, though it suffered a decline for a time in the 1920s when Churchill was Chancellor of the Exchequer, and the USA was pressing hard for the rapid repayment of the UK's First World War debt to the country and for a share of the reparations payable by Germany. Churchill was totally opposed to this, not least because the USA was not a party to the Versailles Treaty and its ancillary structure for the settlement

phase' and in the years that followed changed his attitude to America entirely. If not yet a military superpower, America was clearly a major player in economic and political terms.

In 1929 Churchill paid his first visit to the USA since his 1900 lecture tour – just as the 'Crash' caused him to be all but bankrupt – in an almost conciliatory attempt to get to know the nation better. He visited again in 1931–2, when once more he was using America as a means of providing himself with a living. On that later trip he lectured the length and breadth of North America, met thousands of ordinary Americans and many luminaries, not only developing his liking for America and the Americans, but also his personal trust in the country.

This satirical cartoon by 'Dr Seuss' highlights the isolationist attitude of many Americans at the beginning of the Second World War.

Since 1919, America had stood back from the League of Nations and ushered in an era of isolationism, supported by President Warren Harding immediately after the signing of the Treaty of Versailles. At that time Churchill had presciently, but very optimistically written that Great Britain and the United States had a common purpose which would ensure future global peace. It was a belief that he maintained for the next two decades. When asked by Roosevelt during the Second World War what the new conflict should be called, he replied somewhat bitterly, 'the unnecessary war'. He felt war could have been avoided if the USA had joined the League of Nations, and thus the rearmament of Germany might have been prevented.

The satirical cartoon shown here, drawn by Theodor Geisel ('Dr Seuss'), was published in the daily American newspaper *PM* on 1 October 1941. It perfectly illustrates the sense of American isolationism at this time despite the threat of Hitler being clearly recognised.

When the Second World War began, Churchill and Roosevelt rapidly established a rapport. Any antipathy to the USA was long buried, as Churchill courted the country of which he saw himself as being almost a citizen, having an American mother, something which helped him believe firmly in the 'special relationship' between the two nations, which is still vaunted today. The relationship flourished for the next two years, though with degrees of mistrust dogging senior military figures on both sides of the ocean. Both countries lived up to Churchill's dictum in a speech delivered at Harvard on 6 September 1943, in which he declared that, by working together, nothing would be impossible.

Publicly, the alliance was solid, but cracks were showing: Roosevelt side-lined Churchill in some of his negotiations with Stalin and Churchill himself had separate discussions with Stalin, to draw the lines of areas of influence in post-war Eastern Europe. Nevertheless, the Alliance sustained itself to the end of the war and beyond, though Churchill incurred considerable American ire when he gave his Iron Curtain speech in 1946, though that was soon replaced by widespread respect for his foresight in appreciating the true nature of the Soviet Union.

After Churchill returned to power in 1951, he established a relationship with President Eisenhower, whom he had known well since the Second World War. Despite Eisenhower's appreciation of the man who had backed him as Supreme Commander in Europe, he regarded Britain as having only a fringe part to play in international diplomacy, at first dismissing Churchill's argument for a 'summit' (the term was Churchill's invention) with the Russians, though ultimately agreeing with him.

PHR

The American aviator Charles Lindbergh was one of the most vocal critics of the US becoming involved in European affairs.

53 | Tennis Trophies Won by Frederick Lindemann

One of Churchill's closest friends and colleagues was Professor Frederick Lindemann, a British physicist who served as his chief scientific adviser throughout the Second World War. The pair had first met in 1921, with their friendship being so firm that Churchill's biographer Martin Gilbert has described Lindemann as being 'as close to Churchill in thought, proximity and ideas as any other individual'. Churchill himself was no scientist, but his keen enthusiasm for technological innovation, a shared privileged background and a common loathing of Hitler's Nazism drew the two men together.

They first met through Clementine, who partnered with Lindemann in a charity tennis match. Shown here are a number of tennis trophies won by Lindemann, a formidable player who even competed at Wimbledon. Yet it was not just his sporting prowess which impressed Churchill, who was immediately taken by 'The Prof's' ability to condense complicated scientific ideas in an understandable way. His First World War service at Farnborough's Royal Aircraft Factory also interested Churchill greatly. The two men would establish a firm friendship.

Although having much in common, Churchill and Lindemann differed

Efficient collection of information helped Churchill to make quick and effective decisions during the war.

greatly in terms of their characters, beliefs and attitudes. Churchill was an extremely sociable person, enjoying nothing better than sharing food and drink, and surrounding himself with his family. Lindemann, by comparison, was a vegetarian teetotaller who did not smoke and was a lifelong bachelor.

Lindemann was also much more right-wing in his politics than Churchill, even accepting some of the beliefs of the Nazism to which Churchill was so opposed; he supported the then fashionable idea of eugenic sterilisation while generally despising the working classes, homosexuals and people of

Lindemann (on the left) joins Churchill to watch a demonstration of anti-aircraft defences in Norfolk, 18 June 1941.

colour. Many considered him to have an unpleasant arrogant personality, and his sallow appearance and habitual dark clothing led one of his students to compare him to Dracula. Yet his loyalty and generosity towards Churchill ensured that he would remain a close confidant.

Lindemann joined Churchill on a road trip through Europe in 1932, which made both men realise the extent to which Nazism was beginning to take hold in Germany. Throughout the decade, he would support Churchill's calls for Britain to build up its defences in readiness for another war, and when Churchill went to the Admiralty in 1939, he brought Lindemann in as an unpaid expert; then, when Churchill became Prime Minister in 1940, Lindemann was officially appointed as his chief scientific adviser.

Reporting directly to Churchill in both roles, Lindemann established a new 'S Branch' to distil thousands of sources of data into understandable statistics, with the aim of managing the different ministries and prioritising wartime efficiency. The ability this gave Churchill to make quick, informed decisions proved incredibly valuable, although other scientists sometimes questioned the data that Lindemann supplied. Lindemann was also a strong supporter for experimental weaponry, including the atomic bomb, yet discouraged Churchill from working too closely with the Americans until such collaboration was inevitable. He also initially refused to accept the possibility that the Germans had developed rocket weapons, believing that such long-range missiles were unachievable.

Lindemann was made Baron Cherwell of Oxford in 1941 and the following year appointed Paymaster General, retaining this post until the end of the war. When Churchill returned for a second term as Prime Minister in 1951, Lindemann similarly returned to his earlier role, this time in the Cabinet. In 1956 he was made Viscount Cherwell, but died in July 1957 at the age of seventy-one. Churchill, although some eleven years older than 'The Prof', insisted on walking in the funeral procession to pay his final respects.

APR

54 | 'Never was so much owed . . .' Poster

Churchill assumed office as Prime Minister at a crucial moment for his country. Britain's failure to prevent a German invasion of Norway or conduct an effective campaign to repel it had effectively destroyed the previous government under Chamberlain, and the new leader hardly had the chance to catch his breath before a German invasion of France and the Low Countries began on the same day that he came to power – 10 May 1940. The Nazi war machine ploughed through France and Belgium, forcing the Allies back and leading to a calamitous and humiliating evacuation from Dunkirk and other French ports. The consequences of such a retreat were clear. Britain was now isolated in Europe and facing an imminent German invasion.

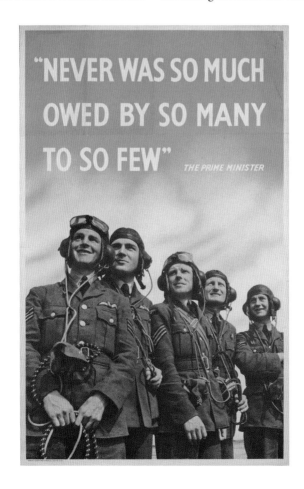

Churchill's stoicism will forever be associated with the Battle of Britain.

Reluctant to proceed with such a major attack, due to all the difficulties that an amphibious landing entailed, Hitler initially hoped to force Britain into submission through an extended aerial campaign. This was intended to crush British resolve to fight on, while destroying the RAF's air defences in preparation for a potential invasion. The Battle of Britain would therefore decide not only whether a German invasion could proceed as planned, but also whether the British people would be ready and willing to stand up to such a threat. It would be a crucial test of Churchill as a war leader.

Even before attacks from the Luftwaffe began in earnest, Churchill delivered one of his most famous speeches in which he called for the nation to brace itself for the onslaught yet to come, and for the British people to conduct themselves in such a manner that future generations would recall the battle as 'their finest hour'.

The Battle of Britain would begin in July 1940. Churchill's plea was met by both the RAF, who doggedly stopped the Luftwaffe from gaining an advantage in the battle, and, from September that year, the populations of British towns and cities, who put up with the seemingly endless German bombing raids during the Blitz. A second influential speech would follow on 20 August in which Churchill memorably paid tribute to the fortitude of the Royal Air Force, coining one of his most famous turns of phrase that never 'was so much owed by so many to so few'.

The popularity of Churchill's words, and in particular his use of the term 'The Few' to describe the RAF pilots and crew who were largely responsible for the positive outcome of the battle, led to its use for numerous propaganda purposes including a famous RAF wartime recruitment poster shown on the previous page. The phrase also alludes to Shakespeare's King Henry V who, when delivering his famous St Crispin's Day speech before the Battle of Agincourt, rallies his 'low rated English' troops by describing them as 'We few, we happy few, we band of brothers'.

The crucial moment in the Battle of Britain arrived on 15 September, later known as 'Battle of Britain Day', on which the Luftwaffe launched their largest mass bombing attack yet, only to be decisively defeated by the RAF's defences. While bombing raids on Britain would continue, any hopes by Germany of quickly beating the nation into submission were soundly dashed. Although not an outright victory for Britain in the widely understood sense, the positive outcome of the battle meant that Britain had survived long enough to begin fighting back. It bolstered Churchill's reputation as a strong leader who was exactly the right figurehead for the country at that point.

APR

Churchill inspects home defence troops.

55 | Air Raid Siren, Cabinet War Rooms

After failing to defeat the RAF in the Battle of Britain, the Luftwaffe turned to night-bombing raids against London and other British cities. The 'Blitz', beginning on 7 September 1940, aimed to disrupt war production and break the nation's resolve, and as the end of the year approached, the raids became ever more intense.

It was in preparation for such attacks that construction of the Cabinet War Rooms (CWR) began in 1938, providing a safe underground facility in Whitehall for

Further construction in the CWR added thirty-four new underground rooms to house Joint Planning, Joint Intelligence and London Control Section (who had responsibility for devising deception operations), as well as a telephone exchange, first-aid room, canteen and suite for use by Churchill and his staff. These were only used occasionally, however, since the worst of the Blitz had passed by the time they were ready.

It was crucial for British morale to remain buoyant in the face of the repeated heavy bombing raids, and Churchill was

---

As war leader, Churchill helped the British people to endure the hardships of the Blitz.

---

the government and military leadership to conduct the war. Due to the Blitz, the majority of War Cabinet meetings in October and November 1940 took place there; eventually one in ten War Cabinet Meetings was held there, but Churchill spent only the occasional night in his underground bedroom.

As the bombing continued, it became evident that Churchill could no longer stay in safety at 10 Downing Street and so offices and private rooms were prepared in the building above the CWR. In December 1940 Churchill, Clementine, and his personal map keeper, Captain Richard Pim, moved into what would become known as the No. 10 Annexe.

adamant that he should play a full part in keeping the British people's spirits up. He made sure that he was frequently seen in public, notably remaining in London despite the bombing (along with the King and other members of the Royal Family), while also travelling widely across the country to visit factories, shipyards, bombed cities and military bases. Regularly filmed for newsreels and reported by the press, such visits proved vital in demonstrating Churchill's strong leadership at a time of great uncertainty about the future.

True to his nature, Churchill showed little concern for his own safety. When a raid was expected, he would often go

This air raid siren from the Cabinet War Rooms was activated by turning its handle to warn of imminent bombing, and then to announce the 'all clear'.

Churchill visits the ruins of Coventry Cathedral on 28 September 1941.
The city had suffered terribly from enemy raids, with its Cathedral
symbolic of the immense destruction caused.

up to the Whitehall roofs in order to watch it unfold. However, he was far from foolhardy; in September 1940 he discovered that the CWR was not totally bomb-proof and immediately authorised an additional concrete slab to be installed above the site as extra protection.

With London suffering what turned out to be its last heavy raid of the Blitz on 10 May 1941, the CWR survived intact. In fact, few high explosive bombs fell near to the site. For the following few years, the War Cabinet could largely resume their meetings at 10 Downing Street or the House of Commons, and it was not until the new threat from V-weapons appeared in June 1944 that the CWR would host them again.

Churchill had always expressed confidence that Britain could resist the Blitz, but believed that true victory over Nazi Germany could only happen once he had the full support of the United States. One hurdle had therefore been passed, but a greater one remained in his sights.

APR

56 | A22 (Churchill) Infantry Tank

Britain had been one of the pioneer developers of tank warfare during the First World War, with Churchill himself an enthusiastic advocate for armoured vehicles. Although the interwar years had seen Britain's initial burst of experimentation diminish in the face of disarmament and economic retrenchment, this changed as another European conflict seemed to appear more likely and plans were put in place to mechanise the country's armed forces. Crucially, however, an initial specification for a new tank in 1939 called for the kind of armoured vehicle that would be most suitable for the style of trench warfare familiar from the First World War: something which could cross wide trenches and rough ground potted with shell craters in order to attack a fixed defensive line.

After the fall of France in 1940 it became obvious that trench warfare was now an unlikely scenario and the new tank's specification was therefore refined, with designs commissioned from Vauxhall Motors and ordered into production by Churchill himself as speedily as possible. With a German invasion of Britain imminently expected, time was of the essence. This hasty introduction meant that when the first of the new A22 tanks rolled off the production line in June 1941, they proved unreliable and suffered numerous mechanical faults.

Churchill gave his name to one of the most successful armoured vehicles used by the Allies during the Second World War.

The tank was, of course, named after Churchill as the British Prime Minister who was in office at the time of its introduction. Such a tribute was also in some way an acknowledgement of his longstanding promotion of tank warfare, as well as recognising that it was he who had pushed through the A22's early development. Realising the difficulties experienced with the early models, Churchill famously joked to Field Marshal Jan Smuts that they had named the tank after him because it was 'no damn good'.

But soon a major programme of modifications was put into place which saw the A22 Churchill take on a number of improvements which made it ready for battle. It was used offensively for the first time in the Dieppe Raid of August 1942, and then employed on a small scale at the Second Battle of El Alamein in October of the same year. By the end of the campaign in North Africa the idea of the heavily armoured infantry tank had fallen out of favour, with mobility now being prioritised over armour. Although due for retirement in 1943, the Churchill tank was granted a reprieve after proving itself in the hilly terrain of Tunisia, and production therefore continued, perhaps at the cost of other more promising vehicles still in the development stage.

A further improved model of the A22 Churchill, the Mark VII, was used extensively throughout North-West Europe from D-Day onwards along with other specialist variants. Indeed, the Churchill proved to be the most famous British infantry tank in use throughout the war, seeing action in almost all the major campaigns. Several hundred examples were even sent for the use of Soviet forces on the Eastern Front.

APR

This Churchill tank has been adapted to include a flamethrower weapon.

57 | Map Room, Cabinet War Rooms

When the Second World War broke out, the British authorities were embarrassingly short of relevant maps, resulting in a scouring of libraries and stores to support the map rooms of the military.

Churchill, as a trained soldier, was not only aware of the value of maps, but was, it is fair to say, obsessed with them. Apart from the facility they gave to track events – and younger generations are less aware of the level of precision that not only longitude and latitude, but their subdivisions into 'minutes' allowed – they also provide an instant 'picture', in lieu of copious prose. Churchill was bombarded by paper – and famously insisted memoranda should not run to more than half a page, a rule he himself broke frequently – and preferred the instantaneity and the avoidance of thinking processes that the visual information on a map provides.

When he came to office as First Lord of the Admiralty in September 1939, he established, as he had done when First Lord in the First World War, a Map Room at the Admiralty, which he could consult at any time of day or night. He recruited a personal Map Keeper, Captain Richard Pim, RNVR, who served him both there and subsequently when he took on the office of Prime Minister,

Entrance to the Map Room.

Churchill had a lifelong obsession with maps.

right through to his resignation in July 1945. When the Cabinet War Rooms were opened for use in late August 1939, the one absolutely intrinsic part of the operation was the establishment there of a Map Room, manned day and night by officers of the three services, and accessible to a restricted and very senior clientele at any hour of any day. The duty officer there would be responsible for maintaining up to date visuals of all the military campaigns of the war (including the Pacific and Russian theatres) and for submitting a daily 'sit-rep' to Churchill, the Chiefs of Staff and the King by 9 a.m. Typically, the report was never allowed

to run further than two pages, which resulted, on one occasion when an over-zealous officer reported at length on a naval engagement, in it being returned to him with the offending piece crossed out in Churchill's dreaded green ink and a note demanding 'no trench raids please'.

When Churchill migrated from his subterranean lair to the largely unprotected ground floor of the GOGGS (Government Offices Great George Street) building above, in December 1940, he had

a personal Map Room established there, just feet from his new accommodation. Captain Pim made sure his master was well served with maps and data, and its outer office became Churchill's regular place of work. Indeed, when monitoring the results of the 1945 General Election as they became known, he did so from his Map Room, which, as the war in the Far East was still being fought, continued to constitute his battle HQ after VE-Day.

When Churchill visited President Roosevelt in Washington after the USA joined the war in December 1941, he took with him a whole team of map keepers and a welter of maps, with which he could be kept up date on all aspects of the progress of the war, and set up a base in the Monroe Room of the West Wing of the White House. Roosevelt was so impressed by the facility that, on Churchill's departure, he expressed regret at the loss of the map room, whereupon Churchill readily offered to leave a map officer behind to establish a map room for the President. This was to become, though in a different location in the West Wing, the map room that exists there today.

The importance of maps to Churchill is clearly illustrated by his use of them at the Cairo conference of 1921, which redrew the map of the Middle East, and in his dealings with Stalin in the famous 'percentages agreement' reached by the two of them in Moscow in October 1944. This divided the post-war continent of Europe into zones of influence, a decision that was to become the basis for the division of Europe until the fall of the Berlin Wall in 1989.

PHR

The Map Room on display to the public today includes a map illustrating the world situation after Victory over Japan in 1945.

58 | Ship of State Poem

Soon after Churchill's appointment as First Lord of the Admiralty in September 1939, President Franklin D. Roosevelt penned the first of his notes to Churchill, a correspondence that, by the death of the President in April 1945, amounted to 1,161 messages from Churchill to Roosevelt and 788 from FDR in return, averaging an exchange every two or three days over the whole period. Later in life, Churchill compared his 'courting' of the President to a lover flattering his mistress, and he certainly did everything within his powers to please the American leader.

Despite a forthcoming election, due in November 1940, and a nationwide disapproval of any American involvement in a European war, Roosevelt did all he could to offer support to the UK in the early months of the war. In March 1941 he signed into law the Lend-Lease Act whereby America gave Britain massive material support and, in July 1941, the USA 'garrisoned' the neutral strategic territory of Iceland, which the British had occupied since 10 May 1940, but which stretched their resources to breaking.

On 20 January 1941 Roosevelt sent a personal letter to Churchill quoting the famous lines from Longfellow's poem, *The Building of the Ship*: 'Sail on O ship of state, sail on, O union strong and great!' Churchill was deeply moved by this massive expression of support from the US President, and later had the text printed as a card, which they jointly signed at their first meeting.

On 17 July 1941 a physically frail, but mentally robust American, who was to become vital to Churchill's long-standing efforts to bring the USA into the war as Britain's ally, paid his second and most important visit to the UK. This was Harry Hopkins, who was to be Roosevelt's personal representative to Churchill and his eyes and ears on exactly what was happening in the UK, and the working of the Lend-Lease agreement. He and Churchill hit it off from their first meeting, which was not surprising, given Hopkins's broadcast on the BBC shortly after his arrival, announcing to the British that President Roosevelt had promised to guarantee the delivery of American supplies to Britain, and ending with the words: 'You are not fighting alone.'

In a meeting with Churchill at Downing Street in late July, on the eve of his travel to Russia, Hopkins told Churchill how glad the President would be to meet Churchill and learn at first hand of Britain's actions and hopes in the war. Churchill grasped the idea immediately and, in a direct call to the president the very next day, agreed to meet Roosevelt off the coast of Newfoundland.

Frantic, ultra-secret planning followed and Churchill embarked on his journey on 4 August 1941 on board the battleship HMS *Prince of Wales* – which had not long before played a major part in the sinking of the German battleship *Bismarck*. In Britain the mission was a very well-kept secret, though Churchill's

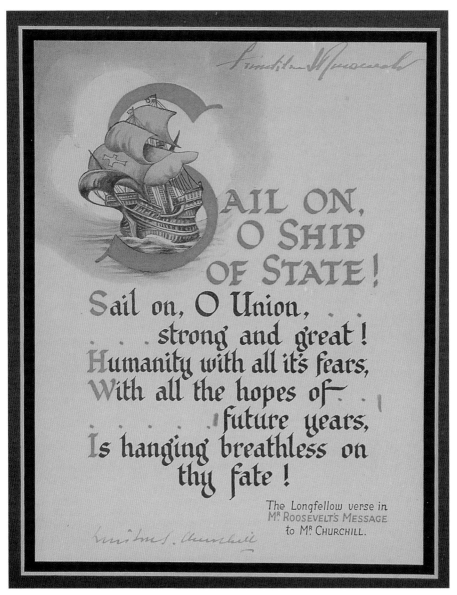

close friend and Minister for Information, Brendan Bracken, had permitted two writers, to join the trip and to report on it subsequently for the British media. Oddly, one of the two, the renowned travel writer H. V. Morton, was an avowed antisemite and Nazi sympathiser. The American media quickly grasped that the President's cover, a fishing trip up the east coast on the Presidential yacht *Potomac*, disguised what they conjectured would be a meeting in North America with the British premier, thus heightening the already massive risk from German U-boat attack.

The two men finally met on board the USS *Augusta* on 9 August 1941 in Placentia Bay off the coast of Newfoundland, where Churchill unintentionally wounded the President, saying how glad he was to meet him

Churchill's first meeting with President Roosevelt led to the signing of the Atlantic Charter.

at last – forgetting they had met in London in 1917. Despite the inauspicious beginning, the two men found a kindred spirit and were soon working out the text of a declaration that came to be known as the Atlantic Charter. Under this both countries vowed that they supported, among other things: no territorial aggrandisement by any country; 'to respect the right of all peoples to choose the form of government under which they live'; freedom of world trade; to establish a peace, assuring all nations of their safety and 'freedom from fear and want'; 'the abandonment of the use of force'.

Though never signed as a formal treaty, the charter was ratified by an emergency meeting of the British War Cabinet, led by the Labour leader and Deputy Prime Minister, Clement Attlee, in London on 12 August, and allegiance to its principles was proclaimed by delegates of ten Allied nations, including the Soviet Union,

on 24 September 1941. The charter was subsequently endorsed by representatives of 26 nations at war with the Axis powers, meeting in Washington on 1 January 1942, an event generally acknowledged as the birth of what, in 1945, was to become the United Nations Organization.

Four months after the summit Britain and the USA formally became allies following the Japanese attack on Pearl Harbor and the subsequent German declaration of war on the Americans.

The day before that declaration, HMS *Prince of Wales*, together with the battlecruiser HMS *Repulse*, were sunk by Japanese aircraft off the coast of Malaya with the loss of over 800 British sailors. Years later, Churchill would recall that this was the greatest shock he received during the entire war.

PHR

Roosevelt and Churchill meet on board the USS *Augusta* in Placentia Bay, Newfoundland, on 9 August 1941.

59 | Enigma Machine

A late-war four-rotor Enigma machine.

In 1974 Group Captain F. W. Winterbotham published a book entitled *The Ultra Secret*. The book was officially sanctioned, and needed to be, as it revealed to the world for the first time the fact that the British had broken many secret German messages sent using Enigma cipher machines, with the decrypted intelligence (classified as 'Ultra') giving the Allies a demonstrable advantage throughout the Second World War. The book contained a number of inaccuracies – as official records were still not available to fact-check, so Winterbotham had to rely on his memory of his experiences. The breaking of

Churchill's deep interest in getting results from new technology led to his encouragement of the secret work at Bletchley Park.

Enigma was not, however, a simple one-off activity – each of the German armed services used numerous radio networks, with individual Enigma 'keys' that had to be broken separately, and then broken again each day.

The work of deciphering the German messages was undertaken at a manor house at Bletchley in Buckinghamshire, which was established in 1938 as the Government Code and Cypher School (GCCS). Just twelve days after Churchill was appointed Prime Minister in May

1940 Bletchley achieved the first major breakthrough, when they began regularly breaking into the Enigma key most used by the German Air Force. Churchill was quick to appreciate the unique value of this intelligence source, which was already providing some information on German troop movements and plans invaluable to the rescue of the British and French forces as they were evacuated from Dunkirk.

Churchill also realised how crucial it was that the successes in breaking the Enigma machine were kept secret,

Hitler's top tank commander General Heinz Guderian looks on while his cipher clerks operate their three-rotor Enigma machine in his command vehicle during the conquest of France in 1940.

A U-boat radio room with a four-rotor Enigma machine in use, *c.* 1943.

as any suspicion by the Germans that their messages had been compromised would completely nullify Allied success. Where this was occasionally flouted, he made sure that the strictures were quickly adhered to. His fears were, on two occasions, fully justified when Allied successes in sinking German ships and submarines led the German Navy to consider – but finally dismiss – the possibility that the Allies had broken Enigma.

Churchill's role in the development and success of the code-breaking was personal and major, as best illustrated by his response to a personal letter from the principal cryptanalysts, begging for more resources. This followed Churchill's only visit to Bletchley on 6 September 1941. Churchill ensured that their requirements were immediately forthcoming, knowing that they were crucial to the development, that had already started, of the electro-mechanical 'bombe' devices that tested possible solutions to Enigma keys far faster than any human methods.

Even faster and more sophisticated bombes were essential to achieving a vital breakthrough, after the German submarine fleet, in 1942, was given a new Enigma machine variant. This added a fourth enciphering rotor to the previous three, increasing the complexity of the process by many times and making the U-boats' 'Shark' Enigma key impenetrable for months on end. At a stroke this reversed Allied successes, leading to massive increases in sinkings of Allied ships. Churchill commented later that the Battle of the Atlantic frightened him the most among the many challenges Britain faced during the war. Improved bombes helped turn the tide during the first half of 1943.

Churchill was aware of the value to the British war effort that breaking Enigma brought, but he also appreciated how important it could be to Britain's allies. When Enigma showed that Germany planned to invade the USSR, Churchill insisted that the information gained should be shared with the Soviets, albeit under the guise of secrets obtained in other ways, some of it supplied by a fictitious 'agent Boniface'. Despite Stalin's initial reluctance to give credence to these reports, Churchill made sure that any information relevant to the Soviets should be shared with them.

When American forces began arriving in the UK from early 1942, Churchill made sure that their commanders had access to Enigma information and

encouraged the adoption of what came to be known as 'the written constitution' of Anglo-American cryptanalysis in June 1943. This co-operation was vital in the Allied operations in North Africa, Sicily, Italy and Normandy. It allowed Churchill to encourage the Allied bombing of targets that represented a serious risk to the USSR's part in the war and, in the absence of a 'second front', to demonstrate that the Allies were doing all they could to assist the Soviets.

All of the work at Bletchley was conducted in the utmost secrecy – and was kept secret for decades after the war. It is little surprise then that Churchill christened the Bletchley teams 'the geese that laid the golden eggs and never cackled'.

PHR

One of the high-speed four-rotor bombes built to counter the upgraded Enigma machines. As a precaution against a possible German air raid this machine was installed at Eastcote, not the main GCHQ base at Bletchley Park.

60 | Churchill's Chair, Cabinet War Rooms

From 1919, even though the British Cabinet established a policy – to which Churchill was a major signatory – of there being no likelihood of a war for the next ten years, attention was continuously given to the

The speculative casualty rate from the eventuality of enemy bombers attacking London (as they had done from 1915 onwards) was of 50,000 casualties per month. By 1936, some two years after the 'ten-year rule' was abandoned, that

---

The frustrations of leadership remain evident from a simple piece of furniture.

---

theoretical effects of a future war, not least the likely toll on human life from the development of aircraft capable of delivering large bomb loads over long distances.

figure had risen to 200,000 per week, of whom 60,000 were expected to be killed. Contrary to popular mythology – aided by Churchill's increasing hectoring of the government – government spending on

The scratch marks seen on the arm rest of Churchill's chair in the Cabinet Room indicate his stress levels.

defence in the 1930s (once the focus on an effective offensive bomber force was dismissed as unachievable) was gradually increased. Ever greater thought was also given to the protection of civilians from bombing raids, a policy made all the more a focus of public demands after the rash statement by the Conservative leader Stanley Baldwin, in 1932, that 'the bomber will always get through'.

A good deal of consideration was given to the protection of the command structure, in the event of London being bombed and, after much argument and a variety of iterations, it was decided in December 1937, to establish a 'Central War Room', which would house the Chiefs and Deputy Chiefs of Staff of the three services, the Joint Planning Committee and the Joint Intelligence Committee. There was a real fear that concentration of personnel in one location would

present an increased risk of their being wiped out and it was only in May 1939 that a decision was taken to house the War Cabinet (the reduced version of the full Cabinet, comprising some six or seven ministers) alongside these bodies, with options to evacuate from central London if necessary, in a suite of concrete-reinforced ministerial war rooms.

The basement of the 'New Public Offices' on the corner of Storeys Gate and Great George Street, was chosen as the location for a Central War Room, as it was convenient for Parliament and No. 10 Downing Street and as the building above – as its name implied, the newest government building in the area – had a steel frame, which, it was thought, might help it to remain standing in the event of a bomb hit. Seen as a temporary solution, not least by the Office of Works, whose archives were removed to accommodate

The Cabinet meeting room,
in the underground War Rooms.

raid on the night of 15/16 October 1940, which seriously damaged the back of No. 10 Downing Street, where he had been sheltering – unharmed – in the basement. Even then, he was a reluctant resident of the CWR and, in December 1940, moved his base and his living quarters to the ground floor of the building, directly above the concrete mantle, and with only shutters on the windows to provide protection. This area, which became known as 'No. 10 Annexe', was where he based himself for the rest of the war, until he resigned in July 1945.

However, during the heavier bombing raids, he would be obliged to meet in the CWR with his War Cabinet and his Defence Committee (his personal coterie for running the war in 1940–2) on well over 500 occasions. Thus, it was his shelter during the intense air raids of the Blitz (September 1940–May 1941) and again when the V-1 flying bombs (also known as 'buzz bombs' or 'doodlebugs') and the V-2 rockets rained down on London between 13 June 1944 and the end of March 1945.

His distinctive wooden chair in the Cabinet Room was positioned directly opposite those of his Chiefs of Staff, who were there to advise the War Cabinet and be part of the executive Defence Committee, but the ebullient character of the Prime Minister made for many abrasive exchanges between these two sides, provoking the 1941–6 Chief of the (Army) General Staff, General Alan Brooke, to complain that the main disadvantage of the CWR was its proximity to Churchill.

Faced with the more measured approach of his Chiefs sitting opposite, the position of the Leader of the Labour Party, Clement Attlee, on his left and

the CWR, their development was haphazard, with the concrete bomb-proof mantle (calculated to stop at least a 250-kg bomb) above it only begun in December 1938. As the historian Richard Holmes aptly described it, this was a 'definitively British' operation.

The site was, nevertheless, ready for occupation at the end of August 1939, just one week before war was declared, but was used only intermittently until the arrival of German air raids in August 1940. Shortly after his appointment as Prime Minister in May 1940, Churchill inspected the rooms and, in the Cabinet Room, boldly declared that this would be from where he would direct the war.

Churchill, however, was not a natural one to seek shelter – as he had shown in the trenches of the Western Front in 1915–16 – and stayed away until forced into meeting there by a German bombing the bombing raids that drove him underground, this forcibly restrained bulldog took his frustration out on his chair, leaving deep indentations in its arms, from banging it with his signet ring and scratching it with his fingernails.

For a man with a frequent penchant for observing the air raids from the roof of the building, this was not his natural lair.

PHR

The rather battered chair that Churchill used during meetings of the wartime Cabinet.

61 | Doodles by Field Marshal Alan Brooke

Alan Francis Brooke was born in Pau in the south of France in July 1883, the son of Sir Victor Alexander Brooke, 3rd Baronet of Colebrooke in County

Louth. Twenty-six Brookes of Colebrooke served in the First World War, twenty-seven in the Second World War. The Brookes were aristocratic, military and thoroughly Irish Protestant.

In his role of Prime Minister, Churchill surrounded himself with strong military advisers.

Fermanagh and Alice Bellingham, daughter of Sir Alan Edward Bellingham, 3rd Baronet of Bellingham in County

Brooke served as an ever more successful artillery officer in Ireland and India and then throughout the First

Doodle of an unidentified subject, drawn by Field Marshal Alan Brooke during a War Cabinet meeting.

World War on the Western Front. He passed through various staff posts, until, in the late 1930s, he became the head of the UK's Anti-Aircraft Command. As war approached in August 1939, he was made Commander-in-Chief of Southern Command and took command of II Corps of the British Expeditionary Force in France and, after being recalled on 29 May 1940, was quickly sent back to Cherbourg, in an effort to build a new second British Expeditionary Force.

It was at this point that he had his first major encounter and run-in with Churchill, who ordered him to hold the line, to make the French feel they were being supported. Brooke, who as a Francophone knew the French well, in all their pluses and minuses, responded that it was 'impossible to make a corpse feel', as the French Army was to all extents and purposes dead. After thirty minutes of argument, Churchill gave way, and allowed the withdrawal Brooke advocated. This was to become typical of their relationship after Churchill appointed him on Christmas Day 1941 as Chief of the Imperial General Staff (CIGS) in succession to General Sir John Dill.

Brooke had previously served as Director of Military Training at the War Office in 1936 and commander of the new Mobile Division in 1938, and so had a deep understanding of the workings of Whitehall. In July 1940 Churchill had appointed him as C-in-C Home Forces in succession to General Ironside, in whom Churchill had lost confidence and, in that capacity he had an office in Churchill's Cabinet War Rooms where he could closely observe Churchill's style and manner.

The other service chiefs did not like the idea of Brooke joining them as head of the Army, dismissing him as too abrupt, over-forceful and tactless. Churchill, legendarily, a man of supreme energy and endless imagination, which led to him challenging his Chiefs at almost every turn, initially also felt unsure of the appointment of someone so tough-minded as CIGS, telling Anthony Eden that he feared they would not get on. But he quickly concluded that, with all his skills and experience, Brooke was the obvious man for the job.

Roosevelt said of Churchill that he was a man who had ten ideas a day, only one of which was any good, but he didn't know which one it was. This was indeed true of Churchill, but is as true of many CEOs or leaders, who rely on their lieutenants to sort their ideas and then share a back and forth to make some of them workable. In the same vein, Brooke complains regularly in his diaries, which were finally published in unexpurgated form in 2001, about Churchill's lack of strategic knowledge. Yet advice on strategy was essentially Brooke's responsibility and neither he nor any Chief would have wanted Churchill dictating strategy. It is true that Brooke, like all the Chiefs, had to argue a case very strongly to win Churchill over, but Churchill claimed to have never over-ruled his Chiefs. The 1992 book by Lord Bramall and Bill Jackson, *The Chiefs*, suggests that 'Churchill's imagination needed no stimulation, only discipline: Brooke provided that discipline.'

Churchill was not at all afraid to get rid of commanders who he felt were not up to the job or were simply misplaced. But it was certainly to his credit that he never appointed 'yes men' and his long-term Chiefs of Staff – Portal (for the RAF), Cunningham (for the Royal Navy) and especially Brooke – were people who stood up to him and whose opinions he respected.

Brooke's copious diaries were written as a personal record for his wife to read after the war, recording, in the heat of the moment, entries that were often critical of Churchill. However, they really reflect the extreme fatigue, stresses and strains of his position. Brooke was not the beneficiary, after the war, of the monetary compensations which had been a long tradition in the British armed forces for its victorious generals. There was no London statue of him until 1993 (it is in Whitehall, by the same sculptor as that of Churchill in Parliament Square).

When a friend said to him about his appearance alongside Churchill on VE-Day that the public probably never realised they were seeing, in him, the man who had done most to win the war against Germany, he replied that, 'The public has never understood what the Chiefs of Staff have been doing in the running of the war. On the whole, the PM has never enlightened them much.'

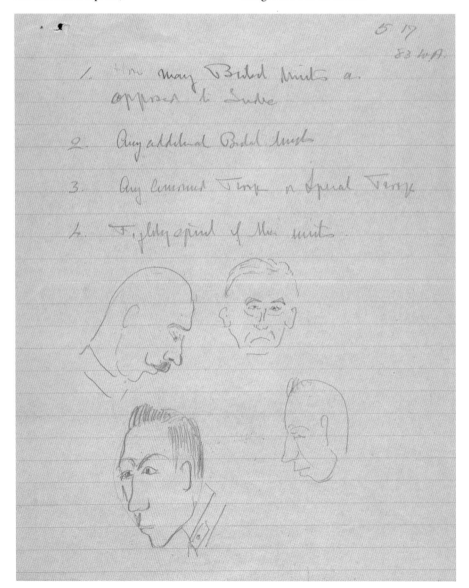

Further doodles by Brooke, plus notes made during a Cabinet meeting.

The doodles shown here were drawn by Brooke during one of the many War Cabinet meetings when he was seated opposite the long-winded Churchill, and were kept as a souvenir by his Military Assistant, Lieutenant-Colonel A. B. Boyle.

It seems that Brooke refrained from sketching the Prime Minister on this occasion.

PHR

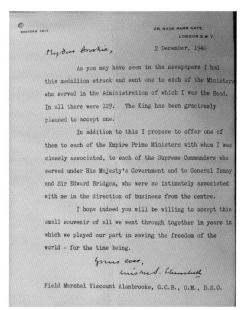

In late 1945 Churchill had a special medallion struck for those who had been part of his wartime government. The medallion presented to Lord Alanbrooke is shown here.

62 | Portrait Photograph by Yousuf Karsh, 1941

O n 4 June 1940 the last British soldier was lifted off the beach at Dunkirk, making a total of some 338,000 Allied troops (including 114,000 French) evacuated from what had seemed only days before a desperate situation. This was the majority of Great Britain's professional army, now totally exhausted, mentally crushed and completely denuded of weaponry, having abandoned some 60,000 vehicles, 2,000 field guns, 90,000 rifles and 600,000 tons of fuel. In addition, since 10 May 1940, the RAF had lost over a thousand aircraft and 1,127 pilots and aircrew.

Before the Dunkirk evacuation was over, Churchill had reluctantly, but wisely, decided against sending more aircraft over to France, concluding that those that were left would be needed for what was expected to be a German onslaught on, and invasion of, the UK. Plans to send new troops to France and form a second British Expeditionary Force were then also abandoned. Among the formations earmarked for this task was

When first visiting Canada in 1900, Churchill immediately fell in love with the country.

the 1st Canadian Division, by now based in southern England. Some units of the division did go to France but were quickly withdrawn.

In part to encourage American support, Churchill had referred in his speeches to Britain fighting 'alone', when in fact the Empire and Commonwealth contributed a sizable percentage of the 11 million 'British' fighting personnel and the more than half a million British and Empire dead in the war, including over 35,000 who served with the Merchant Navy.

On 10 September 1939, Canada joined Britain in the fight against Nazi Germany. The Canadians went on to gift to Great Britain one billion Canadian dollars for the war effort, but, more importantly, more than a million Canadian men and women served in the armed forces during the Second World War, which constituted around 10 per cent of Canada's population; almost all who served overseas were volunteers rather than conscripts. Some 45,000 would be killed and 55,000 wounded.

The Canadians fought in every theatre of war in Europe and, famously, in the ill-thought out and disastrous Operation 'Jubilee', the combined forces attack on Dieppe on 19 August 1942, involving 5,000 British and Canadian troops. The operation was conceived primarily to test German anti-invasion defences, but also gave a very small detachment of American forces their country's first taste of active combat in the European theatre. It was a complete and expensive failure, costing the Canadian contingent 68 per cent of their number, killed, wounded or taken prisoner.

Subsequent enquiries showed that blame for the failure at Dieppe rested largely with the Chief of Combined Operations, Lord Louis Mountbatten, but, in his memoirs Churchill covered up for him, leaving himself as the whipping boy. This resulted, in a similar way to the hostility of many Australians towards Churchill after the failure of the Dardanelles campaign, to widespread Canadian disapproval of Churchill.

Despite the Dieppe raid, Churchill's relations with Canada's Prime Minister, W. L. Mackenzie King, were always cordial and marked by mutual admiration and liking, beautifully illustrated by an occasion when Churchill whirled King around the dance floor at Chequers. The relationship survived many blows, not least Churchill's failure to share with the Canadians any details of the outcome of his meetings with Roosevelt, off the coast of Newfoundland in August 1941.

Largely at the insistence of Roosevelt, the Canadians were excluded from any participation in the Anglo-American summits held at Quebec in August 1942 and September 1944, which established several of the main future strategies for the war. On these occasions, however, Churchill made every effort to keep the Canadians briefed on the conference proceedings and decisions and Britain's High Commissioner to Canada confidently reported back to London that, as a result, Canadian attitudes to Churchill, initially slightly wary and untrusting, were massively boosted by his friendly, approachable and sharing behaviour towards his Canadian hosts.

At D-Day on 6 June 1944, more than 14,000 Canadian soldiers landed in France. 110 Canadian warships participated, together with 10,000 Canadian sailors and 15 fighter and bomber squadrons of the RCAF who fought above them. Churchill was fully aware of the huge contribution to the fighting effort and the scale of Canada's sacrifice in the First World War (more than 660,000 Canadians and Newfoundlanders fought and lost over 10 per cent of their strength) and was profoundly appreciative of their contribution in both of the biggest challenges to Britain's survival in the twentieth century.

Churchill's love affair with Canada – and the words are no exaggeration – began with his first visit there in late December 1900. It was intended as a visit to boost his coffers, with income from an extensive series of speaking engagements, many of which gave Churchill a rough ride over his very active part in suppressing the Boers in the South African War. By contrast, his visit to Ottawa, almost forty years on to the day, was cheered to the rafters (aided in part by his brilliant 'Some chicken, some neck' speech in which he belittled French derision of his decision to resist German aggression). Although he frequently emphasised Canada's status as a dominion which formed the vital link between the UK and the USA, his respect for the country in its own right was unbounded, with him even suggesting to his wife in 1929, that he might emigrate there, should his political career fail.

Perhaps above all we should thank Canada for providing what must be *the* iconic image of Churchill, the famous photograph of him taken by Yousuf Karsh in the chamber of the Speaker of the Canadian House of Commons on 30 December 1941. Karsh's portrait, titled 'The Roaring Lion', sees Churchill giving a strikingly stern expression. Such grumpiness was achieved by Karsh having removed the Prime Minister's cigar from his mouth immediately before taking the photograph.

PHR

An alternative, and lesser-known image from the Karsh photo session, in which Churchill is smiling.

63 | Rota the Lion

In a 1941 cartoon by 'Poy' and an unattributed cartoon in *Punch* in August 1942, Churchill was portrayed as a bulldog, an image which had been first used by Sidney Strube in his famous *Daily Express* cartoon of 8 June 1940 (the 'Go To It' cartoon of bulldog Churchill standing on a model of Britain, glaring towards the continent). The bulldog was understood to take a vice-like grip on an adversary and not let go. Churchill enjoyed many cartoons of himself, but certainly revelled in his bulldog-breed image. It was a

Nelson, and the dynasty of six successive marmalade cats named Jock that had the free run of Chartwell. He populated the pond at Chartwell with rare black swans and stocked it with golden orfe, claiming to another visitor that the fish would come to the edge of the pool to hear him speak (he left out that he also fed them).

Of all the animals that Churchill was given while Prime Minister, two stand out: a platypus and Rota the lion. The platypus, a totemic Australian animal, was actually requested by Churchill from the Australian government in 1943,

---

Although forever associated with a bulldog, Churchill owned many other animals.

---

widely held belief, partly as a result of these cartoon images, that Churchill kept bulldogs, when in fact he only had one once, when he was at Harrow. It comes as a surprise to most people to discover that his most beloved dogs were actually two poodles, Rufus I, and, when he died, Rufus II. He was devoted to both dogs, whose graves can be seen in the gardens at Chartwell.

The Chartwell estate included a farm and Churchill kept animals of all breeds, not least cows, pigs, ducks and chickens. When scratching the back of one of his favourite pigs on the Chartwell farm one day, he remarked to a visitor that 'dogs look up to you, cats look down on you,' but a pig 'looks you in the eye and treats you as an equal'. Churchill was a keen lover of cats, especially the Admiralty cat,

even though its transportation across submarine-infested waters presented enormous difficulties. But no challenge was greater than helping the platypus tolerate such a long journey: it needed a diet of 700 earthworms a day. This had never been done before and in this case too the platypus did not survive, after having its rations cut because of the extended length of the voyage and after the distress of a German submarine attack. Nevertheless, it did serve to improve declining relations between Great Britain and its Australian ally and is sometimes credited with Churchill acceding to Australian Prime Minister Curtin's many pleas for help in re-arming Australia.

London Zoo had built a special enclosure for the platypus, but had

Following his death, Rota the lion was stuffed and exhibited in the town of St Augustine, Florida, where he remains in a local museum.

more luck with Rota the lion. Rota had been won as a cub in a bet by a George Thompson of Pinner in North London in the 1930s and kept as a pet by him in his garden. With the reductions in food rations in 1943, Thompson donated the lion to the London Zoo, but urged them to give it to the 'lionhearted' Churchill, to mark Britain's military successes in North Africa. This the Zoo agreed to do, prompting Churchill both to pay visits to 'his' lion, but also to remark to the zoo that, though he had no use for a lion at that time, situations might arise, when he might need it to bring his Cabinet to order. After its death in 1955 Rota was stuffed and is now displayed in the Lightner Museum in Florida.

Churchill enjoyed his rural retreat and when his period out of office permitted him the time, he revived a pre-war interest in encouraging butterflies to populate his garden and also bred bees. Animals were always a source of great comfort – and, on their death, real grief – to Churchill.

PHR

Churchill visits Rota at London Zoo, 26 July 1943.

64 | SIGSALY

A close link between Britain and the United States was of immense importance to Churchill, who knew that American involvement in the war was essential for victory. Key to this was his communication with US President Franklin D. Roosevelt. Technology listener. Instead, the two leaders usually communicated by encrypted telegram but it was clear that a more secure form of communication was needed.

The answer would be a secret project begun in October 1940, enabling secure telephone conversations to be transmitted across the Atlantic. This came to be called

---

Churchill's desire for secure communication with Roosevelt led to a technological innovation.

---

available at the beginning of the war allowed for secure phone calls to be made. These could theoretically be unscrambled by an enemy (and some eventually were) but not be understood by a casual SIGSALY (a codename rather than an acronym) and relied on extremely large machines, weighing around 50 tonnes each and requiring a team of signallers to operate them.

The large SIGSALY equipment filled a whole room.

The Transatlantic Telephone Room at the underground Cabinet War Rooms,
where the siren-suited Churchill could conduct private conversations with President Roosevelt.

Twelve SIGSALY terminals were created in total during the war, with each costing around $1 million (at 1943 values). In order to establish the transatlantic link between the two countries, the first machine was set up in the Pentagon while the second, because of its size, was installed in London, deep below Oxford Street in the basement of Selfridge's department store.

Ultimately, further extensions were installed across London including the US Embassy in Grosvenor Square, at 10 Downing Street and in the still-surviving underground Cabinet War Rooms. This last extension was kept in a cupboard made to look like a toilet for Churchill's private use; such was the clandestine nature of SIGSALY that its function was hidden even from those

as a digital packet to an identical receiving machine. It would then be decoded and reconstructed into the original voice transmission. Anybody listening in on the transmission would hear nothing but a continuous buzzing noise. SIGSALY was therefore often referred to by the nickname 'Green Hornet' (after the original American radio series of the same name, which was popular at the time).

The system was indeed secure, for after the war it was discovered that the Germans had recorded SIGSALY transmissions but been unable to decode them.

The first SIGSALY conference call took place on 15 July 1943 between Churchill and General Dwight D. Eisenhower. The first time that Churchill spoke with Roosevelt using the system was in April 1944, but while he and the President held several further conversations via SIGSALY, the bulk of their communication tended still to be via encoded messages. Churchill did, however, speak to Roosevelt's successor, Harry S Truman, on numerous occasions by SIGSALY, including to convey his condolences after Roosevelt's death.

The fact that the United States was willing to devote such massive resources in terms of manpower, time and money to install the SIGSALY system indicates the importance with which the two nations' 'special relationship' was regarded.

APR

who worked at secret sites. In total, the terminals carried at least 3,000 conversations during the war and the system's further installations across the world – including Paris, Australia and the Philippines – demonstrate the conflict's global nature.

SIGSALY worked by splitting a voice at one end of the call into twelve separate sound channels; ten accounted for speech while two controlled pitch and tone. Each of these channels was separately encrypted fifty times every second, before being sent

65 | Avenue Winston Churchill Street Sign

I t is ironic, given his later love affair with the country, that, as a seventeen-year-old in December 1891, Churchill tried to get out of being sent to stay with a French family to learn French. He did learn French: both his mother and his wife spoke the language fluently, and Churchill himself learnt French well enough to converse in it – though he deliberately and frequently descended into Franglais – and also read French books in the original, not least the many he owned on his hero Napoleon.

Force. After the fall of France de Gaulle became, almost by default, the leader of the French in exile, even though he was scarcely known in France.

Churchill's deep and sincere admiration for France, its history and its culture, was boundless and demonstrated repeatedly, especially in June 1940, as France was overrun by the Germans, when he referred to what he called the 'indissoluble union' of Britain and France. On Bastille Day, 14 July 1940, he broadcast to the people of France his firm belief, when

---

Churchill's sincere admiration for France and its people was boundless.

Both he and Charles de Gaulle, leader of the Free French and future French President, delighted in deprecating his French language abilities, but, as with a lot of aspects of Churchill's life, the mythology was spread by the man himself.

Despite the many issues he had with General de Gaulle, Churchill was as one American academic described him 'an ardent though not uncritical Francophile'. In 1915–16 Churchill fought on the Western Front in France and he later became a lifelong admirer of the French statesman Georges Clemenceau.

His relationship with de Gaulle was less clear cut. In May 1940 Prime Minister Paul Reynaud promoted de Gaulle to the temporary rank of general and then, as a newly appointed Under-Secretary of State, sent him to London to persuade Churchill to reinforce the French Army and Air

there were no grounds for such faith, that their country would once more serve as a defender of freedom. Such faith was frequently challenged during the Second World War by the stubborn, chauvinistic and often petty behaviour of de Gaulle, provoking Churchill to such levels of rage against him that Churchill's staff genuinely feared real violence might occur in one particular meeting of the two men – in fact it was conducted amicably despite the hostility which preceded it. Churchill – and still more so Roosevelt, who nurtured a deep mistrust of de Gaulle – did not help matters by keeping details from de Gaulle of operations on which he felt he should be consulted, not least in the sinking of the French fleet at Oran and Mers El Kébir in 1940, armistice negotiations with the Vichy French in the Levant in June 1941, and the British invasion of Madagascar

VILLE DE
CHARENTON-LE-PONT
AVENUE
WINSTON CHURCHILL
Homme politique Britannique
1874.1965

This street sign from a suburb of Paris illustrates the affection which many liberated French people had for Churchill.

in May 1942. Even Operation Torch, the Anglo-American invasion of Vichy-occupied North Africa was kept secret from him – at Roosevelt's insistence and against Churchill's wishes.

The details of the planned D-Day operations were only revealed to de Gaulle two days before they began and he was prohibited from sharing the information with anyone. De Gaulle felt he was due greater respect and regard as the leader of the French in exile and tried to prevent Eisenhower from instructing the French people on civil administration. De Gaulle deliberately kept secret the text of the broadcast he was to give to the French after the invasion, but Churchill need not

have feared the worst, as it graciously and sincerely thanked the British for their efforts in the liberation of France. As with the sinkings at Oran and Mers El Kébir, in the end de Gaulle came down firmly in favour of the British.

The problem of relations between Churchill and de Gaulle stemmed, as much as anything, from their similar self-belief and often truculent manners. At one point de Gaulle was prompted to say he 'could not care less whether or not Britain won the war ... all that mattered was that France be saved'. For his part Churchill was once so enraged by the French leader that he hinted that, like Joan of Arc, he might be burned at the stake. Such outbursts were the results of frustration and bombast by both men, but Churchill made clear that, in reality, he saw de Gaulle as a man of destiny (as he saw himself), that he 'understood and admired' de Gaulle (while disliking his arrogant demeanour). He also needed de Gaulle to enter Paris at the head of the victorious Allied forces on 19 August 1944, in order to avoid any possibility of the Communists, who were a major influence in the French Resistance, gaining too much of the credit. When the two men marched, as Churchill had anticipated some four years before, together down the Champs Elysées on 11 November 1944, the vocal support for Churchill from the Parisian populace was unprecedented in any of Churchill's popular receptions.

This affection for Churchill among the people of France is reflected in their adoption of his name for many street signs throughout the country. The particular example shown on the previous page originates from a street in Charenton-le-Pont, a suburb of Paris.

As if to demonstrate the mutual admiration of the two, on 6 November 1958 de Gaulle presented Churchill with the Croix de la Libération, an order created by de Gaulle himself in 1940 to recognise 'distinguished or exceptional services by French citizens or foreigners who aided the liberation of France'. On Churchill's death de Gaulle wrote to Queen Elizabeth saying of Churchill. 'In the great drama he was the greatest of all.'

PHR

The most famous of the many roads called
Avenue Winston-Churchill is in central Paris,
shown here with the Hôtel des Invalides in the background.

66 | Poster for the Film *Henry V* (1944)

In part due to his habit of going to bed very late at night – often 2.00 or 3.00 in the morning – one might assume that Churchill worked hugely long days and he often did. He would have meetings – albeit rarely Cabinet meetings, which generally took place at more civilised hours – at times when most people would expect to be in bed. After the war, he was in the habit of dictating text for his memoirs/histories to his brood of highly qualified scribes between midnight and 3 a.m. But often, even during the war, his late nights would be spent watching films.

threw at her, while her stoical husband, played by Walter Pidgeon, without fuss, took his small boat to what turned out to be the small ships rescue of the troops from Dunkirk in 1940. These 'ordinary' (in Hollywood's terms) heroes embodied and advertised to the populace the values, the attitudes and, above all, the spirit of defiance that Churchill wanted to nurture in the British people.

A visit to the cinema also provided an opportunity for the general population to escape from the stresses and privations of war. Although radio and newspapers were regular sources of news, the cinema

---

As a means of relaxation, Churchill loved the cinema.

Incredibly, it is said he watched *Lady Hamilton / That Hamilton Woman* – the story of Lady Hamilton and Admiral Lord Nelson, starring the husband and wife team of Vivien Leigh and Laurence Olivier – seventeen times during the war. Viewing the film now, it's not hard to see why he so enjoyed it, especially the scene that must have excited and inspired him most, where Nelson, faced with an Admiralty Board about to negotiate peace terms with Napoleon, pleads 'You cannot make peace with dictators; you have to destroy them, wipe them out.'

Another favourite was the 1942 romantic film *Mrs Miniver*, which showed a stalwart Greer Garson as a mother undaunted by the many and sometimes personally tragic challenges that the war

newsreels were an immensely popular medium for public information (albeit somewhat out of date).

Churchill, ever aware of his image and the power of the media, cultivated the silver screen to get his messages across to a wide audience. He first appeared on film in the late 1930s, claiming a skill at presenting himself on film, though in fact his appearance and style could best be described as bumptious.

The supreme example of his use of cinema as a means of communicating a message of resilience is Laurence Olivier's 1944 version of Shakespeare's *Henry V*, which Churchill persuaded Olivier to make. The film shows the plucky underdog British faced with the overwhelming might of the confident

French and gaining victory at Agincourt despite the odds.

Churchill was thoroughly familiar with the deeply inspiring words that Shakespeare has Henry deliver to his troops: 'and gentlemen of England now abed, shall think themselves accurs'd they were not here, and hold their manhoods cheap whiles any speaks that fought with us upon Saint Crispin's day'. The parallels with 1940 and the messages of that time are obvious, as perhaps is the conceit of Churchill in wishing to see himself in the guise of a heroic warrior king, personally inspiring his nervous subjects.

Churchill cultivated friendships with stars whose films he frequently enjoyed at night in war-torn London, not least Charlie Chaplin (despite his strong left-wing views), the Marx Brothers and Orson Welles. He was also friends with many of the great film and theatre directors of the time, especially Alexander Korda, for whom he wrote three screenplays, though, sadly, none of them ever made it to the screen.

At least Churchill has gained screen time since then in the form of the many stars who have played him in feature films and who continue to keep his reputation high.

PHR

67 | Bowker Hat

Of all the famous faces of history, in any era, Winston Churchill's must surely be one of the most familiar and most easily recognised. Clearly, his stature as one of the most important figures in modern times makes this inevitable, but it should also be noted that Churchill was one of the first and greatest masters of 'spin', who carefully and deliberately nurtured his own image.

Churchill's hats remained an important part of his wardrobe, with his Bowker being a particularly common sight when the Prime Minister was photographed out and about during the war. A cross between a bowler and a homburg, Churchill increasingly favoured this

particular style of headwear, finding it more suitable on many occasions than the formal top hat due to its being softer and more comfortable to wear.

We inevitably picture him with his iconic cigar in his mouth, and, despite the hardships of life during the Second World War, the general public wanted to see their leader with his (expensive Cuban) cigars. Even German propagandists exploited this association, changing the words to the popular wartime song 'The Man with the Big Cigar' in order to make detrimental references to Churchill. Churchill would generally ensure that all his appearances in public and many in private, as well as the artistic, promotional and even parodic depictions (such as in cartoons),

Churchill's image remains one of the most easily identifiable in history.

---

recorded him as he wished to be seen. And the cigar was intrinsic to that.

One of the best examples of Churchill's management of his image came in 1928, when a photograph was published of him, dressed in his archetypal, workaday siren suit (as opposed to his later well-tailored 'evening dress' versions), building a wall at his country residence, Chartwell. At the same time, the *Daily Mail* published an image of his membership card for

the Amalgamated Union of Building Trades Workers, which he joined that year and where his occupation is listed as 'bricklayer'. The ploy failed badly, as members of the union, disgusted at a politician who was generally seen as being anti-working class being allowed to join their union, forced the union leaders to cancel his membership. Neither the image, taken on his estate, nor the visual of the pass could have been made without not

Churchill raises his Bowker hat in salute during an inspection of the 1st American Squadron of the Home Guard at Horse Guards Parade in London, 9 January 1941.

simply his permission, but his direction. Churchill wanted people to think of him, not as an aristocrat (which he most certainly was, being the grandson of a duke), but as a man with the common touch.

In a similar vein, in the famous poster headlined 'Let us Go Forward Together', Churchill is not only wishing the populace to get the full force of his words and give their all for the common cause, but also to be portrayed as a man of the people. The images of him on the hustings in the 1920s and again in 1945, which show him on a cold/wet day without a hat (in an age when hats were an important part of an outfit), are deliberately aimed at letting people know (especially in 1945 when he was seventy) that here was a man not afraid of a bit of bad weather.

The image which remains his single most iconic portrait, is that of him seated and looking suitably severe in the photograph taken of him in Ottawa just after Christmas 1941 (and the entry of the USA into the war) by Yousuf Karsh. Churchill later told Karsh (whose lasting reputation was made by this one image) that he had 'caught the roaring lion in me'. The tag of the leonine image thus became forever attached to Churchill and was later reinforced by William Manchester's global bestseller biography, *The Last Lion*. Churchill had actually given himself the tag, when modestly explaining that victory in 1945 was attributable to the people, who had the lion's heart, while he had only been called upon to give the roar.

Whether we think of him as a lion, as a bulldog, as a sentimentalist or a hot-blooded warrior, Churchill ensured that his legacy would be as he intended, with an image moulded by himself.

PHR

68 | General Montgomery's 'Short Snorter'

G eneral (later Field Marshal) Bernard Montgomery was a successful career military officer who by 1942 had worked his way up the ranks to lead the British Eighth Army in the Western Desert of North Africa. Something of a protégé of General (also later Field Marshal) Alan Brooke, Montgomery (who was popularly known as 'Monty') sported a brash personality, and this lack of tact and dislike of diplomacy could easily cause annoyance to those around him.

Churchill had already been warned of Montgomery's 'eccentricities' by the time that he first got to know the general, over dinner in a hotel in Brighton in the summer of 1940. He was shocked

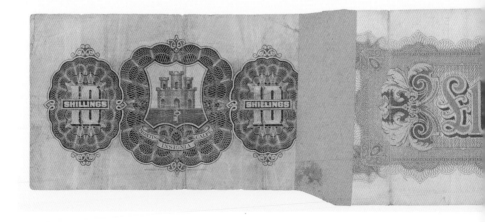

to his core when Montgomery declared that he avoided alcohol and smoking in order to achieve 100 per cent fitness, with Churchill allegedly retorting that he himself drank as much brandy and smoked as many cigars as he could get, which had made him 200 per cent fit.

Any uncertainty over Monty's fitness to lead, however, was removed after the British success in the Second Battle of El Alamein in November 1942, which was a clear turning point in the North African campaign. Montgomery continued to command the Eighth Army during the Allied invasions of Sicily and Italy, before taking charge of all the Allied ground

forces during the D-Day landings of June 1944 and subsequent Normandy campaign.

Churchill may sometimes have found Montgomery difficult to deal with, but it was certain that he greatly admired him as a military leader. One of the rare occasions on which the Prime Minister questioned his general's wisdom was during the planning for D-Day, when Monty to Churchill's dismay had arranged for as many as 2,000 officers and clerks to be part of the invasion force simply to keep records.

The signed banknotes shown here are known as a 'short snorters' and one

The three bank notes which form Montgomery's 'short snorter', their reverse shown below.

Churchill's relationship with one of his most important generals
was both fractious and friendly.

---

belonged to Monty. The tradition of signing a banknote appears to have begun in the 1920s to mark a shared aircraft flight, but by the time of the Second World War this had developed into a game based on the idea of an exclusive club of limited membership. One signatory could challenge another to produce his 'short snorter' at any time, and if he were unable to do so, a forfeit (often involving alcohol or money) would be required. In this particular case, the exclusive club appears to have included Churchill, Eisenhower, George VI and other notable personalities.

After the end of the war the two men remained in contact, exchanging letters on a regular basis and often visiting each other. An abrasive quality can certainly be seen in some of their correspondence – with Churchill questioning Monty's wisdom at getting involved in political matters – although their continued friendship was reflected in them holidaying together on occasion. Montgomery continued to visit Churchill at Chartwell throughout the elderly statesman's final years, and witnesses describe the field marshal as being moved to tears on seeing his old leader in such an aged condition. While the two men were poles apart in terms of their personalities, they remained a successful wartime partnership.

APR

Montgomery, Churchill, and the young exiled King Peter of Yugoslavia in 1941,
while Montgomery was commanding part of the defending forces in southern England.

69 | The Sword of Stalingrad

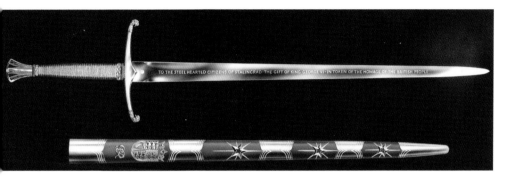

osef Stalin became General Secretary of the Communist Party of the USSR in 1922. As General Secretary, Stalin was a member of the ruling Politburo and after Lenin's death in 1924 he gradually took over the leading position in the Soviet government, shaping the nation's economic and social development and its international position during the 1930s.

A hallmark of Churchill's life and career was his fundamental hatred of Bolshevism, yet, in the Second World War, the two men worked together as allies in a very *Realpolitik* sense. Churchill's philosophy in war had at its core the

historic saying that 'my enemy's enemy is my friend'.

When Hitler invaded the Soviet Union on 22 June 1941 Churchill's private secretary, Jock Colville, recorded in his diary that the Prime Minister coined one of his most famous quotes, in justifying an alliance with Russia, with the words: 'If Hitler invaded Hell, I would at least make a favourable reference to the Devil in the House of Commons.'

Churchill found much to dislike in what he knew about Stalin's government of the USSR in the 1930s, but he went along with the Western media's paternalist

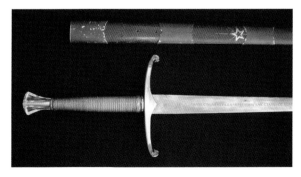

The inscription on the sword's blade, in both English and Russian,
forms a tribute to the citizens of Stalingrad.

Churchill's relationship with Stalin proved crucial to the war.

characterisation of the Soviet leader as 'Uncle Joe' and praised Stalin for his strength, courage and humour. He was determined to forge an alliance with Stalin and to convince him of the value of such a friendship to the war.

Churchill knew that the sheer size of the Soviet Union and the resources needed to fight a war on that front demanded that Hitler commit vast amounts of men and materiel which might otherwise be used elsewhere. Yet he also knew of the massive cost in lives that this resistance imposed on the USSR.

The first meeting of the two men came in mid-1942, following Soviet Foreign Secretary Molotov's visit to Churchill in June that year, when they established good relations and a belief in Churchill's mind that his Soviet ally trusted him. He met Stalin in Moscow on 12 August 1942. Stalin had long been demanding a 'second front' in Europe, to take the heat off the Red Army forces in the east fighting and finally overwhelming Germany's armies. But Churchill had to tell him that a second front was not a feasible option at that time.

Stalin actually had an inherent mistrust of Churchill, even choosing to disbelieve Churchill's feeding to him information that would have warned him of an imminent German invasion in June 1941. He insulted Churchill and railed against Great Britain's 'cowardice' in not launching a second front, to which Churchill responded with eloquence and frankness, but threatened to go home and abandon the meeting. Only after a subsequent *tête à tête* in Stalin's apartment, accompanied as ever by copious amounts of drink, food and verbal sparring, did the two men finally bond,

leaving Churchill subsequently elated and proclaiming Stalin a 'great man'.

Stalin had long refused to fly and had last left Russia in 1912, but he agreed to meet Churchill and President Roosevelt in November 1943 at Tehran, a location chosen for its ease of access for the Soviet leader. At Tehran Roosevelt did not help Churchill's cause, negotiating one to one with Stalin, establishing cosy relations with him and effectively side-lining and even belittling Churchill and Great Britain. In the midst of this Churchill seized the high ground, presenting a gift from the King to Stalin, the 'Sword of Stalingrad', to honour the city's resistance to the German siege, bringing tears to Stalin's eyes and leading him to give Churchill a great bear hug.

In October 1944 Churchill turned the tables on Roosevelt and met one to one with Stalin in Moscow, where he proposed the famous 'percentages' post-war division of Europe into zones of influence. Churchill was aware of his relatively rogue actions, telling Stalin that the Americans and Roosevelt would be shocked by such a division, though in fact Stalin's own plans for Europe were already a *fait accompli*. He solidly refused to negotiate on the future of Poland, where the Soviets had pointedly not gone to the assistance of the Warsaw Uprising that summer. Roosevelt too held back on providing assistance for fear of upsetting Stalin, while Churchill at least argued strongly with Stalin in an attempt to guarantee independence for Poland after the war.

Churchill's next meeting with Stalin, still reluctant to leave the USSR, was to be at Yalta in February 1945, which Churchill dubbed the 'riviera of Hades'. Stalin and the now ailing Roosevelt continued their

Churchill presents the Sword of Stalingrad to Stalin, while Roosevelt looks on.

courtship and, though Stalin pompously praised Churchill as 'a man who is born once in a hundred years', he continued to distrust him. Stalin remained firm in his view that Poland should be under Soviet control, while Churchill was obliged to accept his promise of free elections there after the war.

At the next Allied conference, in the Potsdam district of Berlin in July 1945, the US president was Truman and Churchill was in the midst of an election at home, which he and the leader of the Labour Party, Clement Attlee, both believed he would win easily. Churchill complained to Stalin about the closing off of Eastern Europe, with a phrase that he was to revise and revive the very next year concerning an 'iron fence' that had been installed around Soviet territory. Shortly after this Churchill and Attlee returned to London, where Churchill was to find that he had been defeated in the election and would not be returning to Potsdam. While he and Stalin were never to meet again, this, of course, was far from the end of his public opposition to the Soviet leader.

PHR

AND MAY GOD DEFEND THE RIGHT

While the best-known Churchill Toby jug perhaps remains the one of Churchill with hat and cigar shown at right, the earlier version above depicts him as First Lord of the Admiralty.

70 | Churchill Toby Jugs

Such is the prevalence of souvenirs and other objects associated with Churchill that a unique term – 'Churchilliana' – is often used to describe them. One of the most popular Churchill mementos is the Toby jug, a pottery jug usually in the form of a seated person or at least the head of a famous individual. The original design of a fat, cheerful man wearing a tricorn hat and holding a mug of beer in one hand was popularised by Staffordshire potters in the 1760s, and it is no surprise that the Toby jug's links with British tradition and jovial good humour could easily be applied to the character of Winston Churchill.

The first Toby jugs known to have been directly inspired by Churchill were a pair produced in 1927 by W. H. Goss of Longton, portraying him in his role as Chancellor of the Exchequer. The previous year he had introduced a tax on the turnover from betting, and the jugs make reference to this; the tax proved so unpopular that it was scrapped in 1930. It is likely that First World War-era jugs were also at least in the planning stage, yet Churchill's disgrace over the Dardanelles affair may have put an end to his appeal in pottery form.

It would really be the Second World War when Churchill Toby jugs became widely available, with the finest examples being sold for large amounts, even at a time of wartime austerity. Their modern-day value can be similarly high. A limited edition of 350 jugs designed by the Royal Staffordshire Pottery in Burslem and depicting Churchill in his uniform as First Lord of the Admiralty were originally advertised by Harrods for the relatively high cost of five guineas each in 1941; in 2002, an example of the same model would be sold for $2,750.

One of the souvenirs most commonly associated with Churchill is the Toby jug.

One of the best known examples of the Churchill Toby jug is one produced by the Royal Doulton company. Their Churchill jug was first produced in 1940 and sold to commemorate the occasion of his becoming Prime Minister that same year. Designed by Harry Fenton, the Royal Doulton jug proved so popular that it was reintroduced at the end of the war in different sizes and would enjoy the longest production run of any such Churchill souvenir, its production only coming to an end in 1991.

Produced to capitalise on the popularity of Britain's war leader, but often retained and handed down as tokens of Britain's wartime spirit, Churchill souvenirs proved immensely popular throughout the war and, indeed, have continued to be so in more recent years as collectables. With his immediately recognisable image, smoking a cigar and often giving the 'V for Victory' gesture, Churchill remains one of the easiest historical figures to represent. The ongoing appeal of 1940s nostalgia and the close association of Churchill with anything from that wartime period ensures that his image will remain with us as representative of that particular era.

APR

71 | Portrait by Douglas Chandor, 1946

On 17 December 1903 the brothers Orville and Wilbur Wright achieved the very first manned flight of a heavier than air aircraft, at Kitty Hawk in North Carolina. The science of flying developed rapidly in the years that followed and Churchill, a keen supporter of modern technological development and also a fearless adventurer, was quick to join the ranks of those who risked their lives – and early aviation was an extremely risky affair – by embarking on flying training in 1912. He was an irrepressible enthusiast for flying and was said to have undertaken up to ten flights a day.

Churchill expressed huge interest in flying, despite never qualifying as a pilot.

As First Lord of the Admiralty from 1911, and aware of the potential of aviation in a war situation, Churchill applied his enthusiasm to encouraging the development of military flight. In 1912, a sub-committee of the Committee of Imperial Defence recommended the establishment of a Royal Flying Corps, which would exploit aviation for its military potential, though then and for some time afterwards the priority was to be to use aircraft to guide artillery fire and to observe enemy movements on the ground. The RFC originally had two branches – a Military Wing which was part of the Army, and a Naval Wing. With Churchill's support the latter became a more independent force in July 1914, called the Royal Naval Air Service (RNAS).

Churchill never qualified as a pilot, having reluctantly agreed in 1913 to his wife's pleas to give up the dangerous occupation of flying. But he continued to fly (with a qualified pilot) during the First World War, coming close to death on one occasion, when his aircraft's engine died mid-flight, causing it to plunge towards the sea, before springing back to life in the nick of time (Churchill wrote that he had had no fear of death at that moment, which so typified his whole life).

After returning from his service on the Western Front, following his fall from glory because of the failed Dardanelles campaign, he was given the office, in 1917, of Minister of Munitions, in which capacity he boosted the country's air resources. From 1919 to 1921 he served as the first Secretary of State for Air, overseeing the newly formed (April 1918) Royal Air Force, an amalgam of the RFC and the RNAS, as an independent military arm. He was also responsible for the development of civil aviation, and the first scheduled British commercial flights between London and Paris were begun on his watch in May 1919.

The facility that the new aerial weapon offered for military actions rather than just reconnaissance, was rapidly realised by both sides, though Germany, with its Zeppelin and Gotha air raids in particular, showed how aircraft allowed the war to be taken directly to the front door of the enemy. By the time of the Second World War aircraft had been massively improved on all sides, making enemy raids on the homeland an inevitability – with Stanley Baldwin admitting publicly in 1932 that 'the bomber will always get through', meaning civilian casualties would be unavoidable. Churchill, being out of office in the 1930s, could do little more than shout and bluster – as he did on a major scale – in an attempt to reverse defence cuts (that he himself had promoted just a few years beforehand as Chancellor of the Exchequer) and re-arm in readiness for another major conflict.

His campaigning made his return to government on the outbreak of war in September 1939 inevitable and Prime Minister Chamberlain brought Churchill back once again as First Lord of the Admiralty. When he succeeded Chamberlain as Prime Minister on 10 May 1940, the day of the beginning of the German *Blitzkrieg* on Western Europe, he quickly made the British people aware of the scale of the task that faced them, with a rare case of a politician offering only 'blood, toil, tears and sweat', rather than the customary optimistic spin that politicians today put on bad news stories. When the British Expeditionary Force was being evacuated from Dunkirk, he sensibly, but much to the chagrin of his French ally, held back from sending all the RAF's fighter forces to ensure the country had at least some hope of defending itself, against an inevitable German onslaught.

In a speech delivered in Parliament on 20 August 1940 he paid tribute to the heroism and sacrifice of the RAF fliers, whom he described as 'the few'; indeed the majority of them were scarcely out of their teenage years. The speech was to become a by-word of English rhetoric and to become the label by which the Battle of Britain fighter pilots are known. Yet Churchill's tribute applied also to Bomber Command, and he continued to place faith in the Allied bomber offensive later in the war to lay the ground for eventual victory.

The RAF in its turn repaid the debt of honour to Churchill by granting him the honorary rank of air commodore (the Army equivalent would be brigadier) of No. 615 (County of Surrey) Squadron, which was based just twenty miles from Chartwell. He wore the uniform with real pride on many occasions during the Second World War, more especially after King George VI granted him his RAF 'wings' (though he had never qualified as a pilot) on the twenty-fifth anniversary of the establishment of the RAF on 1 April 1943.

Churchill wears this RAF uniform in the portrait shown here, painted by Douglas Chandor in 1946. The artist had been commissioned the previous year by President Roosevelt to paint 'The Big Three' at the Yalta conference; although he completed sketches of both Roosevelt and Churchill at that time, Stalin proved unavailable and so the full painting was never finished

PHR

The artist Douglas Chandor (1897–1953) specialised in portraiture. Born in England, Chandor lived in Texas later in life.

72 | Tehran Conference Commemorative Scarf

C hurchill helped establish a series of conferences throughout the Second World War which saw him journey around the globe to meet with other Allied leaders to plan grand strategy. In this he was dramatically different to Stalin, who was reluctant to leave Moscow, and Roosevelt, whose disability made travel difficult. But it did not stop Churchill from meeting both leaders individually on separate occasions: Roosevelt on several instances beginning in August 1941 in

in Egypt shortly before) and bears background images depicting Cairo and Tehran.

Tehran was the first opportunity for Roosevelt to shake hands with the Soviet leader. Arriving with different objectives, all three agreed to commit to establishing the long-called-for Second Front at the earliest opportunity, which would involve a cross-Channel invasion of North-West Europe scheduled for May the following year. They also debated operations against Japan as well as the post-war fate

---

The conference in Tehran proved to be one of the most important wartime meetings for the Allied leaders.

Newfoundland, and Stalin first in Moscow in August 1942. But the initial occasion when all three of them would meet together would be at Tehran, in Iran, on 28 November 1943.

The Tehran conference would last for four days and proved to be a particularly exciting opportunity – not only for progress to be made in the Allied war strategy, but in terms of the boost to morale and confidence which seeing 'The Big Three' leaders together brought to the Allied cause. As such, much was made of the meeting in all forms of media, while souvenirs were produced and sold as a means of commemorating the important event. The decorative scarf shown here, for example, depicts the Big Three as well as the Chinese leader Chiang Kai-shek (who had met Churchill and Roosevelt

of Europe, in particular the question of Poland's borders.

One tense moment occurred when Stalin suggested executing between 50,000 and 100,000 German officers in order to prevent another war, which led to Roosevelt jokingly suggesting that only 49,000 deaths might be required. Churchill stormed out of the room in disgust, aware that Stalin had already ordered mass executions at sites such as Katyn and so was fully capable of what was being suggested; Stalin had to lead him back into the room, explaining that he had made a joke in poor taste. Churchill suspected that Stalin had rather been testing the reaction he received to such a suggestion.

Over the course of the war, there would be a distinct shift in the relationship between the Big Three. Stalin's actions before the conflict, when he had formed an alliance with Hitler, led both Churchill and Roosevelt to hold deep suspicions towards him. Yet they would work together for the greater good, in order to beat the larger threat from Nazi Germany. Roosevelt in particular laboured hard to court Stalin's support, which annoyed Churchill at times. Britain lacked the vast resources of both the United States and Soviet Union, and was therefore always going to be the junior partner in such an alliance. But Churchill's strong personality and presence ensured a more equal consideration for British interests.

APR

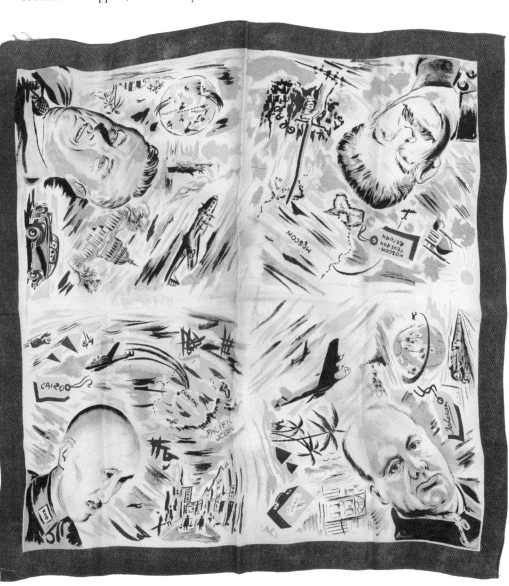

Souvenirs like this commemorative scarf proved popular during the war, often being sold to raise money for war-related charities.

73 | Bottle of Pol Roger Champagne

Churchill drank from at least the time he left school and famously claimed he overcame a dislike of whisky when, in the Army in India, he claimed his drink options were reduced to tea, tepid water and lime or tepid water and whisky. He opted for the last and never looked back. It is known that his staff would customarily place a well-watered whisky – ten parts water, one part whisky; known

top *cuvée*, matured over ten years, as the Cuvée Sir Winston Churchill, and the neck label still bears his image. Among the many quotes by Churchill referencing champagne, perhaps the most famous was his claim that he could not live without it: 'In victory I deserve it. In defeat I need it.'

Despite his catalogue of daily alcohol consumption, Churchill was never recorded as having been seen to behave in an obviously drunken manner. His

---

Of the many characteristics attached to Churchill's persona, most prominent would be his capacity for strong drink.

---

to his staff as 'mouthwash' – next to his bed in the morning. He would sip his 'mouthwash' all day long, but, despite his taste for whisky (mostly Johnny Walker Black Label), the drink with which Churchill is most associated is champagne and he is said to have drunk champagne at lunch and dinner on a regular basis.

Pol Roger was his favourite champagne – he once described the house as 'the most drinkable address in France'. After his death the company put a black edge around the label of every bottle exported to the UK: a residual shading is still to be found on the labels. In honour of their best customer, Pol Roger also named their

famous exchange with Bessie Braddock MP might indicate otherwise, but Churchill claimed to hold drunkards in contempt and further declared that he had taken more from alcohol 'than alcohol has taken out of me'. His apparently prodigious consumption was deceptive, given the length of his working day. A probably apocryphal quotation has nevertheless a ring of truth about it: when asked how he continued to function, despite his drinking, he simply replied: 'practice'.

PHR

74 | HMS *Belfast*

The opening of the long awaited Second Front in Europe on 6 June 1944 (D-Day), with the Allied landings in Normandy, was a key turning point in the course of the Second World War. In many ways those landings were a culmination of considerable effort made by Churchill to foster relations between Britain and the United States, leading to both nations' forces fighting side by side against a common enemy.

But the course of planning had been far from smooth. Roosevelt and Stalin

The cruiser HMS *Belfast*, now permanently moored in the Thames near Tower Bridge.

Churchill's enthusiasm for being at the heart of the action could sometimes lead to controversy, as shown at the key moment of D-Day.

had been pushing for the Second Front to be launched sooner, while Churchill and his Chiefs of Staff had always preferred a more cautious approach, aware of the need for long preparation for such an operation and wary of revisiting the high casualty rates which had so characterised the stalemated battles of the Western Front in the First World War. This more careful attitude had allowed industrial production in the United States and Britain to be boosted while masses of troops and equipment were transported to the UK in readiness for the invasion.

The key factor in ensuring that the Western Allies remained united throughout this joint endeavour was the strong relationship between their respective leaders, Churchill and Roosevelt, although by 1943 Britain (and therefore Churchill) was certainly the junior partner due to the greater resources at the disposal of the Americans.

Churchill could sometimes be the very definition of a 'loose cannon' who would suddenly offer alternative scenarios and ideas that were ill thought-through and far from helpful to the bigger picture. It was therefore often necessary for his various service chiefs to rein him in and discourage such rashness. As D-Day approached, he was still discussing a potential invasion of Norway as well as an Allied landing at Bordeaux, but such ideas were successfully stifled before they could cause too much concern.

Yet Churchill's unorthodox attitude could also prove of great benefit to military planning. He was a strong supporter of the elaborate D-Day deception plan, Operation Fortitude, which proved remarkably successful in convincing the Germans that any Allied

invasion would be centred on either Norway or the Pas de Calais region of France rather than Normandy. His enthusiasm for secret behind-the-lines operations was well known, while his long-standing fascination with new technology and innovation encouraged multiple developments in connection with D-Day. The amphibious nature of the landings necessitated the design and production of new vehicles and equipment as well as the adaptation of existing ones, including the duplex drive (DD) swimming tanks, vehicles specially designed to detonate mines, tanks with mounted flamethrowers to clear enemy pillboxes, and armoured vehicles designed to demolish concrete obstructions. Among the most admired innovations were the Mulberry harbours, temporary artificial harbours floated into position to meet the need for port facilities at the landing beaches. These were made from huge concrete assemblies and other specially manufactured components so that supplies and reinforcements could be landed readily, before French ports had been liberated and put back into use.

Churchill had accepted that the Supreme Commander of the Allied Expeditionary Force should be an American, and President Roosevelt selected Dwight D. Eisenhower for this vital role. Perhaps it was a feeling that he had been generous in supporting the alliance and sacrificing any say in this important decision that encouraged him to assert a claim to be at the heart of the action on the day itself. This was a clear personality trait of Churchill, who never shied away from danger and always wanted to be at the centre of any military operation, despite the fact that his involvement often only frustrated those involved. He therefore announced to Eisenhower that he would personally attend the invasion, and be on board the cruiser HMS *Belfast* to view the landings from as near as possible to the beaches. Expecting resistance to the idea, Churchill even threatened to commission himself into the Royal Navy and therefore justify his presence on one of its ships.

Eisenhower and the British Chiefs of Staff were faced with an awkward situation. Their strategy for keeping the Prime Minister out of trouble was therefore to appeal to the King, who had planned to accompany Churchill on D-Day, but was persuaded otherwise. The King wrote to Churchill twice, mere days before D-Day, to ask him to reconsider, suggesting to Churchill that his presence aboard *Belfast* would add immeasurably to his own anxieties and put Churchill's Cabinet colleagues in a very difficult position which they would justifiably resent.

The royal pressure encouraged Churchill finally to concede that his duty was to remain at home. HMS *Belfast* was to be among the first ships to bombard the Normandy coast in preparation for the landings, and would therefore become an obvious target for the German guns – a dangerous position at the best of times, let alone with a maverick like Churchill on board. But he still could not resist travelling to Normandy at the first opportunity, some six days later on 12 June, to view the beachheads for himself and converse with the troops.

APR

Churchill is helped onto the Mulberry Harbour moored off
Arromanches, Normandy, on 21 July 1944,
shortly after the D-Day landings.

75 | Churchill's Cigars

The young Winston Churchill began experimenting with smoking while still at school. Initially he tried cigarettes, but graduated to cigars, until his mother wrote disapprovingly and offered him incentives to discourage the habit. Then, shortly before his twenty-first birthday in 1895, when he went to Cuba to report on the occupying Spanish forces' efforts to suppress a revolution, he took up cigar-smoking again and never looked back. He gained and maintained a taste for good Cuban cigars, which lasted the rest of his life, though he sometimes had to make compromises.

In the 1930s, out of office and finding it difficult to make ends meet (despite earning massive fees for speaking in the USA and for writing newspaper and journal articles on almost every subject imaginable), he ordered cheap American cigars by the thousand.

Soon after the outbreak of the Second World War he took up smoking expensive Cuban cigars (in 2023 'Churchill' cigars were £40–£50 apiece), many of which were given him by well-wishers. Churchill ensured that he would scarcely ever be pictured or seen in public without a cigar, between his lips or in his hand. The result was that, a lot of the time, the cigar he had going went out and he is seen to have chewed at the end of it. The result, as any cigar aficionado would know, is that the cigar would get wet and its taste would be spoiled, with the result that his stubs would be several inches long. The 'ashtray' – really a steel bin – in his room at the Cabinet War Rooms had to be big enough to make sure, when he tossed them away, that they would not land on the carpet.

The original cigar on display at the Churchill War Rooms was given to the CWR by his secretary, Elizabeth Layton

Churchill's cigar butts were often retained as souvenirs. *Above*, the cigar kept by Elizabeth Layton; *top*, an example acquired during his travels.

A fondness for smoking cigars was always part of Churchill's image.

(later Nel), who wrote a summary of its pedigree – she caught it when, in a moment of celebrating a victory in Italy in 1944, he threw it in the air.

Churchill's most favoured cigar dealer was Robert Lewis (now Fox) in St James's, where he regularly ordered and even tested for them some of the finest Cuban cigars of the day. His favourite brand was Romeo y Julieta, but Churchill was not averse to smoking many other first-class brands.

In 1941 the National Tobacco Commission of Cuba gifted Churchill a very large consignment of cigars, which sent up red flags with the Security Service, MI5, who feared that attempts might be made to use a cigar to poison Britain's grandee Prime Minister. Having tested several and found them harmless (but having destroyed them in the process), MI5's Victor Rothschild reported the results to Churchill, who, by then, had already smoked or given away many of the gifted stock.

PHR

This cigar box, which belonged to Churchill, was
kept by his personal valet, Norman McGowan
and later sold at auction in 2021 for £79,000.

76 | The Freedom Portrait by Frank Salisbury, 1944

C hurchill was granted the Freedom of the City of London on 30 June 1943, an honorary recognition which in the Prime Minister's case was linked to his devotion to the capital city throughout the Blitz and other wartime struggles. The artist Frank Salisbury was commissioned to paint a large work featuring multiple figures to commemorate the event, and asked Churchill to sit for him. However, on this occasion the Prime Minister was reluctant to spare the time and his likeness had to be based on photographic references.

Salisbury was in many ways the obvious choice to paint Churchill, since he was a traditionalist who specialised in portrait painting and large canvasses of historic events. He had received much acclaim for his works on both sides of the Atlantic, and this success brought not only considerable wealth but the opportunity to mix with the most influential figures in society. He remained determined to paint Churchill from life, however, and would continue to request a personal sitting.

Clementine was rather critical of Salisbury, taking a dislike to him and feeling that he had painted her husband on several occasions without permission. There was almost certainly an element of resentment on her part, based on the fact that Salisbury had seen great success and popularity, including most notably within the Royal Family, at a time just before the war when Churchill was suffering in

Frank Salisbury (1874–1962) was an English artist who also worked extensively in the USA. As well as his commercially successful paintings, he was also noted for his interest in stained glass.

Churchill sat for a portrait painting only once during the Second World War.

the political wilderness. It is therefore somewhat ironic that Salisbury's famous portrait depicting Churchill in informal style wearing his siren suit was for many years displayed prominently in the main reception room at Chartwell, years after the artist himself was actively discouraged from entering the house.

Given his wife's mixed feelings about Salisbury, the pressures of war and his own characteristic reluctance to sit still for very long in any circumstances, Churchill remained unwilling to devote much time to sitting formally for any portrait. But he eventually agreed to Salisbury's request and visited the artist's home studio in Hampstead on 24 November 1944, where he sat for half an hour. Clearly the experience was not too uncomfortable for the Prime Minister, since he would pose again for Salisbury on five other occasions

after the war – albeit for similarly short periods.

With the finished portrait painted in a traditional style and depicting the subject smiling in a determined fashion, Churchill himself approved of the work and considered it a good likeness. Salisbury retained *The Freedom Portrait* himself but incorrectly dated the painting to 24 October, which subsequently led to some confusion. Historians initially presumed that the painting could not have been painted from life, since Churchill was overseas on that date. It was only many years later that a comparison of Churchill's diary and Salisbury's published memoir indicated that it was created following an actual sitting.

APR

77 | *Allies* Sculpture by Lawrence Holofcener

While the 'Special Relationship' between the United Kingdom and United States had been recognised long before the Second World War, based upon the two nations' common language and heritage, such a rapport had cooled somewhat since the end of the First World War. Many in Britain believed that the United States was no longer a reliable ally, pointing to the question of war debts, naval rivalry and the effects of the Depression. Equally, many Americans recognised that their past relationship with the UK had been based just as much on rivalry as friendship.

The outbreak of the Second World War brought the two nations together in a stronger manner. The Fall of France in 1940 meant that Britain would now need to coordinate its military efforts in an unprecedented way with its Empire and Commonwealth, while securing aid from the still neutral United States in order to continue involvement in the war. In due course, once it became clear that a greater alliance was needed to beat the Axis, Churchill concentrated on gaining an American commitment to join the fight. He devoted much effort to establishing a good relationship with the Americans and key to this would be a bond with their President, Franklin D. Roosevelt. In many ways, Churchill was the ideal person to forge such a link, since his mother had been an American citizen and he held a long-standing affinity for the USA.

Churchill's friendship with Roosevelt was key to strengthening the 'Special Relationship'.

Between September 1939 and the President's death in April 1945, Churchill and Roosevelt exchanged some 1,700 letters and telegrams and in addition the two met on eleven occasions. The two leaders did bear some misgivings towards each other. Roosevelt felt that Churchill epitomised the worst of British aristocracy and imperialism, while Churchill had written a number of articles criticising Roosevelt's politics, especially his famous New Deal. Yet they enjoyed each other's company and forged a friendship which, although not resolving all their differences of opinion, certainly contributed to the spirit of cooperation. In his eulogy following the President's death, Churchill declared that in Roosevelt the United Kingdom had lost the greatest friend it had ever known.

When the Bond Street Association of shops and businesses decided to commission a sculpture to mark the fiftieth anniversary of the end of the Second World War in 1995, their desire was to avoid the usual formal style of such tributes in favour of something more intimate, which would appeal to the London district's many international visitors. The American-British artist Lawrence Holofcener therefore created *Allies*, a life-size sculpture in bronze depicting Churchill and Roosevelt chatting on a bench. Located in a pedestrian section of London's New Bond Street, the piece has proved very popular with tourists over the years. The fact that anybody can sit on the bench between the two figures and pose for photographs makes the sculpture a particularly appealing one, with the way in which the figures' knees have been polished to a shine by frequent handling indicating its popularity.

APR

Roosevelt and Churchill during the Casablanca conference, January 1943.

78 | VE-Day Microphone

The press, Churchill wrote in an article for *The Inlander*, the journal of the University of Michigan, in February 1901, offers unique career opportunities, like no other profession. Writing for the press

Although he abandoned his military commission to take up the far more profitable pursuit of journalism, to report from the fighting in South Africa in 1899, he enjoyed the rare privilege – especially after his celebrated escape

---

An experienced journalist himself, Churchill's relationship with the media was sometimes fraught.

---

certainly afforded Churchill a lifestyle in keeping with his aristocratic pedigree and indeed, at various times, was instrumental in his financial survival.

Like his father before him, Churchill saw journalism as a means both of supplementing his income which, whether in the Army or in politics, never seemed to suffice to fund his extravagant tastes and lifestyle, and as a means of self-promotion. The vast variety of the subjects on which he wrote implied he saw himself as an authority on most topics, though he often hired amanuenses, not least his very talented private secretary, 'Eddie' Marsh, to write articles for him, when he had taken on more than he could accomplish in the time available.

from captivity there – of combining a commission (albeit unpaid) with work as a reporter. This gave him a unique status from which to command very large fees, ever aware of the value of his name, as much as his location. Churchill, both through his mother and in his own right, was exceptionally well connected, which among other things led him brazenly to join the generals at their dinner to celebrate the relief of Ladysmith in February 1900, exaggerating his part for public consumption and self-aggrandisement. He knew all the major 'press barons' well and was close friends with Lord Northcliffe (sometime owner of the *Daily Mirror*, *The Times*

'The price of freedom is eternal vigilance.'
Though often attributed to Churchill, the origin of this advice is unclear.

and the *Daily Mail*, among other publications), Lord Camrose (owner of the *Daily Telegraph*), Lord Riddell (owner of the *News of the World*) with Max Aitken (Lord Beaverbrook, owner of the *Daily Express*) and the Astors, sometime owners of *The Times*. He wrote for most of Fleet Street, but despite his connections to, and even friendships with the owners, the press did not always treat him kindly, with Lord Beaverbrook in particular, making plain his absolute disagreement with him in the 1930s over Churchill's stance on rearmament and the possibility of war.

His relationship with the BBC, and in particular with its General Manager in the 1930s, John (later Lord) Reith, was a bitter one. The BBC had been established in 1922 as a commercial enterprise and did not become a government-backed corporation until 1927. At the time of the general strike in 1926 it was just months away from the date for the renewal of its government-granted commercial licence and was being careful not to be seen as being in any way in conflict with the government of the day.

Reith himself firmly believed in the BBC holding a position that demanded it be neutral in political matters, but, during the strike, the ebullient Chancellor of the Exchequer,

Winston Churchill, took control of the government-sponsored *British Gazette* and used it to argue vehemently against the strikers. He felt the BBC too should support the government position against the strikers, and when Reith insisted on BBC neutrality, Churchill famously criticised this impartiality by comparing the strikers to a fire and the government to the fire brigade.

In 1928, shortly before an election, Churchill broadcast what Reith considered to be a strongly biased political message. Thereafter, he was not allowed to broadcast his views on the radio for some years.

Reith turned down Churchill's cheeky offer to pay £100 to be allowed to speak for thirty minutes in December 1929 and two years later the BBC refused to allow him to broadcast his views on the self-government of India, while the subject was still being debated in Parliament. Though he participated in round-table discussions on the radio, he was not allowed to broadcast his views on the economic crisis in 1932. His first chance to speak on the issue of India came on 29 January 1935, in a broadcast that Reith dismissed as 'disappointing' and 'bombastic'.

Many of Churchill's broadcast wartime speeches as Prime Minister were 'retakes' of earlier parliamentary speeches, and as such often lacked the vigour and emotion

This Grampian-type radio microphone is believed to have been used by Churchill during the VE-Day service of thanksgiving held at St Margaret's Chapel in Westminster.

Churchill broadcasts to the nation from the Cabinet Office on the afternoon of VE-Day, 8 May 1945.

of the original. One 1942 attempt by Churchill to persuade Parliament to allow limited broadcasting of speeches recorded live in Parliament failed (Commons and Lords debates were only broadcast [on radio] for the first time in 1978).

Despite having Reith in his government (initially as Minister of Transport in 1940), and his tireless use of the airwaves to speak to the nation, Churchill's feelings about the BBC were still critical: he described the BBC, according to Reith's memoirs, as 'an enemy within the gates, continually causing trouble'. Yet he made much use of the BBC broadcasting equipment installed in the underground War Rooms.

His broadcasts during the 1945 election campaign were widely considered to have been poor, and after losing the election, he turned down nine invitations to speak on the radio. After television returned to the air in 1946, he showed a deep aversion to the medium, appearing only once, in November 1954, to speak a few words as part of a programme on his eightieth birthday. A TV screen-test in 1955 was a failure, with him seeming pompous and unrehearsed, which added further to his aversion. He opposed the introduction of commercial television in the 1950s and even tried to block the television broadcast of the Queen's coronation in 1953 (but was over-ruled by the monarch herself). It is ironic that the live TV broadcast of his funeral in January 1965 was watched by over 300 million people worldwide and became a deeply memorable part of the lives of almost everyone who saw it.

PHR

79 | Douglas C-54 Skymaster EW999

A clear illustration of the 'special relationship' between Britain and the United States, as well as the rapport between the respective leaders of both nations, was President Roosevelt's gift to Churchill of an impressive new transport aircraft for his personal use. The President already had his own four-engine Douglas C-54 Skymaster transport, named *The Sacred Cow*, and it was therefore appropriate for Churchill to be given the same kind of aeroplane. Roosevelt's aircraft had been symbolically named after an Athenian galley used exclusively by Greek statesmen on their voyages to consult the oracle.

Despite the personal intentions behind the gift, the aircraft was in fact treated as part of the Lend-Lease programme in which war supplies and materiel were

---

The aircraft type chosen to transport Churchill and Roosevelt symbolised their 'special relationship'.

---

sent to America's allies to assist their involvement in the war. Arriving in Britain in the summer of 1944, the empty shell of the aircraft was transferred into the care of the Royal Air Force's No. 24 Squadron, based at Hendon, which had

The Douglas Skymaster presented to Churchill by President Roosevelt.

President Harry Truman continued to use the same C-54 Skymaster aircraft as President Roosevelt for a time; this aircraft is shown here in 1947.

responsibility for transporting VIPs such as the Prime Minister.

Work then began on fitting out the Skymaster, with Churchill's personal directive on the matter being to make it look 'British'. This resulted in construction of a separate stateroom including two beds, a conference room, galley and washroom, all decorated in a sumptuous manner with state of the art sound-proofing. Indeed, the sound-proofing was so effective that Churchill complained that the bedside clock in his stateroom was keeping him awake at night with its loud ticking. The toilet could also boast the world's first electrically heated seat. More than three and a half tonnes of special fittings were added to the aircraft in all, with the soft furnishings alone valued at £10,000. One American journalist was so impressed with the interior that he described it as resembling 'the drawing-room of an English castle'.

Both Churchill and his wife used the Skymaster on numerous occasions from November 1944, to travel to overseas conferences and official meetings. The Yalta conference was a particularly notable occasion, as Roosevelt's Skymaster appeared together with Churchill's and formed part of an aerial cavalcade designed specifically to impress their Russian hosts. Later that year the aircraft also flew Clementine to Moscow for her trip as Patron of the Red Cross Aid to Russia Fund.

Churchill's final use of the Skymaster was to take him to the Potsdam conference in July 1945, and afterwards there followed some discussion about sending it to California for a $100,000 overhaul. Yet Churchill's defeat in that year's elections effectively scuppered any ideas that he may have had to retain the aircraft, with Attlee's Labour government hardly keen to spend such sums on luxurious personal transport when their priority was the rebuilding of the nation. It was therefore decided to return EW999 to the United States, as part of the original Lend-Lease arrangement.

The aircraft's final official flight involved transporting General George C. Marshall to China in December 1945 (as part of a failed diplomatic mission), during which it was involved in a minor accident that left it too damaged to consider repair. Its ignoble end was therefore on top of a Chinese scrapheap.

APR

80 | Churchill's Potsdam Conference Map

The Potsdam conference that began on 17 July 1945 would be the final joint meeting of the Big Three, with President Harry S Truman taking the place of the late Franklin D. Roosevelt. Now that Germany had been defeated, important issues needed to be discussed including the administration of captured territory as well as how the borders of post-war Europe would be determined.

Potsdam would be a difficult experience for Churchill, as halfway through the conference the results of the British General Election became known, leading to his replacement by the new Prime Minister, Clement Attlee. Yet while he was still in power and in attendance, Churchill was able to influence some key decisions that would have a lasting impact on Europe in particular.

powers only from their own occupation zone.

Churchill's personal map keeper, the redoubtable Captain Pim, organised travelling maps, usually A0-sized wooden folding frames with handles, which Churchill's staff would carry with them when accompanying the leader on his travels in the Second World War. The most significant of these by far is the map shown overleaf, which Churchill used at the conference to mark out the agreed zones of the planned post-war occupation of Europe. The map shows the eastern, Russian-occupied zone; the American zone in southern Germany (with an area carved out for the French); the British zone in the north (with an area carved

---

Decisions made by the Big Three impacted the post-war layout of Europe.

Germany would be demilitarised and split into different zones of occupation managed by the Americans, British, French and Soviets. The country would be run by an Allied Control Commission made up of the four occupying powers, with Germany's educational and judicial systems purged of Nazi influence and its society reshaped on democratic lines. The question of economic reparations from Germany was also much debated, with an agreement being reached that reparations should be exacted by the occupying

out of Land Bremen to give the American forces a port facility) and the subdivision of Austria.

The biggest stumbling blocks at Potsdam involved the post-war fate of Poland, most notably the revision of its borders and those of Germany. Poland had already been much debated at both the Tehran and Yalta Conferences. In exchange for the territory which it had lost to the Soviet Union, Poland was to be compensated in the west by large areas of Germany up to the Oder–Neisse Line, the border along two key rivers. Yet the Poles, as well as the Czechs and Hungarians, had begun to expel their ethnic German

The Big Three – Churchill, Roosevelt and Stalin – meet in person together for the last time at Yalta. The next conference, in Potsdam, would see Harry S Truman as President of the United States.

minorities and both the Americans and British were extremely worried that a mass influx of Germans into their respective zones could cause problems. A request was therefore made to Poland, Czechoslovakia and Hungary that such expulsions be temporarily suspended, only to be resumed in due course once they could be 'effected in an orderly and humane manner'. On the vexed question of what constituted a 'democratic Poland', the Soviets and the Western Allies were never going to agree.

The greatest outcome of these decisions made at Potsdam was to split Europe into a capitalist West and communist East, and the differences between them would soon become even more evident as the 'iron curtain' (as Churchill himself would define it in March 1946) began to fall across the continent, creating a clear ideological, political and military split. In a speech at the University of Zurich in Switzerland on 19 September 1946, Churchill advocated 'a kind of United States of Europe' as a remedy to the tragic state in which the Second World War had left the continent. He wanted to see past glories restored, amidst assured peace and prosperity. He described the solution as requiring nothing more than the will of the populations and as a first step towards this, Churchill claimed that it was vital for France and Germany to work together, while Great Britain would be one of the influential supporters of the 'new' Europe.

Churchill had the foresight to see how Europe could only move forward by choosing (to quote earlier Prime Minister William Ewart Gladstone) a 'blessed act of oblivion' and not look back on the 'horror of the past'. Yet his simple vision of a united Europe, at peace with itself, would prove difficult to realise.

APR / PHR

81 | 1945 General Election Poster

Under the British political system, when a prime minister resigns from office there is no absolute necessity to call a General Election and, most commonly, the ruling party simply appoints a successor. In May 1940 Churchill succeeded Neville Chamberlain without an election.

The coalition government that Churchill formed in 1940 was known as the 'National Government', since it encompassed not just the ruling Conservative Party, but also the main opposition, Labour, together with some a senior Labour figure, were being put forward as potential successors to him, even during the war. When Germany invaded the USSR in June 1941, making the Soviets into allies of Britain, there was a surge of interest in communism in the UK, but also a general swing to the left among voters sympathetic to the suffering of the Soviet people.

Many Labour supporters decried the compromises that the leadership, under Deputy Prime Minister and Leader of the party, Clement Attlee, was obliged to agree as part of the coalition. Cripps was seen as the spearhead of the left in

---

Despite leading his country to victory in the war, Churchill was immediately voted out of office.

Liberals. Although no serious challenges were made to Churchill's position, he did undergo – usually at his own insistence – several votes of confidence (by which, under the British political system, a leader can be pressured to resign) in May 1941, January 1942, July 1942, March 1944 and December 1944, all of which he won with massive majorities. The votes were generally occasioned by setbacks in the Allies' progress in the fight against Hitler and in the war against Japan, each of which Churchill defended with typical rumbustiousness and wit.

But the votes signalled a degree of impatience with Churchill, especially within his War Cabinet, where individuals, not least Sir Stafford Cripps, 1942, just as it was growing in popularity in the country. But he was the polar opposite of Churchill – a devout Christian who abstained from alcohol and was a vegetarian – and whose character was famously criticised by Churchill as being full of the virtues which he disliked.

It was through Cripps that the left channelled its increasing demands for a commitment to a more egalitarian society after the war, which Churchill dismissed as a distraction with an element of woolly idealism. But such demands continued to increase as the war progressed and especially as victory seemed more likely. The Home Intelligence Division's report in November 1942 found that a majority of Britons supported five main tenets of

"LET US GO FORWARD TOGETHER"

a post-war society: a living wage for all workers; the good of the community being placed above profit; financial security for those unable to work; decent housing for all; equality of access to education for all. A separate report by William Beveridge, a former civil servant and head of the London School of Economics, set out a blueprint for post-war social policy and supported all these aims, along with the creation of a national health service and free medical care for all.

When the Beveridge Report was issued on 2 December 1942, it was like a bombshell. Because the report and its ideas attracted widespread public support in its vision for a post-war world, the Conservatives, fearing a public backlash, nominally supported a Commons motion accepting the report's findings. In light of this, Churchill finally spoke on the radio on 20 March 1943 of a 'four-year plan', which would support the creation of a national health service, higher education for all and full employment. However, he offered no detail and privately dismissed Beveridge and what he considered the report's unrealistic aims. Although Labour members of the War Cabinet shared Churchill's fear of promising people things which could not then be delivered because of lack of funds, they insisted that Churchill sign up to a committed strategy and not simply make theoretical preparations.

Churchill tended to pass domestic policy off to Clement Attlee (who held office as Deputy Prime Minister), while he concentrated on the military prosecution of the war and maintenance of the Grand Alliance. By 1945, the swell of support for a more egalitarian society after the war, combined with increasing demands from Labour members in the country for their leadership to disassociate itself from Churchill's and the Conservative Party's half-hearted support for post-war societal changes, led to increasing demands for the party to quit the Great Coalition and to demand an election, the first since 1935. Churchill tried to convince Attlee to stay in the coalition till the war had been won on all fronts, but the Labour Party's National Executive insisted on Labour leaving the coalition and forcing a General Election.

Churchill formally resigned as Prime Minister on 23 May 1945, just fifteen days after VE-Day, and was formally asked by the King to form a 'caretaker' National Government (essentially a Conservative one) until the General Election results were in. The election was held on 5 July 1945, but the count had to be delayed until 26 July to allow the 'khaki vote' – the votes of those serving in the forces overseas – to be counted. Churchill, more as a sop to democratic processes than any fear that he would lose the election, invited Attlee to join him at the conference of the Allies being held at Potsdam at that time.

Churchill went back to London for the results of the election, but fully expected to be returning as Prime Minister after the votes had been counted. Attlee himself hoped to be able to whittle away some of Churchill's support, but consistent with the general view, expected to be roundly defeated.

In fact the Labour Party won the election with an absolute majority over all other parties of 136, one of the greatest landslide victories of twentieth-century British politics. Churchill's ill-judged speech accusing Attlee of planning to use 'Gestapo' methods of government if elected did nothing to help his party. Churchill won his own seat comfortably, but the country had, as he said, given him 'the order of the boot'.

A famous poster of the time depicted the nation waving goodbye to him … but making clear he would be back. And in 1951, he was.

PHR

82 | Order of Leopold

In March 1944, reflecting on the award of medals and ribbons, Churchill made the point that there was no perfect solution as to how and to whom such awards should be given, concluding that the authorities should simply try to please the most people while aiming to disappoint the fewest.

Though he was awarded thirty-seven orders, decorations and medals between 1895 and 1962, he sometimes felt, with real justification, that he had been overlooked for bravery awards for his deeds in action.

As a civilian 'embedded' journalist in Army uniform, his bravery and dogged determination unquestionably helped the escape of the engine and tender of the train in which he was travelling when it was

attacked by the Boers in 1899. No medal ensued, probably as result of his critical reports on Kitchener in Sudan; Kitchener had become chief of staff in South Africa, and thoroughly disliked Churchill.

The first medal that he was awarded was the Spanish Red Cross (1st Class) of the Order of Military Merit, which was given to him for his part – albeit as a war correspondent – while with the Spanish forces in Cuba in November and December 1895.

His letters home from Cuba exhibit a sangfroid and even excitement at coming under fire that he showed in the most dangerous of situations that he was to face in future. Indeed, after fighting on the North-West Frontier of India in 1897, he revelled in being mentioned in the Commander-in-Chief's despatches.

As an esteemed war leader, Churchill received a wealth of honours and decorations.

Churchill was many times accused of being a 'medal hunter', and it is the case that he tried hard to obtain a commission to fight in South Africa in order to merit a campaign and even a bravery award. As late as 1902, two years after his return from the South African War, he wrote to the Secretary of State for the Colonies, Joseph Chamberlain, to make a case for an award for his actions at the train crash in South Africa, but to no avail.

Churchill showed great courage during the fighting at Diamond Hill on 12–13 June 1900, (now serving as an officer of the South African Light Horse, though still a war correspondent). Again, despite Churchill being put forward for an award by his commanding officer, Lord Dundonald, no decoration ensued.

For his service on the Western Front in the First World War, he received the 1914–15 Star, the British War Medal and the Victory Medal, and, in the Second World War, the regulation service medals: the 1939–45 Star, the Africa Star, the Italy Star, the France and Germany Star, the Defence Medal and the War Medal.

Although he never received the recognition his bravery merited, he went on to be awarded the highest decorations, including, in 1923, the Order of the Companion of Honour and, in 1946, the Order of Merit. Churchill also received numerous decorations from European countries, including the Order of Leopold shown here, the oldest and highest order of Belgium. The Grand Cordon is the highest class of this award, and was given to both Churchill and Eisenhower in 1945 in recognition of their roles in liberating Belgium. Churchill also received the Medaille Militaire and Croix de Guerre from the French government in May 1947, while in 1953 he accepted from Queen Elizabeth II the most distinguished recognition of all, the Order of the Garter.

Churchill was given no awards by the USSR and, apart from the Distinguished Service Medal awarded to him in 1919, he received no other decoration from the United States. This omission was finally rectified by President John F. Kennedy, when, in April 1963, he awarded Churchill the very rare honour – he was only the second person in history to receive the this, after the Marquis de Lafayette in 1784 – of honorary citizenship of the United States.

PHR

83 | Church of St Mary the Virgin, Aldermanbury

Churchill led Britain to victory in the Second World War, yet failed to retain power in the 1945 General Election. When he was voted out of office, it was a particularly low point in his life and any opportunity to influence the development of the post-war world was now seemingly dashed. Yet his standing in the United States remained high as one of the Big Three, and it would be there that Churchill would seize the first opportunity to present his views on the world stage about the expansionist aims of the Soviet Union.

Out of many written invitations he received to speak, Churchill accepted one from Franc L. 'Bullet' McCluer, president of Westminster College in Fulton, Missouri, which came with an added postscript from the US President Harry Truman entreating him to accept. On 5 March 1946, reporters from all over the world therefore gathered to witness

The Church of St Mary the Virgin, Aldermanbury, now relocated to Fulton, Missouri.

The site of one of Churchill's most famous speeches has been commemorated by a special memorial.

Churchill receive an honorary degree and deliver what would become known as his 'Sinews of Peace' address.

The speech was delivered in the college's gymnasium due to the larger than expected crowds, and with Truman at his side Churchill began to talk about the post-war balance of power. After he made reference to the Soviet expansion from the Baltic to the Adriatic as an 'iron curtain' descending across the continent, the phrase was subsequently adopted in a much wider manner as a perfect representation of the political and ideological boundary now separating Europe. Churchill's identification of the separate alliances on each side of the 'curtain' has since been regarded as marking the beginning of the Cold War. He had in fact coined the term before, mentioning the phrase in a pair of telegrams sent to Truman at the end of the war, but this was the first time that it had been expressed so publicly.

Proud of its association with Churchill and his famous speech, in 1961 Westminster College began to look for some way to commemorate the event in the long term. It was discovered that an opportunity had arisen to save the remains of the seventeenth-century church of St Mary the Virgin, Aldermanbury, located in the City of London and gutted by incendiary bombing during the 1940 Blitz. Representative of the bombed buildings then still all too common in the capital, the church had an impressive history, having already been rebuilt on its medieval foundations following destruction in the Great Fire of London in 1666. The original twelfth-century church was reputed to have been where John Milton was married and Shakespeare may also have worshipped there.

Churchill himself approved of the idea, and in 1965 the Sir Christopher Wren-designed church was deconstructed, brick by brick, and relocated on the Fulton campus, where it was then fully rebuilt and restored to its former glory. It now remains as an impressive tribute to Churchill, symbolising the reconstruction process that saw wartime rubble transformed as part of the new direction of the post-war world.

APR

The Westminster College gymnasium at Fulton, Missouri.

84 | *History of the Second World War, 1948–53*

With his long-standing habit of writing historical studies informed by his own experiences and perspective, Churchill intended to write a history of the Second World War from its very beginning. He was, however, very aware of the difficulties he would face in covering such a wide-ranging and modern war, since most documentary evidence would still be confidential. As Prime Minister, he therefore ordered that 'personal minutes' were regularly prepared for him, covering the previous week's meetings, memoranda, correspondence and key information, and which he could save for future reference. He also came to an understanding with the new Attlee government in 1945 that allowed him privileged access to relevant paperwork.

Churchill chose expressive titles for his six volumes of World War Two history: these are first editions of *The Gathering Storm*, *Their Finest Hour*, *The Grand Alliance*, *The Hinge of Fate*, *Closing the Ring*, and *Triumph and Tragedy*, published during 1948–53.

Churchill at his desk in Chartwell.

Shortly after his return from speaking at Fulton, Missouri, in March 1946 Churchill began his war history, which would keep him occupied for some years to come. With a team of research assistants at his disposal who would compile documentary evidence into a chronological order, Churchill would merge these papers with his own records while also appealing to many friends and colleagues for their own personal contributions and perspectives. He then began the process of writing the text, dictating to a team of secretaries often late into the night and then constantly correcting the typed drafts. This process of revision continued well into the proof stage for each book, with the surviving proofs being full of Churchill's handwritten corrections and last-minute changes.

Despite the books undergoing such a long and laborious process of development (or perhaps because of it), *The Second World War* appeared relatively quickly, in six volumes, over the period 1948 to 1953. The series sold well, in both Britain and the United States, with a combined first printing of over 800,000 copies. Trading the literary rights to his books for double the salary he would have made as PM, Churchill's earnings from the series ensured that his earlier financial problems were permanently erased. For perhaps the first time during his life, he could now live an extravagant lifestyle without concern.

Churchill's extremely long and detailed books gave the impression that they were a definitive account of how events had transpired since the end of the First World War up to July 1945, yet they can better

Churchill's memoirs of the Second World War helped to define his place in its history.

be regarded as serving to illustrate the author's own perspective on the conflict. They are more like personal memoirs concerned with Britain's role in the war than a truly unbiased global account. Indeed, the books are most relevant to the time in which they were written, and as such there are key omissions due to certain sensitive topics still remaining confidential, such as Bletchley Park's code-breaking and the development of the atomic bomb.

Ultimately, *The Second World War* was Churchill's interpretation of the events he influenced and experienced, cementing his own role both in the war and in wider history. Yet his informed opinion ensured that the books would remain a crucial source for studying the war, until later research could reveal a wider and somewhat less biased international perspective.

APR

85 | Horse-Racing Colours

Churchill's interest in horse-racing was a family trait, with his father Randolph being a prominent owner for a time after his retirement from politics, while Winston's maternal grandfather, Leonard Jerome, operated his own racecourse in the United States. One of Lord Randolph's horses, a black filly named L'Abbesse de Jouarre, proved to be a very successful investment; she won some £10,000 for him during her racing career, and it is

Churchill's subsequent posting with the Hussars to India did not prevent him from pursuing further equestrian exploits. As a member of the regimental polo team, he took part in several races on his pony Lily, although the pair could only achieve third place at best. His polo team did, however, win the Indian inter-regimental cup. His racing colours were four pink and chocolate brown squares with chocolate sleeves and cap, inherited from his father, with the same colours reappearing on

---

Churchill found great success as an owner and breeder of race-horses.

---

tempting to imagine that this inspired in his teenage son a lasting fascination for the sport.

Quite apart from the family influence, Churchill had always expressed a fondness for horses and enjoyed riding at every opportunity. On deciding to join the military, he perhaps naturally gravitated towards a cavalry regiment – against the wishes of his father, as some evidence suggests. His riding skills were recognised at Sandhurst, when he came second in the annual horsemanship examination, with an impressive mark of 199 out of 200.

In early 1895 Churchill began to try steeplechasing, despite his mother's concerns that the danger involved in the sport made it 'idiotic'. Borrowing a fellow subaltern's horse, he rode under the name 'Mr Spencer' in the 4th Hussars Subalterns' Challenge Cup, achieving third place.

the scarves worn by students at today's Churchill College, Cambridge.

Further horse-racing would have to be put on hold as Churchill embarked on a series of journalistic excursions to military hot spots throughout the world, before beginning his long career in politics. He did, however, have a further brush with the equestrian world during his time as Chancellor of the Exchequer in 1925, when he briefly introduced a very unpopular tax on betting which enraged the horse-racing fraternity and led to its swift repeal. He subsequently introduced the 'totalisator', still current today and now known as 'the tote', a system of registering bets and displaying the odds which successfully removed the more rowdy element prominent at racecourses.

Following the Second World War, Churchill was persuaded by his son-in-law, Christopher Soames, whom he

Churchill's horse-racing colours were inherited from his father Lord Randolph.

had taken on as his Farm Manager at Chartwell after the war, to buy a race-horse to assuage the pain of his defeat at the polls in 1945. The first horse he acquired was Colonist II, which the renowned trainer Walter Nightingall bought in 1949 despite its unprepossessing form. Clementine considered horse-racing an unfitting occupation for a prominent politician, expressing the fear that owning a race-horse might be frowned upon by the electorate as elitist. Yet the horse went on not only to win thirteen of the twenty-four races that he ran, making £12,000 in prize money, but also attracted a wide popular following to the point that

Lord Derby suggested the Tory slogan for the next election should be 'The Conservatives and Colonist'. Churchill received the honour in October 1950 of being elected to the elite Jockey Club, just as his father had before him some seventy years previously.

In response to the suggestion that he should put Colonist II out to stud, Churchill joked that he was afraid of the Prime Minister of Great Britain leaving himself open to the accusation of benefiting from such 'immoral' earnings. He finally sold Colonist II in December 1951 at the Newmarket bloodstock sales, while on the very same day, another of Churchill's horses, named Pol Roger after his favourite champagne, came a close second at Windsor races. Of Colonist II one racing correspondent wrote that, 'No horse in living memory has put up such a sequence of wins in good class races in one season.'

Horses trained by Walter Nightingall won seventy-two races for Churchill, with one of Churchill's horses winning the Irish 1,000 Guineas in 1955, a race that Churchill was unable to attend, being among the runners himself – for the General Election that year (which he won). He continued taking a keen interest in the sport for the remainder of his life, which undoubtedly endeared him to Queen Elizabeth II, who stabled some of his horses and was among the keenest followers of the sport in the country. Churchill only gave up his involvement in horse-racing completely in 1964, the year before his death at the age of ninety.

APR / PHR

Churchill pets his horse 'Canyon Kid' after a win at Windsor, 31 May 1950.

86 | Festival of Britain Programme, 1951

In 1947 the Labour government began to consider the possibility of staging a festival to mark the upcoming centenary of the Great Exhibition of 1851, although this time celebrating Britain's own achievements rather than those of its wider Empire and Commonwealth. The stated purpose of what would be called the Festival of Britain was to provide a national celebration, helping the British people to forget the austerity still prevalent since the war and to show how much the country had progressed in terms of recovering from the conflict. Privately, it was also felt by the government that they were losing support and needed something to boost public confidence.

The Festival of Britain opened on 4 May 1951 with various celebrations taking place across the country and a main centrepiece exhibition on the South Bank in London. The Festival showcased the inventiveness of British technology and science while also promoting national examples of innovation in architecture and the arts. The exhibitions and events ran for a full five months across the summer of 1951, before the Festival closed at the end of September.

The event was generally considered a great success, proving extremely popular with visitors and having generated confidence in British technology, engineering and the arts. While the festival had always been planned to be a temporary one, with its deconstruction beginning in the final days of the Labour government still in power, many historians have since argued that Churchill, as

Churchill greets the King and Queen at the grand opening of the Festival of Britain.

SOUTH BANK EXHIBITION
LONDON
19
51
FESTIVAL OF BRITAIN
GUIDE PRICE 2/6

Churchill had an interesting relationship with the 1951 Festival of Britain.

Leader of the Opposition, had been rather hostile towards the idea.

Yet, despite any concerns he may have had regarding the rationale behind the Festival of Britain, Churchill was happy to take the opportunity to contribute to it in a personal manner. The South Bank exhibition included a corrected proof of a volume from his Second World War memoirs, as well as a personal cigarette box (which was embarrassingly lost by the organisers and never returned). Churchill also entered one of his race-horses in the Festival of Britain Stakes at Ascot and gave every indication of enjoying his visit to the South Bank once it opened. He apparently took childish delight in trying out the 'state of the art' escalators, the like of which had never been seen before in Britain.

Based on our understanding of his character, it is likely that Churchill regarded the Festival of Britain as being a form of Labour propaganda, serving as a means to publicise their vision for a new Socialist Britain. While it celebrated the country's achievements since the war, these were achievements made without Churchill as the nation's leader, and so it is not too surprising that he may have refrained from offering too much support for the project. Churchill had always held the main instigators of the Festival, Herbert Morrison and Gerald Barry, in low personal esteem, and so while he did not openly criticise the venture, he was far from vocal about supporting public spending on such a vast scale.

But by the end of the year, the South Bank site had been levelled with only the Royal Festival Hall being retained as a permanent reminder of the event.

APR

87 | Conservative Election Poster, October 1951

Churchill was only a month away from his seventy-seventh birthday when he took on the role of prime minister for another, final term. The General Election in October 1951 saw the Conservatives win with an overall majority of seventeen seats, and for Churchill it was an opportunity to put his defeat in 1945 to rest for good. Churchill's wartime reputation and charisma had proved vital to the electoral success. A radio party political broadcast he made is widely regarded as one of his most effective speeches since the war, in which he described the difference between the Conservative and Labour outlooks as

to power for as long as he could, knowing that this would be his final opportunity to lead the country. But for somebody with such an impressive reputation, the only direction for Churchill was downwards.

Churchill's main preoccupation throughout his second term as prime minister was foreign affairs. He remained concerned about the potential for nuclear war and saw international cooperation against the threat of the Soviet Union as being the best security for peace. He therefore pursued a strengthening of the 'special relationship' with the United States as he had done during the war, making four transatlantic visits to that end. Yet he struggled to reach agreements

---

Churchill's second term as Prime Minister was his final opportunity to lead the country.

---

being either 'on the ladder' or 'in the queue' to prosperity.

Yet he was well past the age at which most people retire, and his health remained a worry throughout this second premiership. Even King George VI expressed concern at Churchill's wellbeing, yet passed away himself in February 1952. Many within the Cabinet presumed that Churchill would only remain in office for a few months, yet his retirement was continually delayed for a number of years, partly due to the health problems suffered by his intended successor, Anthony Eden. Churchill himself appeared determined to hang on

with Presidents Truman and Eisenhower over a number of key issues, including American military commitments in West Germany and the Middle East. Churchill had difficulties with many foreign policy issues because he still regarded Britain as a superpower rather than a junior partner.

Churchill's only notable worry regarding domestic policy was over housing, in which he made some progress with the replacement of slums and built a considerable number of new homes – some 300,000 – on a yearly basis. Yet the country's day to day administration was largely left to others, and a certain amount of internal rivalry existed between Eden,

Macmillan and Churchill himself, which made matters difficult at times.

Churchill suffered a minor stroke in February 1952 and a more serious one in June 1953, after which his health began to deteriorate more noticeably. Aware himself that he was slowing down both mentally and physically and could no longer fulfil the role of prime minister as he should, he finally resigned on 5 April 1955 and handed power over to Anthony Eden. Despite his already advanced age, however, Churchill would live on for almost another full decade.

APR

Churchill and Clementine campaigning in his Woodford constituency in 1951.
The Woodford constituency was created in boundary changes before the 1945 election. Churchill had previously represented Epping but continued as Woodford's MP from 1945 until he retired in 1964.
The Woodford constituency itself was abolished in 1964 so Churchill was its only MP ever.

88 | Queen Elizabeth II Coronation Memorabilia

I n 1877 the Earl of Aylesford, a close friend of the Prince of Wales (the future King Edward VII), threatened to divorce his wife, citing Lord Randolph's elder brother, the Marquess of Blandford, for having committed adultery with her. In a misguided attempt to protect the family name, Randolph then threatened to make public compromising correspondence between Lady Aylesford and the Prince. Though divorce proceedings were quietly dropped, Randolph was then shunned in society and virtually 'exiled' to Ireland for three years. A reconciliation was achieved some eight years later, but the memory of the incident not only lived long in the Royal Family's memory, it also coloured the name of Churchill for many decades afterwards.

By the time of the Second World War that stigma was still there, but made worse for Winston by his support for Edward VIII, to enable him to remain King and marry the American divorcée Wallis Simpson. After the abdication, Edward became the Duke of Windsor and his brother, always previously known as Bertie, became King George VI. A rather withdrawn individual, with a stammer, which reflected a lack of self-confidence, Bertie had no wish to be king, but was forced into it by the abdication, leaving a deep resentment towards Churchill and his support for Edward.

The precise proceedings of the meeting between the King and Churchill at which he formally asked Churchill to become Prime Minister and form a government are uncertain, made more so by Churchill's own various versions of the event. Certainly Churchill was not the King's first choice (which was Lord Halifax, who was a close friend), not least given his reputation as emotional, volatile and mercurial and there was no great warmth between them

The accession of the new monarch was hailed as the beginning of a 'new Elizabethan age' and celebrated in Coronation memorabilia like this loving cup.

A strong supporter of the Royal Family, Churchill developed close relationships with several British monarchs.

THIS LOVING CUP
IS TO
COMMEMORATE
THE CORONATION OF
QUEEN ELIZABETH II
AT
WESTMINSTER ABBEY
2 JUNE 1953
Edition Limited to 1000.
This is N° 712.

(and even less so between Churchill and George's wife, the later 'Queen Mother').

This difficult start to their relationship – though George had met Churchill while on officer training at the Royal Naval College Dartmouth in 1911, when Churchill visited as First Lord of the Admiralty – was soon put behind them, as both men realised their value to each other and the need each had of the other. Churchill, a staunch monarchist, believed the monarch was there to rule, but not to govern and though he welcomed the King's keen interest in the planning, prosecution and events of the war, holding at least weekly briefings together, he would never allow the King to interfere in governance. A simple example came very soon after Churchill's appointment as Prime Minister, when the King sent him a telegram expressing his earnest wish not to see the maverick Canadian press magnate, Lord Beaverbrook (Max Aitken) appointed to Churchill's Cabinet. In August 1940 Churchill did just that, reinforcing the dividing line between a constitutional monarch and an elected prime minister.

One of the best-known images of the King from that period is of him with his Queen and his daughters – and accompanied by Churchill – on the balcony of Buckingham Palace, on VE-Day, 8 May 1945, being lauded by tens of thousands of well-wishers on the Mall. There was only one other occasion in history when such an assembly and public demonstration of support had occurred: in 1938, when the then Prime Minister, Neville Chamberlain, returned from doing a deal with Hitler to avoid war and joined the King and Queen on the balcony of Buckingham Palace, being cheered to the heights by the milling masses below.

By the time of the King's death in February 1952, he and Churchill had developed a genuine and deep mutual admiration and friendship. The new monarch, the King's elder daughter Elizabeth, was only twenty-five when she ascended the throne and she came to rely on elder statesman Churchill for guidance, wisdom and counsel. Her coronation on 2 June 1953 was commemorated by a multitude of objects such as the loving cup shown here, with the youthful nature of the new ruler suggesting a fresh start for a country still recovering from war. Churchill for his part adored the new queen.

When Churchill finally resigned as Prime Minister in 1955, Her Majesty paid the unique honour of visiting him at 10 Downing Street for a dinner to mark the occasion. She further reinforced her appreciation of, and respect for, the nation's greatest statesman when she insisted, long before his death, that in due course he be given a state funeral, an honour normally reserved for ruling kings and queens. It was also no accident that, in September 2022, Her Majesty's cortège, carrying her body to Westminster Abbey, for the final obsequies, passed directly under the shadow of the statue of her favourite Prime Minister.

PHR

The new Elizabeth's portrait decorates the opposite side from her long-ago predecessor.

89 | Churchill's Standard as Knight of the Garter

King George VI died on 6 February 1952. Churchill was devoted to the monarchy and was deeply upset at the news. He and the King had together been the figurehead leaders for their nation throughout the Second World War, and George VI's death undoubtedly reminded Churchill of his own mortality. Churchill's affection and support for the monarchy was now concentrated on the new ruler, Queen Elizabeth II. As Prime Minister he would enjoy the role of acting as formal adviser to the 25-year-old Queen, and took every opportunity to guide her through the first years of her reign.

At the very end of the war Churchill had been offered the Order of the Garter, the highest British civilian or military honour. Founded in 1348, the Order consists of the monarch and only twenty-five knights, and has commonly been awarded to those who have held public office, contributed in a particularly strong way to national life or served the sovereign in a personal capacity. Yet, despite the great honour, Churchill had felt reluctant to accept the Order from

George VI at that time due to having just been voted out of office at the General Election of 1945. Why should he accept the Order of the Garter, when the country had just given him 'the order of the boot'?

But the new Elizabethan era and his return as political leader of the country made him see things differently. When offered the honour again by the new Queen, he swiftly accepted and was knighted on 24 April 1953. It would therefore be *Sir* Winston Churchill who attended the coronation on 2 June. The cloth standard showing Churchill's status as a Knight of the Garter is now displayed

at Chartwell; by tradition the insignia of the order are returned to the monarch after the recipient's death, but the Queen gave special permission for an exception to be made in Churchill's case.

The coronation itself was a lavish spectacle, the biggest public celebration since the end of the war. Churchill would never let such an opportunity pass him by without influencing its organisation, and his love for pageantry and ritual was well-suited to the extraordinary event. His influence extended from determining who should ride in which carriage as part of the formal processions, the appropriate

Churchill in the robes of a Knight of the Garter, photographed with his son Randolph and his grandson, Randolph's son Winston, shortly before the Coronation ceremony, 2 June 1953.

Britain's new monarch persuaded Churchill to accept her nation's greatest Order of Chivalry.

dress for members of his Cabinet, and even the choice of national anthems to be played. His attempt to prevent the televising of the ceremony failed, however, in the face of strong public opinion.

Churchill's own attendance at the coronation was greeted warmly by the crowds, impressed by his red velvet Order of the Garter robe and white-plumed hat. Yet his jovial manner throughout the day perhaps hid the stress which he had been experiencing over that period. Preparing for the coronation had been work enough,

yet his attendance was also required at the conference of Commonwealth Prime Ministers being organised at the same time, and he had effectively been running the Foreign Office while Anthony Eden was absent through illness. Some three weeks after the coronation, Churchill's work levels likely influenced his third stroke, which would prove to be the most serious suffered so far.

APR

90 | *Life* Magazine, 2 November 1953

Although Churchill's reputation is primarily based on his work as a statesman, throughout his life he also produced a prodigiously large body of writing. By the time of his death, he had written some 6.1 million words, published in 37 books (more than Shakespeare and Dickens combined, according to the biographer Andrew Roberts).

While Churchill made a brief attempt early on in his career to write fiction in the form of a single novel, *Savrola*, and a short story, his output was primarily non-fiction and largely based on historical (or then contemporary) subjects with which he was connected. Indeed, his early military experiences and the success of his published first-hand reports from the battlefields encouraged him to take advantage of similar opportunities throughout his long life.

Churchill's literary career began with an account of a military campaign on the North-West Frontier of India (*The Malakand Field Force*), published in 1898, while his first major book came seven years later, with an epic biography of his late father, *Lord Randolph Churchill*. A further multi-volume biography of another relative was published between 1933 and 1938, as he tackled the life of his distant ancestor, the first Duke of Marlborough.

But it would be Churchill's histories of the First and Second World Wars for which he would be best remembered. *The World Crisis* appeared as four volumes between 1923 and 1929, while his Second World War memoirs ran to six volumes published between 1948 and 1953. He also covered the earlier period of British history up to 1900 in his *History of the English-Speaking Peoples* (1956–8), the

Clementine dines with King Gustav VI Adolf of Sweden at the Nobel Prize banquet, 10 December 1953.

Churchill's reputation as a writer was cemented by his award of the famous Nobel Prize in 1953.

---

writing of which preoccupied him during his first years of retirement.

All of Churchill's writing was characterised by colourful descriptions and narrative, and since many of his books and accounts were heavily influenced by his own involvement in historical affairs, an inevitable degree of bias worked its way in. Despite this lack of objectivity, however, his works were largely well received at the time of their publication. Churchill's important and influential speeches during the war were also published to great acclaim, with particular recognition being received from North America as well as Britain, and it was almost certainly this element of his writing which led to him being presented with the Nobel Prize for Literature in October 1953.

Churchill happened to be at an international conference in Bermuda at the time of the ceremony in Stockholm at which the King of Sweden was to present the prize, and so Clementine accepted the award on her husband's behalf. The Prize took the form of a copy of Churchill's book *Great Contemporaries*, originally published in 1921 as a collection of short biographical essays on famous people of the time, but specially bound in silver.

There is some evidence to suggest that Churchill was somewhat disappointed with the award, as he had hopes of receiving the Nobel Peace Prize instead, which carried greater clout. That year's award went to George Marshall, in recognition of his plan ('The Marshall Plan') aimed at helping the economic recovery of Western Europe after the Second World War.

APR

91 | Graham Sutherland Portrait Study, 1954

To commemorate Churchill's eightieth birthday in 1954, members of the House of Commons and House of Lords jointly funded the commissioning of a new portrait. The artist chosen was Graham Sutherland, who had been an official war artist known for his modernist abstract landscapes and portraits of public figures. He also had something of a reputation for depicting the subjects of his portraits in realistic terms, 'warts and all'.

The most contentious portrait painting of Churchill had a sad fate.

From the start, Sutherland and Churchill argued about the form the painting should take. Churchill asked to be painted in his robes as a Knight of the Garter; Sutherland insisted on a lack of embellishment with the Prime Minister portrayed as in everyday life, dressed in the sort of suit and bow tie that he regularly wore to attend Parliament.

Sutherland began preliminary sketches in August 1954 at Chartwell, but the final oil painting was completed in his studio,. The first viewing of the finished painting was by Clementine on 20 November. While she recognised the portrait as an accurate one of her husband, she felt that it made him look too cross. With his figure shown slightly slumped in a chair, the painting portrayed Churchill as an old, scowling man. Its dark brown colours added to the overall gloomy atmosphere. On viewing a photo of the painting, Churchill was extremely upset, telling his doctor Lord Moran that he considered it a 'filthy' portrait which made him look like a 'down-and-out drunk'.

As a portrait unapologetically showing an elder statesman, it no doubt reminded Churchill of his own mortality. It also angered him that a tribute from Parliament should depict him as an outdated and crumpled figure, at time when he was still serving as prime minister. It has also been argued that, as a painter himself, Churchill might have been disappointed by the dark style of the portrait, since he himself much preferred to use bright colours in art.

Churchill did, however, manage to contain his feelings at the unveiling at Westminster on 30 November. He had been persuaded to accept the painting in good grace, so as not to disappoint those who had contributed to its cost. In his speech, Churchill referred to the painting as a 'remarkable work of modern art' (which provoked laughter from those who recognised his backhanded compliment). Although originally intended to be hung in Parliament, the painting was instead gifted to Churchill, who stored it at Chartwell, out of sight.

In 1978, it was finally reported that Clementine had had the painting destroyed, soon after its arrival at her home. She had also destroyed portraits by Walter Sickert and Paul Maze that she disliked. Yet some preparatory sketches and studies of the Sutherland work do remain within art collections, as the example shown attests, as the final remnants of what must be the most controversial Churchill portrait of all.

The artist Graham Sutherland (1903–80). Sutherland painted numerous portraits of major public figures in the 1950s; Churchill was not the only sitter who disliked the results.

APR

92 | Amplivox Hearing Aid

Churchill suffered from hearing loss as he grew older and was reluctant at first either to acknowledge the problem or seek a remedy to it. His personal physician Lord Moran first suspected such a difficulty during a telephone conversation in 1944, which the Prime Minister ended in frustration at not being able to hear clearly. Yet it was not until 1950 that Churchill finally submitted to an examination and was found to be suffering from high-frequency hearing loss.

At some point in the early 1950s, Churchill began to wear a hearing aid supplied by Amplivox Limited, a company specialising in such medical technology. He expressed deep gratitude to the company for the benefits he had appreciated from use of the equipment,

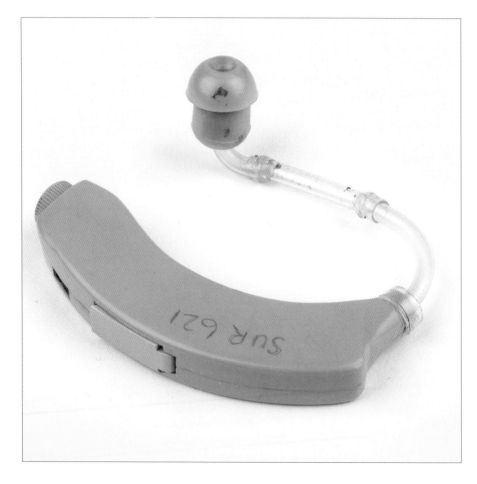

As the symptoms of old age began to make themselves known, Churchill responded with characteristic belligerence.

and wrote warmly to their founder Sir Edwin Stevens, describing the aid as 'wonderful'. Such an endorsement from Britain's great war leader was akin to receiving the royal warrant of approval and suggests perhaps that Churchill himself was fully aware of his own value in making the recommendation.

Yet by all accounts he regarded a hearing aid as a sign of weakness that could be used against him in the political arena. As a result, photographs that show Churchill using an aid are incredibly scarce. This reluctance to seek help meant that by the end of the decade Churchill was suffering from acute deafness which led to sullen silences during mealtimes, a daily occasion when he had previously enjoyed leading any conversation.

Despite entreaties from his family and friends, he refused to use his hearing aid on a regular basis. The turning point that made Churchill realise the necessity of seeking a solution to the problem was a parliamentary debate in the House of Commons in early 1958, during which he struggled to hear much of what was going on.

Unknown to him, however, the public address system happened to have malfunctioned on that particular day, but this unexpected circumstance suggested a potential solution to the problem. Lord Moran seized on this incident as offering a way to improve Churchill's hearing, by using an induction loop system similar to the one in the House of Commons. An amplification system was installed in Churchill's London home at Hyde Park Gate which proved so successful that a similar system was later put into use at Chartwell.

But Churchill's hearing problems were only one of the many characteristics of old age becoming more evident to those who knew him. His poor hearing quite possibly contributed to the gloom that haunted him during the last few years of his life, with the 1960s seeing a much quieter and more insular Churchill whose depression, in the words of one of his biographers, Piers Brendon, 'was to become indistinguishable from senility'.

APR

93 | Churchill's Walking Stick

I n 1966, just a year after Churchill's death, the man who had served as his personal physician from May 1940 onwards, Professor Sir Charles Wilson (ennobled in 1943 as Lord Moran), published a book on Churchill, in which he documented aspects of Churchill's ill health, especially in his declining years.

At the time there was widespread outrage at the possible infringement of patient–doctor confidentiality. Later, controversies developed in which much of what Moran wrote was discredited as unreliable and undocumented. Although Churchill uses the term in one known letter, it was Moran who made a serious issue of Churchill's so-called 'black dog', to describe Churchill's decline in morale at certain junctures in his life. It is now often taken to support claims that Churchill suffered from clinical depression, of which there is no evidence. It is understandable that he should feel, in the loosest sense of the term, 'depressed', after being forced out of office in 1915 and in 1945, and having to transition from an intense eighteen-hour working day and the highest possible level of responsibility to being jobless.

As a teenager he suffered a number of injuries, usually from high-jinks, including falling 10 metres from a tree, while at Harrow School, leaving him with concussion, a ruptured kidney and damage to his cervical spine. He suffered his first bout of pneumonia when only eleven years old, resulting in his being sent to Harrow, rather than his father's old school, Eton, as the climate at Harrow was thought to be less likely to trouble his lungs.

Given the rigours of his wartime routine, it is unsurprising that he suffered other bouts of pneumonia later in life: in London in February 1943 – when his recovery was aided by the newly invented 'antibiotics' – while in Carthage in north Africa in December 1943, an illness that had begun to show itself during the final stages of the Big Three meeting in Tehran, just days beforehand; and again in London in late August 1944. While holidaying on the French Riviera in February 1958, he suffered a bout of pneumonia that was exacerbated and prolonged by the accompaniment of jaundice, rigors and atrial fibrillation. Whereas in 1943, he was, typically, according to Moran, 'in tearing form' within days, his February 1958 bout – at the age of eighty-six – prevented him returning to the House of Commons until late April in that year.

In 1891 Churchill had been diagnosed as having a hernia and was advised to wear a truss, which he soon gave up after he arrived at Harrow and never wore again, until, when on holiday in Italy in September 1945, he was once more obliged to adopt a truss and, some two years later finally underwent an operation to relieve the condition.

Churchill often carried a stick, though usually as a fashion item. The walking stick shown here was given by him to the Countess Clary as a gift when he was visiting a Paris hospital shortly after the Second World War. However, in 1960, after a fall that damaged one of his vertebrae, he relied on a stick more regularly. It certainly was necessary two years later when, at the age of eighty-seven, he was flown home from Monte Carlo on a stretcher to undergo an operation in London for a hip replacement, one of the rare occasions of Churchill having surgical intervention. However, he was showing serious signs of aging and his hip operation necessitated a hospital stay of fifty-four days.

Churchill suffered a number of heart complaints in his later life, the first during his visit to Washington, DC, in late December 1941, following the US entry into the war. Moran was in a quandary as to what to do, knowing that diagnosing Churchill as having a heart condition – which was far from certain – could have seriously endangered the development of the nascent Anglo-US alliance and decided to play the illness down with Churchill and the wider world. The ailment was almost certainly minor.

When in January 1950 Churchill complained of symptoms that could have been the early onset of a stroke – he had had symptoms of a minor stroke just a year before when in Monte Carlo but recovered fully within a week – he refused to slow the pace of his work, instead electioneering around the country. Churchill wrote years later that he probably owed his life to Moran's care, adding that Moran would ignore his instructions to ease up when ill, as he himself would ignore Moran's instructions

Churchill reaches for his cane as he walks with General Montgomery at a North African airfield in early August 1942, shortly after Monty was appointed to command Eighth Army.

Churchill suffered from a number of health scares.

to himself, resulting in them becoming devoted friends.

It seems likely, based on copious examination of Churchill's symptoms and medical diagnoses by a variety of eminent specialists – and throughout his life, from his early youth, all his ailments were attended to by the nation's top specialists – that between 1950 and 1952, Churchill was suffering some reduced cognitive ability and almost certainly what doctors term 'transient ischaemic attacks' or minor strokes. As ever he continued to astonish his doctors, his ministers and his staff with his indomitable energy and powers of recovery.

Sadly, even the bovine constitution of a Churchill had to give way to age and, after he retired from the House of Commons on 27 July 1964, his health went into gradual decline. By his ninetieth birthday in November he was largely bed-bound, his daughter Mary Soames describing him at his celebrations as 'fragile now, and often so remote'. On 11 January 1965 his condition declined further as he suffered a stroke and fell into unconsciousness. He never recovered and passed away quietly on the morning of 24 January, precisely seventy years since his father's death.

PHR

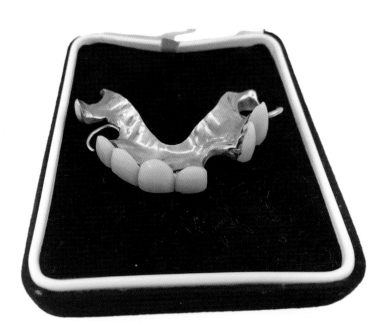

Even the most personal mementos of Churchill command high prices at auction.
This partial set of his false teeth was sold for £18,000 in 2024.

94 | Honorary Citizen of the USA Miniature Book

Churchill's connection with the United States was a strong one, which he did much to foster throughout his life. While much of this 'special relationship' was based on Britain's political and military need for American support, firstly to achieve victory in the Second World War and then to confront what Churchill perceived as the danger of communist aggression in Europe, it is important to remember that Churchill himself had American ancestry and therefore a natural link to the country.

Churchill's mother, Jennie Jerome, was born in Brooklyn, New York, and as a noted beauty and influential socialite did much to boost his early reputation, especially as he entered the political world. Jennie's father, Leonard Jerome, was a famous financier, known as the 'King of Wall Street', who could claim many forebears who had fought alongside George Washington in the War of Independence against the British.

Churchill family tradition suggested that the Jerome branch of the family had perhaps an even stronger link to North American blood, as it was claimed that Jennie's maternal grandmother, Clarissa Willcox, was half Iroquois. This potential link to Native American ancestry was

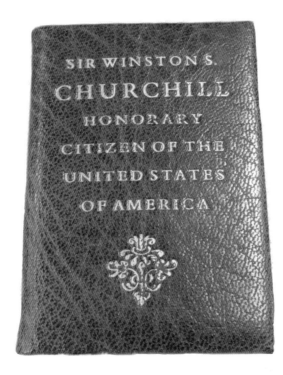

Churchill's American ancestry encouraged lifelong links with the United States.

certainly believed by Churchill's mother and her sister, and for their mother to make such a revelation at a time when Iroquois ancestry would have been regarded as deeply unfashionable remains important. Recent genealogical research has revealed that Churchill could maybe also have laid claim to three ancestors who had sailed to America on the *Mayflower*.

Throughout Churchill's long political career, he was careful to avoid any public criticism of the United States or its people. While visiting the USA – on sixteen occasions between 1895 and 1961, eight times in his role as prime minister (in both peace and war) and almost half of them after 1945 – he would always carefully confine himself to public expressions of support. Yet, in private, he could be much more critical. To trusted confidants, such as George VI or Cabinet colleagues, he could sometimes express severe criticism of the USA and even the

administration of Franklin D. Roosevelt, with whom he outwardly enjoyed an effective working relationship. Much of Churchill's criticism appeared to reflect his frustrations at America's isolationist stance before the war, although even after US involvement in the conflict was established, a certain envy remained of the greater resources at their disposal and their resulting control of the conduct of the war.

But Churchill continued publicly to promote Anglo-American unity because it served Britain's best interests to do so, and his ongoing popularity in the United States is reflected in the way that the nation treated him after the war. Churchill's close relationship with the various US presidents continued. He visited as a personal guest of Eisenhower at the age of eighty-four and was entertained at the White House. His final visit was to New York in 1961, when he

President John F. Kennedy announces Churchill's honorary citizenship at the White House, 9 April 1963.

was offered the opportunity to fly on to Washington DC to meet President John F. Kennedy, but had to decline due to poor health.

The ultimate honour conferred on Churchill by the grateful nation was Honorary Citizenship of the United States, declared by Kennedy on 9 April 1963. This miniature book, containing texts of the Act of Congress, Kennedy's Proclamation plus Churchill's letter in response, was published to mark the occasion as a collectable limited edition.

APR

95 | Sculpture of Churchill's Hand by Oscar Nemon

Many of the most famous artists of the twentieth century portrayed Churchill, each in their own way, producing many of the iconic images we know of Churchill today.

The Churchill War Rooms has on display the earliest known portrait of Churchill, a painting of the four-year-old Winston by the little-known artist P. Ayron Ward. It shows him looking, typically of the age, girlish, with his long red ringlets and frilly collar. A later portrait of him as a young Member of Parliament, painted twenty-two years later by Edwin Arthur Ward, is the first known painting of him as an adult and shows him

very original painting of Lavery, who then went on to produce a further portrait of Churchill in 1916.

Nowhere is Churchill's desperate mood on being forced out of office in 1915 better reflected than in the painting of him by the society painter Sir William Orpen. Commissioned by one of Churchill's friends, the press magnate Lord Rothermere, it stands as one of the great portrait paintings of the twentieth century. It shows him in the Edwardian-style clothing which he favoured when in the House of Commons and was Churchill's favourite portrait, though it haunted him for the rest of his life. It shows the deep disappointment of being

---

As one of the most famous figures of the twentieth century, it is only to be expected that Churchill would be the most portrayed in paintings, drawings and sculpture.

---

looking sophisticated and confident, but sympathetic, wearing, as he was renowned for doing, a smart dress coat and a large bow tie, emulating, as Ward noted, his late father Lord Randolph's dress style.

Churchill himself took up painting in 1915 and, being so well connected socially, he had as his tutors some of the most famous artists of the time. Among these was the Irish-born society portraitist and war artist Sir John Lavery, a near neighbour to Churchill then living in Cromwell Road in London. He was commissioned to paint Churchill while Winston was still First Lord of the Admiralty and Churchill in turn did a

'turfed out' (Churchill's term) of office and the equally deep sense of resilience and determination, as the subject leans forward slightly towards the painter.

Another artist who helped teach Churchill to paint was the renowned master of British post-impressionism, Walter Sickert, whom Clementine had met on a holiday in Dieppe in 1899. The Churchills and Sickert became close friends and Churchill painted Sickert, who in turn painted Churchill (from a photograph) in February 1928, presenting the original ink sketch to the Churchills. Churchill described it as making him look 'crapulous' and 'bilious' and looking 'like a

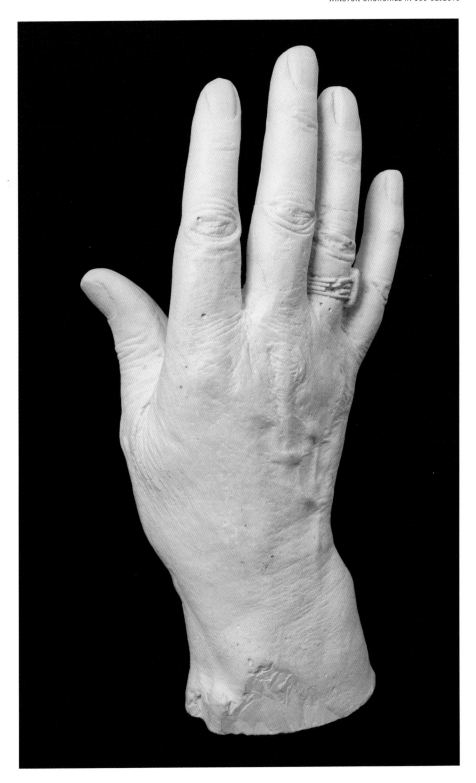

bookie'. His private secretary Eddie Marsh and Clementine thought he resembled the infamous fraudster Horatio Bottomley and Clementine later destroyed the drawing, though Churchill maintained a personal friendship with the painter for the rest of his life.

Another renowned painter of the thirties, William Nicholson, befriended the Churchills, tutored Churchill in painting and, in 1934–5, did a 'conversation piece' of Clemmie and Winston breakfasting together (which they never did) at Chartwell, where it hangs to this day. It has the distinction of being the first portrait of Churchill wearing one of his beloved 'siren suits'.

Many other paintings of Churchill were subsequently executed, not least those by Sir Oswald Birley and Sir William Reid Dick, who had been commissioned by the Royal Academy. But it is in sculpture that Churchill will be best remembered figuratively, not least because so many statues of him were produced all around the world after his death. His cousin Clare Sheridan was an aspiring sculptor to whom Churchill gave a helping hand after the death of her husband (and who later had a passionate affair with Churchill's closest friend, F. E. Smith – later Lord Birkenhead). She produced several outstanding busts of Churchill, including one that was rejected by the Royal Academy Summer Exhibition, a fate she shared with Reid Dick and Sir Jacob Epstein, whose outstanding sculptures met the same rebuff.

The best-known sculpture of Churchill is the twelve-foot statue of Churchill by Ivor Roberts-Jones in Parliament Square in London, which was unveiled in 1973 and shows Churchill in his RAF trench coat (it was originally to be in his Order of the Garter dress but was changed at the request of his widow). Another famous depiction, a life-sized seated sculpture of Churchill by Oscar Nemon, was installed in London's ancient Guildhall in 1955, allowing Churchill to enjoy the rare accolade of having a public sculpture of himself erected during his lifetime. The plaster life cast of Churchill's right hand wearing a signet ring, shown here, was taken during a sitting for this particular sculpture.

Nemon, whom Churchill had first met and befriended in Marrakesh in 1951, was also commissioned by the Queen to sculpt a bust of Churchill, which is housed at Windsor Castle. He sculpted many famous people, including Queen Elizabeth the Queen Mother and Sigmund Freud, and created the statue which still stands in the Central Lobby of the Palace of Westminster, which was unveiled on 2 December 1969. It was the first statue to counter the parliamentary tradition of no likenesses of members being installed until ten years after their death and its left foot has been rubbed to a shiny finish by MPs and the visiting public. It was later reproduced in Toronto, Halifax and Brussels.

Churchill only ever undertook one sculpture himself, when he and Nemon enjoyed a mutual sculpting session. This, however, came to a finish when Churchill made Nemon stand still so that he could finish his work. That unique plaster sculpture of Nemon is on display in London's Churchill War Rooms.

PHR

96 | Letter from President Eisenhower, May 1958

Churchill resigned as Prime Minister on 5 April 1955. He immediately embarked on a holiday to Sicily, spending time painting and playing cards to fill up the days when ordinarily he would have been considering political matters. Yet Churchill's retirement from political leadership did not prevent him from pursuing new projects to keep his mind active. He had much admired the Massachusetts Institute of Technology, established in 1861, which had become a world leader in developing modern technology and science. Churchill decided to set up an equivalent institution in Britain, to encourage further development of the scientific knowledge which had helped to win the war and would need to be fostered if Britain was to continue to play a key role in world affairs.

1958 to declare, 'No other project could so well commemorate for posterity your contributions to your country, to the British Commonwealth and to the Western world.' The college's emphasis on technological and scientific development appealed to Eisenhower and mirrored his own nation's endeavours in this sphere, as he added that, 'In the world I visualise where interchange of scientific information among friends is a matter of course, such a development as is envisioned in Churchill College is bound to have vast benefits for all mankind.'

Churchill College was finally founded by Royal Charter in 1960, with the first students arriving in October of that

---

One of Churchill's greatest historical legacies would be his archive of personal papers, as well as the Cambridge College which houses them.

Churchill's private secretary John Colville offered to take on the not insignificant task of raising the necessary money to start the project, and soon enlisted the support of Churchill's many rich friends and colleagues. These plans would evolve into the creation of a new Churchill College as part of the University of Cambridge.

Churchill's friend Dwight D. Eisenhower, now President of the United States, wrote to him in May

year. Churchill had specifically wanted the college to host a mix of science and humanities students, in order to provide a well-rounded environment for study. Initially all students were male, but Churchill College became the first male college within the University of Cambridge to vote to admit female students, the first of whom arrived in 1972. Today it can boast up to 10,000 alumni worldwide.

A purpose-built archives centre was added to the college in 1973 to house the 3,000 boxes of correspondence and other papers that survived after Churchill's death. This collection covers Churchill's

copy   The White House,
                              Washington.

          12 May, 1958

Dear Winston,

          I have just learned of the plan to establish
at the University of Cambridge a new college to be named
in your honour.   It seems to me that no other project
could so well commemmorate for posterity your contributions
to your country, to the British Commonwealth, and to the
Western world.

          The prospectus of Churchill College appeals
greatly to me, particularly because, as I understand it,
the college will concentrate primarily on the advancement
of technological and scientific education.   We here in
America are working toward the improvement of our own
educational processes in this and other fields, and in the
world I visualise where interchange of scientific
information among friends is a matter of course, such a
development as is envisioned in Churchill College is bound
to have vast benefits for all mankind.

                                        (W.S.C.)

                    2.

          Quite naturally, I applaud the project;   I
know that it will find great popular support in the United
States as well as in your country.

               With warm regard,

                    As ever,

                         IKE   (W.S.C.)

Churchill College, Cambridge, now home to Churchill's
immense collection of private and official papers.

entire life, encompassing his early
childhood letters, drafts of his famous
wartime speeches, and of course his
many essays and books. The preservation
of such papers served as the starting
point for a much wider endeavour – the
establishment of something akin to
the Presidential Libraries of the United
States. The Churchill Archives Centre
now houses the papers of about 600
important political, military and scientific
figures including Margaret Thatcher, John
Major, Ernest Bevin, Admiral Sir Bertram
Ramsay, Field Marshal Viscount Slim,
Rosalind Franklin and Frank Whittle.

Churchill College was dedicated as the
National and Commonwealth Memorial
to Sir Winston Churchill following his
death, and continues to represent an
embodiment of Churchill's vision for how
higher education can benefit society.

APR

97 | Coffin Flag

In the United Kingdom, elaborate state funerals are generally reserved for monarchs but on rare occasions have been given to 'commoners' of particularly high distinction. Churchill's state funeral was arranged for 30 January 1965, adding him to the very exclusive list of other famous British commoners (that is, those not of royal blood) who had received such a tribute in the previous two hundred years: Admiral Nelson, the Duke of Wellington and former Prime Minister Gladstone.

Churchill's state funeral was to be the most elaborate non-royal funeral held in London since that of Sir Douglas Haig in 1928 (which was not a full 'state funeral'). At that time Haig was widely regarded as the man who had won the Great War for his country; now, Churchill would represent the nation's victory during the Second World War. The state funeral of Sir Winston Churchill would prove to be, to date, the last such official ceremony held for a non-royal.

Plans for a state funeral had actually begun quite some time before Churchill's death. In June 1953 the Prime Minister had suffered a serious stroke during a dinner party at Downing Street, which had left him partially paralysed, and although this deterioration in health was kept from public knowledge, one of the few made aware of the truth was the new Queen. She subsequently instructed that plans, codenamed 'Operation Hope

Churchill's coffin, draped with the Union flag, lies in state in Westminster Hall.

Not', should be made in secret for a state funeral to be held on a scale befitting Churchill's eminent place in history, yet it would be another twelve years before such plans were called into action. Churchill himself therefore had the unique opportunity to influence the choice of guests and the order of service to his own ceremony.

It would prove to be the largest state funeral in history, only to be surpassed by that of Queen Elizabeth II herself in 2022. By the Queen's decree, Churchill's body would lie in state in Westminster Hall for three days from 26 January, allowing over 320,000 people to file past and pay their respects. During the lying-in-state, and indeed throughout the entirety of the ceremonials, Churchill's coffin was draped by the Union Flag as a symbol of the nation that he represented so strongly throughout his long life.

On 30 January, the funeral service itself was conducted at St Paul's Cathedral, attended by over 6,000 people and dignitaries from 120 countries. The Queen broke royal protocol not only by attending the service, but by arriving before the coffin and leaving the cathedral after the Churchill family, as a mark of respect. Other prominent guests included Churchill's wartime colleagues

---

Churchill's funeral was on a scale usually reserved for a monarch.

French President Charles de Gaulle and American general and former US President Dwight D. Eisenhower, along with the Prime Ministers of Canada and Rhodesia. Among Churchill's honorary pallbearers were Lord Louis Mountbatten of Burma, the Australian Prime Minister Robert Menzies, and former British Prime Ministers Clement Attlee, Anthony Eden and Harold Macmillan. Broadcast by the BBC, the event was watched by an estimated 25 million people in the United Kingdom, and some 350 million worldwide, making it the most-watched television event up to that date.

The service concluded with the sounding of the Last Post, in the standard way to honour war dead, followed by the Reveille and the bells of St Paul's as a final toll. The final stage of the funeral was now to begin, involving the last journey of Churchill's coffin to the site of his burial, in the family grave at Bladon churchyard, in Oxfordshire.

APR

The launch *Havengore*, seen here in front of the Old Royal Naval College in Greenwich, was used to transport Churchill's coffin during its journey from London to his last resting place.

98 | 'Battle of Britain' Class Locomotive 34051

Churchill's funeral marked the end of an era, as Britain moved on from the memory of the war and said goodbye to the last Victorian statesman who had been so intrinsically linked to the nation's history

steam locomotive would feature as part of a state funeral.

It was Churchill's wish that he be buried alongside his parents. His funeral arrangements therefore required the coffin to be transported from London, where

---

Churchill's final journey was powered by a special locomotive, named in his honour.

---

for the better part of a century. Aspects of the ceremony would reflect this change, since it would be the final time that a

the main procession and ceremony took place, to the small church of St Martin's at Bladon, in Oxfordshire. His coffin was

The nameplate from locomotive 34051.

first moved by gun carriage to Tower Hill where it received a ninety-gun salute from the Royal Artillery, signifying his final age. Churchill is the only commoner ever to receive such a tribute. Then it made its way along the River Thames on the launch *Havengore*, watched by crowds of respectful onlookers. Many people had travelled to London especially for the funeral, camping overnight in the streets in order to ensure a good view of proceedings. As the little vessel passed the London docks, the dockers lowered their cranes in homage. On arrival at Waterloo Station Churchill's coffin was taken by special funeral train to Handborough, the nearest station to Bladon.

The engine chosen for this important task was Southern Railway's locomotive 34051, one of forty-four 'Battle of Britain' class engines built during the immediate post-war period and named in tribute to aircraft or people involved in the defining battle. Appropriately, the engine chosen was the *Winston Churchill*.

The baggage car which carried Churchill's coffin had previously been used for transporting pigeons and vegetables, but was renovated and decorated especially for the funeral. A Pullman carriage (named *Lydia*) was also attached, to carry the Churchill family and other dignitaries. Built in 1925, it had previously served as part of a command train used by Churchill during the Second World War.

As the funeral train made its way to its final destination, the twenty-one stations along the route accommodated thousands of sightseers wishing to pay their final respects. Military veterans stood to attention as the locomotive passed, saluting the man who had led them through the war.

At its final destination, a private service was held at St Martin's Church, with Churchill's grave in the family vault bearing two wreaths – one from his wife, and the other from the Queen. In the following days, it was estimated that some 80,000 people queued to see his resting place. Perhaps surprisingly, the grave suffered long neglect in the years that followed and was only restored in the 1990s by a generous American philanthropist.

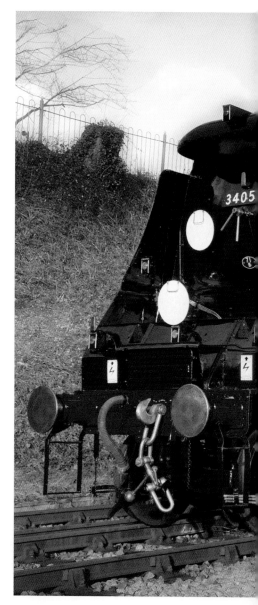

After the funeral, the baggage car which carried Churchill's coffin was transported to the west coast of the United States, where it became something of a tourist attraction at the Pacific Palms Resort in Los Angeles. Similarly, the Pullman carriage also ended up in America and toured the country, remaining at the US National Railroad Museum for over thirty years. The locomotive and the two cars are now fully restored and were displayed back in Britain in 2015 at the National Railway Museum in York, to mark the fiftieth anniversary of the funeral.

APR

99 | Churchill Stamps, 1965

The idea of a possible philatelic tribute to Churchill was first mooted to coincide with his seventieth birthday in 1944, and while nothing came of that idea during the war, the suggestion resurfaced in the 1950s when Churchill was approaching his eightieth year.

The main problem with issuing special Churchill stamps was caused by the international postal regulations in this era. All stamps had to bear the name of the issuing country, with the single exception of Britain, where a portrait of the current monarch was used instead. It was feared that if a stamp bore the image of another person as well as the Queen, it would cause confusion and conflict with the established rules.

However, in April 1964 a series of British stamps was issued to mark the 400th anniversary of the birth of William Shakespeare and these included a portrait of the Bard, setting a precedent for stamps to feature another person in addition to the monarch. The question of issuing stamps to mark Churchill's forthcoming ninetieth birthday in November that same year therefore resurfaced, with much debate ensuing before Prime Minister Alec Douglas-Home quashed the idea. While recognising the intention of issuing a tribute to the great man, it was feared that such a move might be construed as a political one. Churchill himself had previously discussed a proposed statue of Lloyd George but argued that a certain amount of time needed to pass before such a tribute could be deemed appropriate. Despite much public pressure, the idea of a Churchill stamp therefore seemed a non-starter.

However, attitudes changed when Churchill died on 24 January 1965. Impressed by the immediate public reactions of grief, Postmaster General Tony Benn made the decision the following day that two denominations of Churchill stamp would be issued – a 4d.

Churchill received the honour of being only the second non-royal to appear on a British postage stamp.

(inland letter) stamp and another at the 1s. 3d. (airmail letter) rate. The Queen gave her formal approval for the use of Churchill's head alongside her own.

Designs were commissioned almost immediately with the version chosen created by David Gentleman and Rosalind Dease and based on the famous photo portrait of Churchill by Yousuf Karsh. In an unusual move, Clementine was consulted about the designs, and expressed her disappointment that the Karsh photograph was being featured. She did, however, consent to its use since it was one of the most iconic images of her late husband, which people would immediately identify.

The gold commemorative 'stamps', with a certificate of authenticity.

The 4*d*. stamp was printed in gold, with the airmail version in silver and more closely cropped to differentiate it. Both stamps featured a vertical white line separating Churchill from the Queen, in order to avoid the image looking like the Queen was peering over Churchill's left shoulder. The stamps were issued on 8 July 1965 and by the end of February the following year around 145 million of the 4*d*. stamp had been sold, and 8.7 million of the 1*s*. 3*d*. version. Following Churchill's death, the public demand

for 'Churchilliana' soared, and his postage stamps inspired one of the most valuable collectable items: the gold stamp medallions shown here. These were large 18-carat gold replicas of the stamps, produced by the Metalimport Group, with 5,000 made of each version. Sold in a special display case and with a certificate of authentication, such collectables remain much sought after. Examples have recently sold at auction for around £1,000.

APR

100 | Parliament Square Statue, 1973

I t is illustrative of the esteem with which Churchill was regarded during his final years that he was given the opportunity to influence not only his own state funeral, but the site of his permanent statue. Parliament Square, the open green area adjacent to the Palace of Westminster, was subject to plans for redevelopment in the early 1950s, overseen by Churchill as the incumbent prime minister. Looking over a map of the square, he is alleged to have marked a circle in the north-east corner, declaring this to be the site where his statue would go – facing the Big Ben clock tower

when he was inspecting the bomb damage inflicted on the Chamber of the House of Commons by a bombing raid in May 1941. He is shown wearing a military greatcoat, his hand resting on a walking stick and looking ahead, steadfast and determined. During the statue's development process, there were some complaints that the head resembled that of Mussolini rather than Churchill, and the sculptor was therefore tasked with altering it accordingly. The final bronze sculpture was formally unveiled on 1 November 1973 by Clementine, with the Queen in attendance along with the Queen Mother,

---

One of the most famous statues of Churchill remains in Britain's centre of political power.

---

and supervising the deliberations going on inside Parliament. The square was already the site for a number of statues of important former prime ministers including Sir Robert Peel, Benjamin Disraeli and Lord Palmerston.

But it would not be until 1968 that a Winston Churchill Statue Appeal was first established which led to some 4,500 individuals donating in excess of the £30,000 estimated cost for commissioning such a tribute. The artist chosen was Ivor Roberts-Jones, a veteran of the Burma campaign who was already known for sculpting a memorial to one of Churchill's contemporaries, the artist Augustus John.

The statue's pose was based on a wartime photograph of Churchill, taken

the prime minister of the day, Edward Heath, and four former premiers.

Despite the statue being Grade II listed in 2008, the statue has been defaced on a number of occasions, largely due to its location in Parliament Square where political marches are commonly held. One of the most high-profile cases happened in June 2020, when widespread protests highlighting racism were held across the world days after the murder of George Floyd, an African American man, while he was being arrested in the United States on 25 May. A protester sprayed graffiti over the Churchill statue, including the words '… is a racist' after his name on the statue's plinth. Similar damage to other statues across the country led to much

public debate over the appropriateness of their remaining on display; as a result, some linked to controversies such as historic slave trading were removed by their owners. Churchill's statue, however, remained in place following much public support.

The incident did, however, reignite debate concerning Churchill's own views and actions. It is clear that he continues to be a controversial figure, even some decades following his death. With strong views being held on both sides of the argument, Churchill's life and legacy will generate considerable public interest and highlight his undoubted importance as one of the great figures of history. Indeed, he remains the only individual to have three major statues of himself standing in public places in London.

APR

Churchill's statue is positioned so that he seems to keep watch over the Houses of Parliament.

Acknowledgements

The authors and publishers would like to thank the following agencies and individuals for supplying the illustrations used on the pages noted below. Reference numbers are given for images from the collections of the Imperial War Museums (IWM).

Agence Rol: 209
Alamy Stock Photo, Fremantle: 252
Alamy Stock Photo, World History Archive: 6–7
American Museum & Gardens, Bath: 117 below, 118
anglotopia.net: 248
Aperture Photos: 280
Auctioneum, East Bristol: 111
Alexander Bassano: 50
Bing Images: 106
Bing Images/Etsy: 205
Blenheim Palace: 51
bluerobincollectables.com, Yakob Jakubowski-Zentner: 194
Bonhams: 152
British Red Cross Museum and Archives: 90
C & T Auctions: 285 all
Castle Leslie Estate: 11
Christie's Images Ltd. 2023: 266
Churchill Archives: 43, 109, 127, 132, 144, 276
Churchill Book Collector, Marc Kuritz, proprietor, ABAA | ILAB | IOBA: 33, 47 both, 186
Martin Cooper: 32
Cotswold Auction Company: 225, 226, 268
Chris Crowley: 185
cryptomuseum.com: 187
Brian Davis: 281
Dean and Chapter of Westminster: 53, 54

Dr Seuss Collection, Special Collections & Archives, UC San Diego: 150
Doyle Auctioneers & Appraisers: 204
Duke's Auctions: 218–19 all
David Firn: 287, 288
Flickr, tedesco57: 36
Greg Halse: 223
Mark Laban/Hansons Auctioneers: 217 top
Peter Harrington: 49, 103
Heritage Auctions, ha.com: 181
IWM: ii (EPH 001406 B) ix (ZZZ 5426F), xi left (TR 1838), xi right (TR 2842), xii (HU 69983), 3 (IWM_SITE_CWR_000117), 4 (ZZZ 7555D), 12–13 (CM18–03, © Harrow School), 19 & 20 (CM_14_01_F & G), 21 (TR 2275), 22–23 (FIR_010195_D), 24 top (H_002646), 28 both (OMD_005252_A & B, © Churchill Family Collection), 59 (CM_20_02_A), 67 (COM 981 A), 69 & 70 (FIR 3681 C & D), 72 (CM 80 1 D), 81 (Documents.2473 3 & 4), 84 (Documents.10540 A), 93 (Art. IWM_PST 13595), 95 (UNI 12240), 101 & 102 (Documents.17636_2 & 5), 131 (IWM_SITE_CWR_000366), 135 (EPH_000942_C), 136 (COM_1076_A), 137 (CWR_001896), 139 (EPH_001688_A), 142–3 (CM_3_01_A), 147 (CM_20_01_B), 153 (H 10786), 155 (Art.IWM PST 3738), 159 (IWM_SITE_CWR_101_1),

Further Reading

Scarcely a week goes by without the appearance of a new book on Sir Winston Churchill. What follows is, therefore, a necessarily subjective selection of volumes, which I hope will help the keen reader find a source which is reliable, readable and relevant to the particular aspect of Sir Winston's life and achievements that they are seeking information on. I apologise if my selection omits titles which others feel should be included. The list of possible books is essentially endless.

The go-to book(s) for a detailed source of reference, if not for end-to-end reading is the official biography by Martin Gilbert, published in 8 narrative volumes and 21 companion volumes, comprising thousands of background documents. Published under the series title *Winston S. Churchill*, with each volume having its own title, it is an exhaustive source of detail, if, in the case of the narrative volumes, written before much crucial intelligence material, such as Enigma-related items, were released. Sir Martin has also published a handy one-volume version of the biography entitled simply *Churchill: A Life* (1991).

In 2018 the historian (now Lord) Andrew Roberts published his life of Churchill under the title *Churchill: Walking With Destiny*, which, in one (long) volume achieved as comprehensive, thorough and authoritative a study of Churchill's life and work as one could wish for, written in a thoroughly readable and engaging style.

This book was preceded by an abundance of biographies, which all have a value, as each takes an individual stance. One of the finest is:

Winston Churchill: A Brief Life by Piers Brendon (a former Director of the Churchill Archives Centre at Churchill College Cambridge). First published in 1984, it is an outstanding short study of Churchill's life and also a very enjoyable read.

Of the many others the best, to my mind, are:

Churchill: A Study in Greatness by Geoffrey Best (2001);

Churchill by Roy Jenkins (2001). Baron Jenkins of Hillhead was a prominent Labour, Social Democrat and Liberal Democrat politician, and gives useful insights into Churchill's political life;

Man of the Century: Winston Churchill and His Legend Since 1945, by John Ramsden (2002);

Churchill: An Unruly Life, by Norman Rose (1994);

Churchill: A Study in Failure, by Robert Rhodes James (1972).

Many books have been published by people who worked closely with Churchill or were related to him (and crucially knew him in his lifetime. Of these I would single out the following:

A Daughter's Tale, by Mary Soames (2012);

Speaking For Themselves, The Personal Letters of Winston and Clementine Churchill, edited by Mary Soames (1999);

Winston Churchill: The Struggle for Survival, by Lord Moran, published, controversially, in 1966, just a year after Churchill's death by his personal physician from 1940 to 1965;

The Fringes of Power, by Sir John Colville (1986): Colville was Assistant Private Secretary to Churchill 1940–41 and 1943–45 and Joint Principal Private Secretary, 1951–55;

Winston Churchill: As I Knew Him, by Violet Bonham Carter (1965);

Churchill as Historian, by Maurice Ashley (1968). Ashley worked as Literary Assistant to Churchill from 1929 for several years.

For works on individual aspects of Churchill's life, I suggest the following from a welter of such books:

No More Champagne: Churchill and His Money, by David Lough (2015); and *Darling Winston: Forty Years of Letters Between Winston Churchill and His Mother,* by the same author (2018): two eye-opening volumes;

In Command of History: Churchill Fighting and Writing the Second World War, by David Reynolds (2004), an exhaustive study of Churchill as a writer;

Winston Churchill: His Life Through His Paintings by David Coombs and Minnie Churchill (2003);

Churchill and America, by Martin Gilbert (2005), *Churchill in America* by Rober H. Pilpel (1977), and *Churchill and the Jews* by Martin Gilbert (2007) are excellent studies of two very important aspects of Churchill's life. *Forged in War: Churchill, Roosevelt and the Second World War*, by Warren Kimball (1997), and *Franklin and Winston*, by Jon Meacham (2003) give expert insights into relations between President Roosevelt and Winston Churchill.

Two reference sources that I have found indispensable in studying Churchill are:

Churchill By Himself, edited by Richard Langworth (2008) remains the 'bible' of Churchill quotations, albeit with a limited index;

Churchill Style: The Art of Being Winston Churchill, by Barry Singer (2012), a book unsurpassed in answering all those detailed questions about Churchill's tastes, habits, pursuits and peculiarities.

Finally, I have found the website of the International Churchill Society – *winstonchurchill.org* – very helpful for the articles it contains on all aspects of Churchill's long life.

PHR